Fodor's

DEC 1 8 2018

OAHU

D0150848

WELCOME TO OAHU

Oahu is the Hawaiian island that has it all—untouched tropical landscapes as well as a stimulating urban vibe. You can explore the beaches and gentle waves of Kailua, or take in nightlife in buzzing Honolulu (the state's capital), home to a vibrant Chinatown and burgeoning arts scene. Life is still appealingly slow-paced on the northern and eastern shores, where razor-edged mountains descend to spectacular beaches. A thriving traditional culture, plus top-notch historic sites such as the royal Iolani Palace and Pearl Harbor, spice up the mix here as well.

TOP REASONS TO GO

★ **Pearl Harbor:** This historic memorial in Honolulu is a sobering, don't-miss sight.

★ **Waikiki:** Busy but beautiful, with a perfect beach for first-time surfers.

★ **Great Food:** Simple plate lunches, fresh sushi, creative modern Hawaiian cuisine.

★ **Polynesian Cultural Center:** The famous luau provides insight into island culture.

★ **Nightlife:** From upscale jazz bars to local hangouts, Honolulu comes alive after dark.

★ **North Shore:** Shave ice, big waves, pro surfers, and a slower pace add appeal here.

25 ULTIMATE EXPERIENCES

Oahu offers terrific experiences that should be on every traveler's list. Here are Fodor's top picks for a memorable trip.

1 Explore North Shore

Make a day of it when you head to the North Shore. Start off in Kaneohe and drive up Kamehameha Highway all the way to Haleiwa, stopping along the way at fruit stands, shrimp trucks, beaches, world-famous surfing spots (don't miss Waimea Bay), and scenic overlooks. *(Ch. 2)*

2 Watch a Hula Show

If you want a more traditional, less touristy introduction to hula and Hawaiian music, go to the Kuhio Beach Hula Show, free every Tuesday, Thursday, and Saturday evening on Kuhio Beach. *(Ch. 6)*

3 Learn to Surf

Waikiki is still a popular spot to try Hawaii's favorite sport, but White Plains has fewer crowds and great conditions for beginner surfers; you can rent gear or sign up for lessons from the beach recreation stand. *(Ch. 8)*

4 Have a Plate lunch

Everyone should try this Hawaii lunch tradition: an entrée with white rice and a scoop of macaroni salad. It's an island favorite and bargain-priced. *(Ch. 4)*

5 Relax at Kailua Beach

Looking for that idyllic, unpopulated stretch of white sandy beach and Technicolor blue water? Visit Kailua Beach for easy swimming waves and maximum sand. *(Ch. 3)*

6 Paradise Cove Luau

There is no non-touristy luau, but Paradise Cove is where locals like to take visitors for traditional Hawaiian foods (give *poi* a chance) and a genuinely fun experience. *(Ch. 6)*

7 Munch on Malasadas

A must-eat, these deep-fried, sugar-coated doughnuts without holes (first brought to the islands by Portuguese immigrants) are an island fixture. *(Ch. 4)*

8 Byodo-In Temple

Part of the Valley of the Temples cemetery complex, Byodo-In is a smaller version of the 11th-century original in Uji, Japan, but it's every bit as beautiful and peaceful. *(Ch. 2)*

9 Makapuu Lighthouse Trail

Less crowded than Diamond Head, Makapuu (popular with families because of the paved trail) offers an equally beautiful panorama of a different part of Oahu's coastline. *(Ch. 9)*

10 Seek a Waterfall on the Manoa Falls Trail

Manoa Falls is an easy (though occasionally muddy), one-and-a-half-mile rain-forest hike in Manoa Valley with the reward of a 150-foot waterfall at its end. *(Ch. 9)*

11 Explore Chinatown

Oahu's Chinatown is a jumble of the historic and hip, with a revitalized dining scene, plus a mix of galleries, shops, and cultural sites. *(Ch. 2)*

12 Snorkel at Haunama Bay

This nature preserve nestled in a volcanic crater with a vibrant reef is a phenomenal, family-friendly place to see colorful fish and other sea life. *(Ch. 8)*

13 Enjoy Kitsch at La Mariana Sailing Club

Hawaii's tiki era may be over, but La Mariana Sailing Club, a throwback restaurant and tiki bar, carries on the tradition. *(Ch. 4)*

14 Walk Through Waikiki

The best way to people-watch, shop, eat, and sightsee on Waikiki's iconic strip is by foot: skip the traffic, burn off some mai tai calories, and catch the sights you might otherwise miss. *(Ch. 2)*

15 Take a Cruise or Kayak Trip

You've got to get out on the water, whether it's on a sunset catamaran cruise, a whale-watching trip, or a kayak in the Mokulua Islands. *(Ch. 8)*

16 Take Tea at the Moana

Relaxed and refined at the same time, the Moana Surfrider offers high tea on its oceanfront Banyan Veranda, complete with dainty sandwiches, desserts, and a dose of glamour. *(Ch. 4)*

17 Visit Iolani Palace

The only royal residence in the U.S. gives you an introduction to Hawaii's monarchy, which ended with the overthrow of Queen Liliuokalani in 1893. *(Ch. 2)*

18 Eat out in Kaimuki

This unassuming neighborhood east of Waikiki and north of Diamond Head offers a diverse array of restaurants (both upscale and local) in a hip (but not-too-hip) part of town. *(Ch. 4)*

19 Explore the nature preserve at Kaena Point

Striking, stark, solitary: That's what Kaena Point feels like compared to much of bustling Oahu. Take the easy (though not shaded) hike out to the westernmost point of the island that's considered a sacred spot. *(Ch. 2)*

20 Relive History at Pearl Harbor

You can't go to Oahu and skip a visit to Pearl Harbor, where World War II Valor in the Pacific National Monument preserves four different World War II sites, including the the USS *Arizona* Memorial. *(Ch. 2)*

21 Treat Yourself to Shave Ice at Island Snow in Kailua

Matsumoto's on the North Shore may be the most well-known, but we (and former president Barack Obama) prefer Island Snow in Kailua. *(Ch. 4)*

22 Try a Spam Musubi

If you want to eat like a local, you've got to try what is basically Spam sushi—sticky rice with seasoned, fried Spam wrapped up in seaweed and surprisingly tasty. *(Ch. 4)*

23 Visit Doris Duke's Shangri-La

Tobacco heiress Doris Duke's waterfront mansion here was inspired by the Middle East, South Asia, and North Africa. Don't miss it. *(Ch. 2)*

24 Feel the Wind at the Pali Lookout

On especially windy days, you can actually lean up against the wind, and on most days, you get spectacular views. *(Ch. 2)*

25 Watch the Pros Surf at Waimea Bay

Waimea Bay was integral to the early development of big wave surfing, and it's a great place to watch pro surfers to this day. You'll get the best views here during the winter when waves can crest past 20 feet. *(Ch. 9)*

Fodor's OAHU

Editorial: Douglas Stallings, *Editorial Director*; Margaret Kelly, Jacinta O'Halloran, *Senior Editors*; Kayla Becker, Alexis Kelly, Amanda Sadlowski, *Editors*; Teddy Minford, *Content Editor*; Rachael Roth, *Content Manager*

Design: Tina Malaney, *Design and Production Director;* Jessica Gonzalez, *Production Designer*

Photography: Jill Krueger, *Senior Photo Editor*

Maps: Rebecca Baer, *Senior Map Editor*; David Lindroth, Mark Stroud (Moon Street Cartography), *Cartographers*

Production: Jennifer DePrima, *Editorial Production Manager;* Carrie Parker, *Senior Production Editor*; Elyse Rozelle, *Production Editor*

Business & Operations: Chuck Hoover, *Chief Marketing Officer*; Joy Lai, *Vice President and General Manager*; Stephen Horowitz, *Director of Business Development and Revenue Operations;* Tara McCrillis, *Director of Publishing Operations*

Public Relations and Marketing: Joe Ewaskiw, *Manager;* Esther Su, *Marketing Manager*

Writers: Powell Berger, Tiffany Hill, Trina Kudlacek, Chris Oliver, Anna Weaver

Editor: Douglas Stallings

Production Editor: Jennifer DePrima

7th Edition

ISBN 978-1-64097-066-3

ISSN 1559-0771

Library of Congress Control Number 2018946503

SPECIAL SALES

This book is available at special discounts for bulk purchases for sales promotions or premiums. For more information, e-mail SpecialMarkets@fodors.com.

PRINTED IN THE UNITED STATES OF AMERICA

10 9 8 7 6 5 4 3 2 1

CONTENTS

Fodor's Features

CONTENTS

ABOUT
THIS GUIDE

Fodor's Recommendations

Everything in this guide is worth doing—we don't cover what isn't—but exceptional sights, hotels, and restaurants are recognized with additional accolades. Fodor's Choice★ indicates our top recommendations. Care to nominate a new place? Visit Fodors.com/contact-us.

Trip Costs

We list prices wherever possible to help you budget well. Hotel and restaurant price categories from $ to $$$$ are noted alongside each recommendation. For hotels, we include the lowest cost of a standard double room in high season. For restaurants, we cite the average price of a main course at dinner or, if dinner isn't served, at lunch. For attractions, we always list adult admission fees; discounts are usually available for children, students, and senior citizens.

Hotels

Our local writers vet every hotel to recommend the best overnights in each price category, from budget to expensive. Unless otherwise specified, you can expect private bath, phone, and TV in your room. For expanded hotel reviews, facilities, and deals visit Fodors.com.

Top Picks	Hotels & Restaurants
★ Fodor's Choice	🏠 Hotel
Listings	⌐ Number of rooms
✉ Address	♚ Meal plans
✉ Branch address	✕ Restaurant
☎ Telephone	⌂ Reservations
🖷 Fax	👔 Dress code
🌐 Website	⊟ No credit cards
✉ E-mail	⑂ Price
🎫 Admission fee	**Other**
⊙ Open/closed times	⇨ See also
Ⓜ Subway	☞ Take note
⊹ Directions or Map coordinates	⛳ Golf facilities

Restaurants

Unless we state otherwise, restaurants are open for lunch and dinner daily. We mention dress code only when there's a specific requirement and reservations only when they're essential or not accepted.

Credit Cards

The hotels and restaurants in this guide typically accept credit cards. If not, we'll say so.

EUGENE FODOR

Hungarian-born Eugene Fodor (1905–91) began his travel career as an interpreter on a French cruise ship. The experience inspired him to write *On the Continent* (1936), the first guidebook to receive annual updates and discuss a country's way of life as well as its sights. Fodor later joined the U.S. Army and worked for the OSS in World War II. After the war, he kept up his intelligence work while expanding his guidebook series. During the Cold War, many guides were written by fellow agents who understood the value of insider information. Today's guides continue Fodor's legacy by providing travelers with timely coverage, insider tips, and cultural context.

EXPERIENCE OAHU

WHAT'S WHERE

1 Honolulu. The vibrant capital city holds the nation's only royal palace, free concerts under the tamarind trees in the financial district, and the art galleries, hipster bars, and open markets of Nuuanu and Chinatown. It also encompasses Waikiki—dressed in lights at the base of Diamond Head, famous for its world-class shopping, restaurants, and surf—and Pearl Harbor, Hawaii's largest natural harbor and the resting place of the USS *Arizona*, sunk on December 7, 1941.

2 Southeast Oahu. Honolulu's main bedroom communities crawl up the steep-sided valleys that flow into Maunalua Bay. Also here are snorkelers' favorite Hanauma Bay and a string of wild and often hidden beaches.

3 Windward Oahu. The sleepy neighborhoods at the base of the majestic Koolau Mountains offer a respite from the bustling city with long stretches of sandy beaches, charming eateries, ancient Hawaiian fishponds, and offshore islands to explore.

4 The North Shore. Best known for its miles of world-class surf breaks and green sea-turtle sightings, this plantation town also boasts farms, restaurants, and hiking trails.

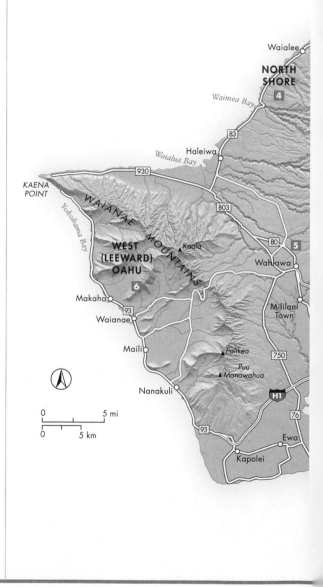

1

5 **Central Oahu.** Although
the interstate cuts through
much of this fertile region, it's
an integral part of Hawaii's
rich cultural history. This
valley, between the Waianae
and Koolau mountain ranges,
is an eclectic mix of farms,
planned communities, and
strip malls.

6 **West (Leeward) Oahu.**
This rugged part of the island
is finding a new identity as a
"second city" of suburban
homes, golf courses, and tech
firms.

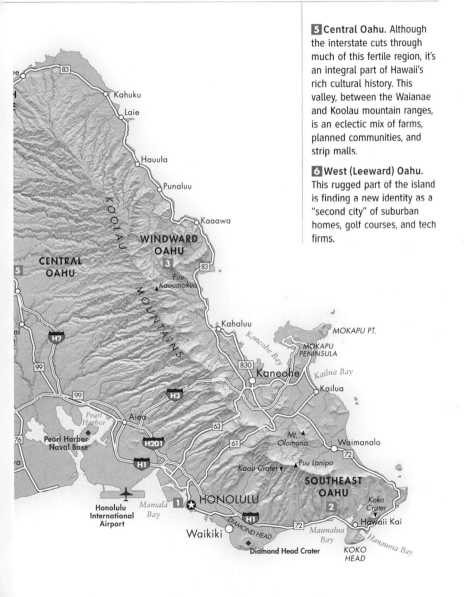

83

Kahuku

Laie

Hauula

Punaluu

K O O L A U

Kaaawa

**WINDWARD
OAHU**

**CENTRAL
OAHU**

3

83

5

Puu
Kaaumakua

M O U N T A I N S

Kahaluu

Kaneohe Bay

MOKAPU PT.

MOKAPU
PENINSULA

H2

830

Kaneohe

Kailua Bay

99

Kailua

99

H3

Pearl
Harbor

Aiea

63

Pearl Harbor
Naval Base

H201

Mt.
Olomana

Waimanalo

76

H1

Puu Lanipo

72

Kaau Crater

**SOUTHEAST
OAHU**

Honolulu
International
Airport

Mamala
Bay

1

HONOLULU

2

Koko
Crater

Hawaii Kai

Waikiki

H1

DIAMOND HEAD

72

Maunalua
Bay

Hanauma Bay

Diamond Head Crater

KOKO
HEAD

OAHU AND HAWAII TODAY

Nicknamed "The Gathering Place," Oahu is the third-largest Hawaiian island, but has 75% of the state's population and is the most developed.

Development

Development remains a huge issue for all Islanders—land prices are skyrocketing, putting many areas out of reach for low-to-middle-income residents. The government, though sluggish to respond at first, is trying to make development in Hawaii as sustainable as possible.

The redevelopment of Oahu's urban Kakaako neighborhood in particular has created many new residential units but few affordable ones. That also applies to the Ward Villages redevelopment, where largely foreign investors and 1 percenters buy condos in multimillion dollar high-rises. The upside? Ward also plans new restaurants, an outdoor movie theater, yoga in the park, and playgrounds. For the last decade or so, Chinatown has been steadily revitalized with art galleries, boutiques, and trendy restaurants moving in, old buildings getting facelifts, and a gradual reduction in crime, but with the inevitable worry that Chinatown is losing its character.

Over on the Windward side, Kailua, once a quiet bedroom community, is seeing more traffic and tourist buses than many would like. The roads into the Lanikai portion of the town's renowned stretch of beach have gotten so busy that parking is now highly restricted. Traffic is becoming a problem on Oahu's other roads that were not designed to accommodate all the new drivers.

Homelessness

Homelessness is not the first thing that comes to mind when you picture Hawaii, but it's a major issue in the Islands, and on Oahu in particular, where most of Hawaii's homeless population is concentrated and where Governor David Ige has declared a state of emergency. The state has the highest per capita rate of homelessness in the country. In areas like Waianae, there are some well-established homeless camps. But in urban areas, the homeless shuffle between one spot or the other as they are evicted from this area or that.

Agriculture and Food

Although *sustainability* is an effective buzzword, 90% of Hawaii's food and energy is still imported. Until fairly recently, most of the land was used for growing pineapple or sugarcane for export, both of which have all but vanished. Emulating how their Hawaiian ancestors lived and returning to simpler ways of growing and sharing a variety of foods has become a statewide initiative. Hawaii has the natural conditions and talent to produce far more diversity in agriculture than it currently does.

Farmers' markets and partnerships between restaurants and local farmers has helped tremendously in this regard. Localized efforts such as the Hawaii Farm Bureau Federation are collectively leading the organic and sustainable agricultural renaissance. Increasingly, sustainable trailblazers enrich the culinary tapestry of Hawaii and uplift the Islands' overall quality of life in both upscale and not-so-upscale establishments.

Oahu is home to many of the restaurants and chefs leading the Hawaii Regional Cuisine food movement with a focus on fresh, local ingredients. Chinatown and Kaimuki in particular are developing into mini food meccas, with new and exciting restaurants and gastropubs. Chefs are expanding and riffing off Hawaiian Regional Cuisine, taking it into new, international, eclectic, and refreshing directions.

Tourism and the Economy

The $14 billion–plus tourism industry represents a third of Hawaii's state income, and much of that is centered on Oahu. This overdependence has caused pretty severe hardship for many Islanders as the financial meltdown of recent years affected tourists' ability to visit and spend. Nevertheless, while tourism is on the rebound, its role is changing.

Belief that an industry based on the Hawaiians' *aloha* should protect, promote, and empower local culture and the environment while providing more entrepreneurial opportunities for local people has become more important to tourism businesses. More companies are incorporating authentic Hawaiiana in their programs and aim not only to provide a commercially viable tour but also to ensure that the visitor leaves feeling connected to his or her host. The concept of *kuleana,* a word for both privilege and responsibility, is increasingly upheld by the tourism industry.

Transportation

It can take awhile to get things done on Hawaiian time. Take, for example, the contentious 40-year development of a mass transit system to ease road congestion on Oahu. After numerous ideas were proposed and rejected over the years, Hawaiian voters approved a $5 billion rail plan in 2008 (its estimated final cost is now closer to $10 billion). Projected for completion in 2025, the elevated rail system will stretch 20 miles, from East Kapolei to Ala Moana Center, with several planned extensions, including one

into Waikiki. The first rail section, from East Kapolei to Aloha Stadium, should open in 2020.

Military

Along with tourism, the U.S. military continues to be a primary economic force in Hawaii. On Oahu in particular, the military's influence is felt even more. Locals aren't always friendly to the military, sometimes seeing them as interlopers on which the island economy is too reliant.

Rise of Hawaiian Pride

After Hawaii became a state in 1959, a process of Americanization began silencing traditions in the name of citizenship. Teaching the Hawaiian language was banned from schools, and children were distanced from their local customs. That process is being slowly reversed.

The people have rediscovered language, hula, chanting, and even the traditional Polynesian arts of canoe building and wayfinding (navigation by the stars without the use of instruments). This cultural resurrection is now firmly established in today's Hawaiian culture, with a palpable pride exuded by Hawaiians young and old.

The Native Hawaiian population is also rising once again, something that hasn't occurred since first contact with Westerners in the late 1770s introduced diseases that devastated Hawaiians. Puuhonua o Waimanalo, with 80 mostly Native Hawaiian residents on 55-acres in Windward Oahu, is held up as one successful example of a Hawaiian settlement created in partnership with the government.

OAHU PLANNER

When You Arrive

Honolulu International Airport is 20 minutes (40 minutes during rush hour) from Waikiki. Car-rental companies have booths at baggage claim; shuttle buses then take you to the car-pickup areas. An inefficient airport taxi system requires you to line up to a taxi wrangler who radios for cars (about $40–$45 to Waikiki). Other options include the city's reliable bus system ($2.75) with stops throughout Honolulu and Waikiki, or the Roberts Hawaii shuttle ($16), which transports you to any hotel in Waikiki. Ask taxi drivers to take Interstate H1, not Nimitz Highway, or your introduction to paradise will be via Honolulu's industrial back side.

Visitor Information

Hawaii Visitors and Convention Bureau. ✉ *2270 Kalakaua Ave., Suite 801, Waikiki* ☎ *800/464-2924 for brochures* ⊕ *www.gohawaii.com.*

Getting Here and Around

You can get away without renting a car if you plan on staying in Waikiki. But if you want to explore the rest of the island, there's no substitute for having your own wheels. Avoid the obvious tourist cars—candy-colored convertibles, for example—and never leave anything valuable inside, even if you've locked the car. Get a portable GPS navigator or make sure your phone has a navigation app, as Oahu's streets can be confusing.

Reserve your vehicle in advance, especially when traveling during the Christmas holidays and summer breaks. This will not only ensure that you get a car but also that you get the best rates. (Cars do sell out during busy periods.) ⇨ *See Travel Smart Oahu for more information on renting a car and driving.*

Island Driving Times

Don't let maps fool you. Although the distance between Waikiki and, say, the North Shore is roughly 40 miles, it may take more than an hour to get there, thanks to heavy traffic, construction, and other factors. Many of Oahu's main roads are a single lane in each direction, with no alternate routes. So if you're stuck behind a slow-moving vehicle, you may have no other choice than to hope it turns soon. Heavy traffic moving toward downtown can begin as early as 6 am, with after-work traffic starting at 3 pm.

Here are some average driving times—without traffic—that will help you plan your excursions.

Waikiki to Ko Olina	1 hour
Waikiki to Haleiwa	45 minutes
Waikiki to Hawaii Kai	25 minutes
Waikiki to Kailua	30 minutes
Waikiki to downtown Honolulu	10 minutes
Waikiki to airport	25 minutes
Kaneohe to Turtle Bay	1 hour
Hawaii Kai to Kailua	25 minutes
Haleiwa to Turtle Bay	20 minutes

Money-Saving Tips

A vacation to Hawaii doesn't have to break the bank. Take advantage of coupons in the free publications stacked at the airport and in racks all over Waikiki. Online sources like Groupon offer discounted rates for everything from dinner cruises to massages. Buy your souvenirs at Longs rather than at shops catering solely to tourists, and you'll likely get the same goods for less money.

You don't need to stay at a pricier waterfront hotel when, in Waikiki, almost all hotels are a short walk to the shore. Access to beaches and most hiking trails on the island is free to the public. For inexpensive fresh fruit and produce, check out farmers' markets and farm stands along the road—they'll often let you try before you buy.

For cheap and quick lunches, consider a food truck. Part of the culinary landscape of Oahu for generations, these lunch wagons—which rove around downtown and other areas—charge substantially less than restaurants. Take advantage of *pau hana* time (happy hour) for cheaper drinks and appetizers at many establishments.

Dining and Lodging on Oahu

If you want to see Hawaii's cultural blending, look no further than its cuisine. From traditional local-style plate lunches to sushi bars to high-end steak houses, there's no shortage of interesting flavors and cuisines. Choosing vacation lodging is a tough decision, but fret not—our expert writers and editors have done most of the legwork.

Seeing Pearl Harbor

Pearl Harbor is a must-see for many, but there are things to know before you go.

Consider whether you want to see only the USS *Arizona* Memorial, or the USS *Bowfin* and USS *Missouri* as well. You can also visit the Pacific Aviation Museum on Ford Island. Allow approximately 1 hour 15 minutes for the USS *Arizona* tour, which includes a 23-minute documentary of the Pearl Harbor attack and a ferry ride to the memorial itself.

You can now reserve USS *Arizona* Memorial tickets online for a certain day for a $1.50 processing fee. If you don't reserve tickets ahead of time, plan to arrive early—same-day tickets for the USS *Arizona* Memorial are free and given out on a first-come-first-served basis. They can disappear within an hour, and your entire party must be present to receive same-day tickets. Take some time to enjoy the upgraded visitor center, which houses two exhibits using state-of-the-art technology to tell the story of the attack on December 7, 1941.

Strict security measures prohibit any sort of bag (purses, backpacks, diaper bags, camera cases—even small ones), although cameras are allowed. Strollers are allowed in the visitor center but not in the theaters or on the shuttle boats. Baggage storage is available for a small fee. Also, don't forget your ID.

Children under four years of age are not allowed on the USS *Bowfin* for safety reasons, and may not enjoy the crowds or waiting in line at other sights.

Older kids are likely to find the more experiential, hands-on history of the USS *Bowfin* and USS *Missouri* memorable. The Pacific Aviation Museum's vintage planes are an added bonus attraction if you have the time.

For more information, visit ⊕ *www.nps. gov/valr.*

OAHU'S BEST BEACHES

The best thing about Oahu's beautiful beaches? Like snowflakes, no two are exactly alike. Some are wide, others are narrow. Some are protected by fringing reefs, and others have huge waves breaking right onshore. *All* are special.

Here are some of our favorite stretches of sand, where you can make your home away from home:

Best for Families
Ko Olina, West (Leeward) Oahu. Four man-made lagoons are totally protected and offer great grassy spots to grab a nap. Plus, Disney's Aulani resort is nearby if the kids get restless and need a Mickey fix.

White Plains, West (Leeward) Oahu. Not only are there bathrooms, barbecues, and picnic tables here—there are even sleeping seals. What more could a kid want?

Best for Big Waves
Haleiwa Alii Beach Park, the North Shore. The Vans Triple Crown of Surfing kicks off at this beach in November, and the small town of Haleiwa is a surfing mecca. From board shops to galleries devoted to inside-the-tube photos, you'll experience the full range of the surfing lifestyle.

Waimea Bay, the North Shore. In summer, snorkeling is great at this beach. But in winter, surf's up, so be careful if you don't know what you're doing. Pros flock here for contests—"the Eddie," a competition honoring big-wave-surfer Eddie Aikau, is held here only when waves are at least 20 feet—and fans flock to watch. Come early in the morning when there are waves and claim your seat on the dunes.

Best for People-Watching
Kuhio Beach Park, Waikiki. Everywhere along Waikiki's shoreline is pretty packed, but Kuhio is home to some of the area's more active, and fit, beachgoers. Nice restaurants and clubs are nearby.

Best for Flying a Kite
Sandy Beach, Southeast Oahu. If you're afraid you'll break your neck bodysurfing in the waves here, retire to the shoreline and watch kites perform acrobatics in the gusts.

Kualoa Regional Park, Windward Oahu. This expansive park gives campers and others plenty of space to spread out and take advantage of the wind with two-handed kites. Chinaman's Hat, an offshore island, provides a great backdrop.

Best for Soft Sand
Ala Moana Beach Park, Honolulu. Just steps away from food and shopping outlets, this beach offers extraordinarily fine sand, though there's little shade. When you get warm, the equally smooth water beckons.

Lanikai Beach Park, Windward Oahu. This spot and adjacent Kailua Beach Park have powdery white sand and some trees for shade. But good luck finding a parking spot on weekends.

Best for Watching the Sun Rise and Set
Bellows Beach, Southeast Oahu (Sunrise). Try camping out (weekends only) at this eastward-facing beach so you can catch the earliest rays. Nearby Waimanalo Beach Park offers another option.

Sunset Beach, the North Shore (Sunset). The name says it all. From here, you can see all the way down the North Shore toward Kaena Point in the west, and enjoy the last rays before the sun dips below the horizon.

KIDS AND FAMILIES

Choosing a Place to Stay

Resorts: All the big resorts make kids' programs a priority. When booking your room, ask about *keiki* (children's) menus at restaurants, free activities on the property, and pools and water parks built specifically for the younger set.

In Waikiki, your best bet for kids is the Hilton Hawaiian Village, where there's a large beach and loads of kids' programs. Also good choices: Waikiki Beach Marriott Resort, Aston Waikiki Beach Hotel, and the Sheraton Princess Kaiulani.

Condos: You can cook your own food and get twice the space of a hotel room for much less. Be sure to ask about the size of the complex's pool and barbecue availability. For the ultimate family condo experience on Oahu, Marriott's Ko Olina Beach Club can't be beat with its sheltered beaches, four pools, barbecues, children's play areas, large kitchens, and an on-site grocery store. In Waikiki, try the the Castle Waikiki Shore and Outrigger Luana Waikiki.

Ocean Activities

On the Beach: In Waikiki, your best beach bets for young children are Kuhio Beach Park and Fort DeRussy Beach Park, both protected from a strong shore break and with a wide stretch of sand, with lifeguards on duty. On the windward side, try Kailua Beach Park, with its shady trees and good bathroom/shower facilities. North Shore beaches are recommended for children only in the summer months, and of these, Waimea Bay, with its wide stretch of sand and good facilities, is best for kids. On the leeward side, Ko Olina's protected coves are great for families with small children.

On the Waves: Waikiki is *the* place for everyone to learn to surf, including kids.

Some hotels, including the Waikiki Beach Marriott Resort & Spa, offer in-house surf schools. Or, for a less crowded surfing experience, head to Barber's Point.

The Underwater World: Hawaii is a great place to introduce your kids to snorkeling. Even without the mask and snorkel, they'll be able to see colorful fish darting around coral reefs, and they may also spot endangered Hawaiian green sea turtles and dolphins. On Oahu the quintessential snorkeling experience can be had at Hanauma Bay, where kids can see hundreds of species of fish in protected waters and enjoy a wide stretch of beach. In summer months only, Shark's Cove on the North Shore is an interesting experience for older kids who already have snorkeling basics.

Land Activities

Oahu is fortunate to have the largest variety of land-based experiences in the Islands. Kids can visit the Honolulu Zoo for twilight tours, touch fishy friends at the Waikiki Aquarium, help in a dolphin training session at Sea Life Park, or husk a coconut at the Polynesian Culture Center. Hoomaluhia Botanical Garden offers wide-open spaces and a duck pond, while Kualoa Ranch is the place for horseback riding.

After Dark

At night, younger kids get a kick out of luau, and many of the shows incorporate young audience members, adding to the fun. Older kids are more likely to enjoy the handful of more modern luau, incorporating acrobatics, lively music, and fire dancers. On Friday, don't miss watching the Hilton Hawaiian Village's free fireworks show at 7:45 pm or 8 pm (varies seasonally) from your beachfront seat.

GREAT ITINERARIES

Highlights of Oahu in One Week

7 Days. With the capital and two-thirds of the state's population, Oahu is a vibrant, ever-evolving island. Cultural, outdoor, historical, culinary, and other adventures abound. From *mauka* (mountains) to *makai* (sea), Oahu is probably the Hawaiian island most likely to please all types of travelers whether you're an outdoorsy type, a beach bum, a foodie, or a family, and a week should give you enough time to see the highlights. You can either use the bus or take taxis while you're in Honolulu, but rent a car to get out of Waikiki and around the island for a true feel for all things Oahu in this one-week highlights itinerary.

Waikiki

Day 1. You'll want to get your beach legs under you after that long flight to Oahu. Given the time difference between Hawaii and the rest of the U.S. (it's 6 hours earlier than the east coast, 3 hours earlier than the west coast), you'll probably be jet-lagged. Use your earlier rising to go grab coffee and head to Waikiki, Sans Souci, or Fort DeRussy Beach. You'll see locals on their morning jogs at Kapiolani Park and catching waves at their favorite shore break. Once caffeinated, hit Kalaukaua Avenue on foot, the best way to shop and sightsee. Got kiddos in tow? Try the Waikiki Aquarium or Honolulu Zoo. Get some refreshments with tea at the Moana Surfrider, the oldest hotel in Waikiki, or mai tais and *pupu* (hors d'oeuvres) at Duke's Canoe Club (a better deal at lunch). In the afternoon, it's time for a surf lesson on the beginner-friendly waves of Waikiki. Finish your day with a surfside dinner at your restaurant of choice to watch the sunset.

Pearl Harbor

Day 2. Give yourself a whole day for Pearl Harbor, in part because the history is so rich and overwhelming and in part because you may be waiting in lines. Just be aware that tickets for the USS *Arizona* Memorial usually sell out early, but you can arrive as early as 7 am. After your ferry ride out to the memorial, you can explore the USS *Bowfin* submarine or take a shuttle to Ford Island and visit the restored USS *Missouri* battleship (the "Mighty Mo"). and the Pacific Aviation Museum. Only the USS *Arizona,* and the Visitor Center, which are operated by the National Park Service are free; the other sights are operated by private entities and charge admission. You won't be allowed to carry bags to any of the sights, so be sure that anything important fits in your pockets; you can pay to store your bags near the Visitor Center. Head back to Waikiki for some late-afternoon beach time and a good dinner; you deserve it.

Downtown Honolulu and Chinatown

Day 3. Cab or bus it to downtown Honolulu for a guided tour of royal residence, Iolani Palace, where you'll get an excellent overview of Hawaii's monarchy era from the early 1800s through its overthrow in 1893. Next take a walk between Honolulu Hale, Kawaiahao Church, Hawaiian Mission Houses Historic Site and Archives, the Hawaii State Capitol, Washington Place, the Kamehameha I Statue, and Aliiolani Hale for historical highlights (several companies offer professionally guided walks of the area). Then keep walking the half mile through Honolulu's business district into Chinatown for lunch at one of its eclectic eateries. Little Village Noodle House is always a good bet. Browse the shops, art galleries, and cultural sites like the Maunakea Marketplace, Chinatown

Cultural Plaza, Izumo Taisha Shrine, and Kuan Yin Temple.

Diamond Head and Kaimuki

Day 4. Today you will go the opposite direction from downtown. Tours of Shangri La, the opulent waterfront home of heiress Doris Duke, with its Islamic art and architecture, book up well in advance, but it's well worth the effort to make an online reservation for a small surcharge. Shuttles to the Kahala home start and end at the Honolulu Museum of Art. After your tour, grab a to-go lunch from Diamond Head Market & Grill, and enjoy it at the picnic tables at Diamond Head State Monument and Park. Then hike the relatively easy 1½-hour trail up and down this dormant volcano. Finish the day with dinner in the emerging foodie neighborhood of Kaimuki.

Kailua and South Shore

Day 5. Head to the Windward side for a stop in Kailua, a once sleepy suburb that's become a popular visitor spot. Go for a swim at quintessential Kailua Beach, then have lunch at Kalapawai Cafe & Deli or Cactus Bistro. Next, drive along the southeastern shore via Waimanalo, and choose your afternoon adventure:

1) do the easy, stroller-friendly hike at Makapuu Lighthouse with great whale-watching views in winter and spring; 2) snorkel at Hanauma Bay State Park, the pristine nature preserve where you'll have more space to swim with the fishies if you arrive after the morning-to-midday rush; or 3) stop at Halona Blowhole and the *From Here to Eternity* Halona Beach Cove nearby.

WEDDINGS AND HONEYMOONS

There's no question that Hawaii is one of the country's foremost honeymoon destinations, but it's also popular for destination weddings.

The Big Day

Choosing the Perfect Place. You really have two choices to make: the ceremony location and where to have the reception. For the former, Oahu boasts offers beaches, sea-hugging bluffs, gardens, private residences, resort lawns, and, of course, places of worship. As for the reception, there are these same choices, as well as restaurants and even a luau. If you decide to go outdoors, make sure to have a backup plan for inclement weather.

Finding a Wedding Planner. If you're planning to invite more than an officiant and your loved one to your wedding ceremony, seriously consider hiring a wedding planner who can help select a location, design the floral scheme, and recommend a florist and photographer. They can also plan the menu and choose a restaurant, caterer, or resort, and suggest any Hawaiian traditions to incorporate into your ceremony.

If it's a resort wedding, most have on-site wedding coordinators; however, there are many independents around Oahu who specialize in certain types of ceremonies—by locale, size, religious affiliation, and so on. Share your budget, and get a detailed proposal—in writing—before you proceed.

Getting Your License. There's no waiting period in Hawaii, no residency or citizenship requirements, and no required blood test or shots. You can apply and pay the fee online; however, both the bride and groom must appear together in person before a marriage-license agent to receive the marriage license at the State Department of Health in Honolulu. You'll need proof of age—the legal age to marry is 18. Upon approval, a marriage license is immediately issued and costs $60. After the ceremony, your officiant—must be licensed by the Hawaii Department of Health—will mail the marriage certificate (proof of marriage) to the state, and you'll get your copy about four months later. For more detailed information, visit ⊕ *marriage.ehawaii.gov.*

Wedding Attire. In Hawaii, basically anything goes, from long, formal dresses with trains to white bikinis. For men, a pair of solid-colored slacks with a nice aloha shirt is appropriate. If you're planning a wedding on the beach, barefoot is the way to go.

Local Customs. The most obvious traditional Hawaiian wedding custom is the lei exchange in which the bride and groom take turns placing a lei around the neck of the other—with a kiss. Bridal lei are usually floral, whereas the groom's is typically made of *maile,* a green leafy garland that drapes the neck. Brides often also wear a *lei poo*—a circular floral headpiece. Other Hawaiian customs include the blowing of the conch shell, hula, chanting, and Hawaiian music.

The Honeymoon

Do you want Champagne and strawberries delivered to your room each morning? A breathtaking swimming pool in which to float? A five-star restaurant in which to dine? Then a resort is the way to go. A small inn is also good if you're on a tight budget or don't plan to spend much time in your room. Or maybe a condominium resort. The lodging accommodations are almost as plentiful as the beaches.

HAWAIIAN CULTURAL
TRADITIONS HULA, LEI, AND LUAU

HULA: MORE THAN A FOLK DANCE

Hula has been called "the heartbeat of the Hawaiian people" and also "the world's best-known, most misunderstood dance." Both are true. Hula isn't just dance. It is storytelling.

Chanter Edith McKinzie calls it "an extension of a piece of poetry." In its adornments, implements, and customs, hula integrates every important Hawaiian cultural practice: poetry, history, genealogy, craft, plant cultivation, martial arts, religion, protocol. So when 19th-century Christian missionaries sought to eradicate a practice they considered depraved, they threatened more than just a folk dance.

With public performance outlawed and private hula practice discouraged, hula went underground for a generation. The fragile verbal link by which culture was transmitted from teacher to student hung by a thread. Even increasing literacy did not help because hula's practitioners were a secretive and protected circle.

As if that weren't bad enough, vaudeville, Broadway, and Hollywood got hold of the hula, giving it the glitz treatment in

an unbroken line from "Oh, How She Could Wicky Wacky Woo" to "Rock-A-Hula Baby." Hula became shorthand for paradise: fragrant flowers, lazy hours. Ironically, this development assured that hundreds of Hawaiians could make a living performing and teaching hula. Many danced *auana* (modern form) in performance; but taught *kahiko* (traditional), quietly, at home or in hula schools.

Today, decades after the cultural revival known as the Hawaiian Renaissance, language immersion programs have assured a new generation of proficient—and even eloquent—chanters, songwriters, and translators. Visitors can see more, and more authentic, traditional hula than at any other time in the last 200 years.

Like the culture of which it is the beating heart, hula has survived.

Lei *poo*. Head lei. In *kahiko*, greenery only. In *auana*, flowers.

Face emotes appropriate expression. Dancer should not be a smiling automaton.

Shoulders remain relaxed and still, never hunched, even with arms raised. No bouncing.

Eyes always follow leading hand.

Lei. Hula is rarely performed without a shoulder lei.

Arms and hands remain loose, relaxed, below shoulder level—except as required by interpretive movements.

Traditional hula skirt is loose fabric, smocked and gathered at the waist.

Hip is canted over weight-bearing foot.

Knees are always slightly bent, accentuating hip sway.

Kupee. Ankle bracelet of flowers, shells, or foliage.

In kahiko, feet are flat. In auana, they may be more arched, but not tiptoes or bouncing.

BASIC MOTIONS

Speak or Sing

Moon or Sun

Grass Shack or House

Mountains or Heights

Love or Caress

At backyard parties, hula is performed in bare feet and street clothes, but in performance, adornments play a key role, as do rhythm-keeping implements such as the pahu drum and the ipu (gourd).

In hula *kahiko* (traditional style), the usual dress is multiple layers of stiff fabric (often with a pellom lining, which most closely resembles *kapa*, the paperlike bark cloth of the Hawaiians). These wrap tightly around the bosom but flare below the waist to form a skirt. In pre-contact times, dancers wore only kapa skirts. Men traditionally wear loincloths.

Monarchy-period hula is performed in voluminous muumuu or high-necked muslin blouses and gathered skirts. Men wear white or gingham shirts and black pants.

In hula *auana* (modern), dress for women can range from grass skirts and strapless tops to contemporary tea-length dresses. Men generally wear aloha shirts, but sometimes grass skirts over pants or even everyday gear.

SURPRISING HULA FACTS

■ Grass skirts are not traditional; workers from Kiribati (the Gilbert Islands) brought this custom to Hawaii.

■ In olden-day Hawaii, *mele* (songs) for hula were composed for every occasion—name songs for babies, dirges for funerals, welcome songs for visitors, celebrations of favorite pursuits.

■ Hula *mai* is a traditional hula form in praise of a noble's genitals; the power of the *alii* (royalty) to procreate gave *mana* (spiritual power) to the entire culture.

■ Hula students in old Hawaii adhered to high standards: scrupulous cleanliness, no sex, daily cleansing rituals, certain food prohibitions, and no contact with the dead. They were fined if they broke the rules.

WHERE TO WATCH

If you're interested in "the real thing," there are annual hula festivals on each island. Check the individual island visitors' bureaus websites at ⊕ *www.gohawaii.com*.

If you can't make it to a festival, there are plenty of other hula shows—at most resorts, many lounges, and even at certain shopping centers. Ask your hotel concierge for performance information.

ALL ABOUT LEI

Lei brighten every occasion in Hawaii, from birthdays to bar mitzvahs to baptisms. Creative artisans weave nature's bounty—flowers, ferns, vines, and seeds—into gorgeous creations that convey an array of heartfelt messages: "Welcome," "Congratulations," "Good luck," "Farewell," "Thank you," "I love you." When it's difficult to find the right words, a lei expresses exactly the right sentiment.

WHERE TO BUY THE BEST LEI

Most airports in Hawaii have lei stands where you can buy a fragrant garland upon arrival. Every florist shop in the Islands sells lei; you can also treat yourself to a lei while shopping for provisions at any supermarket or box store. And you'll always find lei sellers at crafts fairs and outdoor festivals.

LEI ETIQUETTE

■ To wear a closed lei, drape it over your shoulders, half in front and half in back. Open lei are worn around the neck, with the ends draped over the front in equal lengths.

■ Pikake, ginger, and other sweet, delicate blossoms are "feminine" lei. Men opt for cigar, crown flower, and ti leaf lei, which are sturdier and don't emit as much fragrance.

■ Lei are always presented with a kiss, a custom that supposedly dates back to World War II when a hula dancer fancied an officer at a U.S.O. show. Taking a dare from members of her troupe, she took off her lei, placed it around his neck, and kissed him on the cheek.

■ You shouldn't wear a lei before you give it to someone else. Hawaiians believe the lei absorbs your *mana* (spirit); if you give your lei away, you'll be giving away part of your essence.

ORCHID

Growing wild on every continent except Antarctica, orchids—which range in color from yellow to green to purple—comprise the largest family of plants in the world. There are more than 20,000 species of orchids, but only three are native to Hawaii—and they are very rare. The pretty lavender vanda you see hanging by the dozens at local lei stands has probably been imported from Thailand.

MAILE

Maile, an endemic twining vine with a heady aroma, is sacred to Laka, goddess of the hula. In ancient times, dancers wore maile and decorated hula altars with it to honor Laka. Today, "open" maile lei usually are given to men. Instead of ribbon, interwoven lengths of maile are used at dedications of new businesses. The maile is untied, never snipped, for doing so would symbolically "cut" the company's success.

ILIMA

Designated by Hawaii's Territorial Legislature in 1923 as the official flower of the island of Oahu, the golden ilima is so delicate it lasts for just a day. Five to seven hundred blossoms are needed to make one garland. Queen Emma, wife of King Kamehameha IV, preferred ilima over all other lei, which may have led to the incorrect belief that they were reserved only for royalty.

PLUMERIA

This ubiquitous flower is named after Charles Plumier, the noted French botanist who discovered it in Central America in the late 1600s. Plumeria ranks among the most popular lei in Hawaii because it's fragrant, hardy, plentiful, inexpensive, and requires very little care. Although yellow is the most common color, you'll also find plumeria lei in shades of pink, red, orange, and "rainbow" blends.

PIKAKE

Favored for its fragile beauty and sweet scent, pikake was introduced from India. In lieu of pearls, many brides in Hawaii adorn themselves with long, multiple strands of white pikake. Princess Kaiulani enjoyed showing guests her beloved pikake and peacocks at Ainahau, her Waikiki home. Interestingly, pikake is the Hawaiian word for both the bird and the blossom.

KUKUI

The kukui (candlenut) is Hawaii's state tree. Early Hawaiians strung kukui nuts (which are quite oily) together and burned them for light; mixed burned nuts with oil to make an indelible dye; and mashed roasted nuts to consume as a laxative. Kukui nut lei may not have been made until after Western contact, when the Hawaiians saw black beads from Europe and wanted to imitate them.

LUAU: A TASTE OF HAWAII

The best place to sample Hawaiian food is at a backyard luau. Aunts and uncles are cooking, the pig is from a cousin's farm, and the fish is from a brother's boat.

But even locals have to angle for invitations to those rare occasions. So your choice is most likely between a commercial luau and a Hawaiian restaurant.

Some commercial luau are less authentic; they offer little of the traditional diet and are more about umbrella drinks, spectacle, and fun.

For greater culinary authenticity, folksy experiences, and rock-bottom prices, visit a Hawaiian restaurant (most are in anonymous storefronts in residential neighborhoods). Expect rough edges and some effort negotiating the menu.

In either case, much of what is known today as Hawaiian food would be as foreign to a 16th-century Hawaiian as risotto or chow mien. The pre-contact diet was simple and healthy—mainly raw and steamed seafood and vegetables. Early Hawaiians used earth ovens and heated stones to cook seafood, taro, sweet potatoes, and breadfruit and seasoned their food with sea salt and ground kukui nuts. Seaweed, fern shoots, sweet potato vines, coconut, banana, sugarcane, and select greens and roots rounded out the diet.

Successive waves of immigrants added their favorites to the ti leaf–lined table. So it is that foods as disparate as salt salmon and chicken long rice are now Hawaiian—even though there is no salmon in Hawaiian waters and long rice (cellophane noodles) is Chinese.

AT THE LUAU: KALUA PORK

The heart of any luau is the *imu*, the earth oven in which a whole pig is roasted. The preparation of an imu is an arduous affair for most families, who tackle it only once a year or so, for a baby's first birthday or at Thanksgiving, when many Islanders prefer to imu their turkeys. Commercial luau operations have it down to a science, however.

THE ART OF THE STONE
The key to a proper imu is the *pohaku*, the stones. Imu cook by means of long, slow, moist heat released by special stones that can withstand a hot fire without exploding. Many Hawaiian families treasure their imu stones, keeping them in a pile in the backyard and passing them on through generations.

PIT COOKING
The imu makers first dig a pit about the size of a refrigerator, then lay down *kiawe* (mesquite) wood and stones, and build a white-hot fire that is allowed to burn itself out. The ashes are raked away, and the hot stones covered with banana and ti leaves. Well-wrapped in ti or banana leaves and a net of chicken wire, the pig is lowered onto the leaf-covered stones. *Laulau* (leaf-wrapped bundles of meats, fish, and taro leaves) may also be placed inside. Leaves—ti, banana, even ginger—cover the pig followed by wet burlap sacks (to create steam). The whole is topped with a canvas tarp and left to steam for the better part of a day.

OPENING THE IMU
This is the moment everyone waits for: The imu is unwrapped like a giant present and the imu keepers gingerly wrestle out the steaming pig. When it's unwrapped, the meat falls moist and smoky-flavored from the bone, looking just like Southern-style pulled pork, but without the barbecue sauce.

WHICH LUAU?
Most resort hotels have luau on their grounds that include hula, music, and, of course, lots of food and drink. Each island also has at least one "authentic" luau. For lists of the best luau on each island, visit the Hawaii Visitors and Convention Bureau website at ⊕ *www.gohawaii.com.*

MEA AI ONO: GOOD THINGS TO EAT.

LAULAU
Steamed meats, fish, and taro leaf in ti-leaf bundles: fork-tender, a medley of flavors; the taro resembles spinach.

Laulau

LOMI LOMI SALMON
Salt salmon in a piquant salad or relish with onions and tomatoes.

POI
Poi, a paste made of pounded taro root, may be an acquired taste, but it's a must-try during your visit.

Lomi Lomi Salmon

Consider: The Hawaiian Adam is descended from *kalo* (taro). Young taro plants are called "keiki"–children. Poi is the first food after mother's milk for many Islanders. Ai, the word for food, is synonymous with poi in many contexts.

Not only that, we love it. "There is no meat that doesn't taste good with poi," the old Hawaiians said.

But you have to know how to eat it: with something rich or powerfully flavored. "It is salt that makes the poi go in," is another adage. When you're served poi, try it with a mouthful of smoky kalua pork or salty lomi lomi salmon. Its slightly sour blandness cleanses the palate. And if you don't like it, smile and say something polite. (And slide that bowl over to a local.)

Poi

E HELE MAI AI! COME AND EAT!

Local-style Hawaiian restaurants tend to be inconveniently located in well-worn storefronts with little or no parking, outfitted with battered tables and clattering Melmac dishes, but they personify aloha, invariably run by local families who welcome tourists who take the trouble to find them.

Many are cash-only operations and combination plates, known as "plate lunch," are a standard feature: one or two entrées, two scoops of steamed rice, one scoop of macaroni salad, and—if the place is really old-style—a tiny portion of coarse Hawaiian salt and some raw onions for relish.

Most serve some foods that aren't, strictly speaking, Hawaiian, but are beloved of ka-

maaina, such as salt meat with watercress (preserved meat in a tasty broth), or *akubone* (skipjack tuna fried in a tangy vinegar sauce).

MENU GUIDE

Much of the Hawaiian language encountered during a stay in the Islands will appear on restaurant menus and lists of luau fare. Here's a quick primer.

ahi: *yellowfin tuna.*

aku: *skipjack, bonito tuna.*

amaama: *mullet; it's hard to get but tasty.*

bento: *a box lunch.*

chicken luau: *a stew made from chicken, taro leaves, and coconut milk.*

haupia: *a light, pudding-like sweet made from coconut.*

imu: *the underground oven in which pigs are roasted for luau.*

kalua: *to bake underground.*

kimchee: *Korean dish of fermented cabbage made with garlic, hot peppers, and other spices.*

Kona coffee: *coffee grown in the Kona district of the Big Island.*

laulau: *literally, a bundle. Laulau are morsels of pork, chicken, butterfish, or other ingredients wrapped with young taro leaves and then bundled in ti leaves for steaming.*

lilikoi: *passion fruit, a tart, seedy yellow fruit that makes delicious desserts, juice, and jellies.*

lomi lomi: *to rub or massage; also a type of massage. Lomi lomi salmon is fish that has been rubbed with onions and herbs; commonly served with minced onions and tomatoes.*

luau: *a Hawaiian feast; also the leaf of the taro plant used in preparing such a feast.*

luau leaves: *cooked taro tops with a taste similar to spinach.*

mahimahi: *mild-flavored dolphinfish, not the marine mammal.*

mai tai: *potent rum drink with orange liqueurs and pineapple juice, from the Tahitian word for "good."*

malasada: *a Portuguese deep-fried doughnut without a hole, dipped in sugar.*

manapua: *steamed Chinese buns filled with pork, chicken, or other fillings.*

niu: *coconut.*

onaga: *pink or red snapper.*

ono: *a long, slender mackerel-like fish; also called wahoo.*

ono: *delicious; also hungry.*

opihi: *a tiny limpet found on rocks.*

papio: *a young ulua or jack fish.*

poha: *Cape gooseberry. Tasting a bit like honey, the poha berry is often used in jams and desserts.*

poi: *a paste made from pounded taro root, a staple of the Hawaiian diet.*

poke: *cubed raw tuna or other fish, tossed with seaweed and seasonings.*

pupu: *appetizers or small plates.*

saimin: *long thin noodles and vegetables in broth, often garnished with small pieces of fish cake, scrambled egg, luncheon meat, and green onion.*

sashimi: *raw fish thinly sliced and usually eaten with soy sauce.*

ti leaves: *a member of the agave family. The leaves are used to wrap food while cooking and removed before eating.*

uku: *deep-sea snapper.*

ulua: *a member of the jack family that also includes pompano and amberjack. Also called crevalle, jack fish, and jack crevalle.*

EXPLORING
OAHU

Updated by
Tiffany Hill

Oahu is one-stop Hawaii—all the allure of the Islands in a plate-lunch mix that has you kayaking around offshore islets by day and sitting in a jazz club 'round midnight, all without ever having to take another flight or repack your suitcase. It offers both the buzz of modern living in jam-packed Honolulu (the state's capital) and the allure of slow-paced island life on its northern and eastern shores. It is, in many ways, the center of the Hawaiian universe.

There are more museums, staffed historic sites, and guided tours here than you'll find on any other island. And only here do a wealth of renovated buildings and well-preserved neighborhoods so clearly spin the story of Hawaii's history. It's the only place to experience Islands-style urbanity, since there are no other true cities in the state. And yet you can get as lost in the rural landscape and be as laid-back as you wish.

Oahu is home to Waikiki, the most famous Hawaiian beach, as well as some of the world's most famous surf on the North Shore, and Hawaii's best-known historical site—Pearl Harbor. If it's isolation, peace, and quiet you want, Oahu might not be for you, but if you'd like a bit of spice with your piece of paradise, this island provides it.

Encompassing 597 square miles, Oahu is the third-largest island in the Hawaiian chain. Scientists believe the island was formed about 4 million years ago by three shield volcanoes: Waianae, Koolau, and the recently discovered Kaena. Recognized in mid-2014, Kaena is the oldest of the three and has long since been submerged 62 miles from Kaena Point on Oahu's northwestern side. Waianae created the mountain range on the western side of the island, whereas Koolau shapes the eastern side. Central Oahu is an elevated plateau bordered by the two mountain ranges, with Pearl Harbor to the south. Several of Oahu's most famous natural landmarks, including Diamond Head and Hanauma Bay, are tuff rings and cinder cones formed during a renewed volcanic stage (roughly 1 million years ago).

The northern and eastern sides of Oahu—and of each Hawaiian island—are together referred to as the Windward side, and generally have a cooler, wetter climate. The island's southern and western sides are commonly called the Leeward side, and are typically warmer and more arid. The island's official flower, the little orange *ilima,* grows predominantly in the east, but lei throughout the island incorporate ilima. Numerous tropical fish call the reef at Hanauma Bay home, migrating humpback whales can be spotted off the coast past Waikiki and Diamond Head December–April, spinner dolphins pop in and out of the island's bays, and the 15 islets off Oahu's eastern coast provide refuge for endangered seabirds.

Oahu is the most visited Hawaiian island because early tourism to Hawaii started here. It's also the most inhabited island today—69% of the state's population lives on Oahu—due to job opportunities and the island's military bases. Although Kilauea volcano on Hawaii was a tourist attraction in the late 1800s, it was the building of the Moana Hotel on Waikiki Beach in 1901 and subsequent advertising of Hawaii to wealthy San Franciscans that really fueled tourism in the Islands. Oahu was drawing tens of thousands of guests yearly when, on December 7, 1941, Japanese Zeros appeared at dawn to bomb Pearl Harbor. Though tourism understandably dipped during the war (Waikiki Beach was fenced with barbed wire), the subsequent memorial only seemed to attract more visitors, and Oahu remains hugely popular with tourists—especially the Japanese—to this day.

HONOLULU

Here is Hawaii's only true metropolis, its seat of government, center of commerce and shipping, entertainment and recreation mecca, a historic site, and an evolving urban area—conflicting roles that engender endless debate and controversy. For the visitor, Honolulu is an everyman's delight: hipsters and scholars, sightseers and foodies, nature lovers, and culture vultures all can find their bliss.

Once there was the broad bay of Mamala and the narrow inlet of Kou, fronting a dusty plain occupied by a few thatched houses and the great Pakaka *heiau* (shrine). Nosing into the narrow passage in 1794, British sea captain William Brown named the port Fair Haven. Later, Hawaiians would call it Honolulu, or "sheltered bay." As shipping traffic increased, the settlement grew into a Western-style town of streets and buildings, tightly clustered around the single freshwater source, Nuuanu Stream. Not until piped water became available in the early 1900s did Honolulu spread across the greening plain. Long before that, however, Honolulu gained importance when King Kamehameha I reluctantly abandoned his home on the Big Island to build a stately compound near the harbor in 1804 to better protect Hawaiian interests from the Western incursion.

Two hundred years later, the entire island is, in a sense, Honolulu—the City and County of Honolulu. The city has no official boundaries,

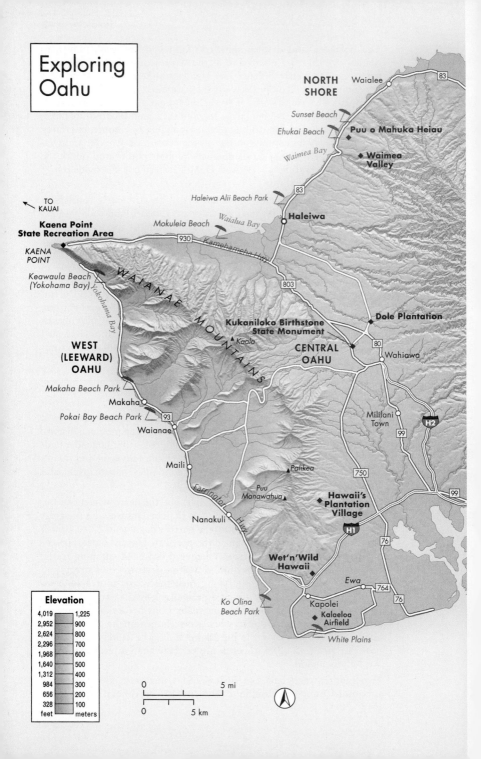

Exploring Oahu

NORTH SHORE

Waialee

83

Sunset Beach

Ehukai Beach

Puu o Mahuka Heiau

Waimea Bay

◆ **Waimea Valley**

← TO KAUAI

Haleiwa Alii Beach Park

Kaena Point State Recreation Area

KAENA POINT

Mokuleia Beach

Waialua Bay

930

Kamehameha Hwy

Haleiwa

83

Keawaula Beach (Yokohama Bay)

Yokohama Bay

803

Kukaniloko Birthstone State Monument

▲ *Kaala*

Dole Plantation ◆

80

Wahiawa

WEST (LEEWARD) OAHU

WAIANAE MOUNTAINS

CENTRAL OAHU

Makaha Beach Park

Makaha

Pokai Bay Beach Park

93

Mililani Town

H2

Waianae

99

Maili

▲ *Palikea*

750

Puu Manawahua ▲

Hawaii's Plantation Village ◆

99

Farrington Hwy

Nanakuli

H1

76

Wet'n'Wild Hawaii

Ewa

764

Ko Olina Beach Park

Kapolei

76

◆ **Kalaeloa Airfield**

White Plains

Elevation

feet	meters
4,019	1,225
2,952	900
2,624	800
2,296	700
1,968	600
1,640	500
1,312	400
984	300
656	200
328	100

0 — 5 mi

0 — 5 km

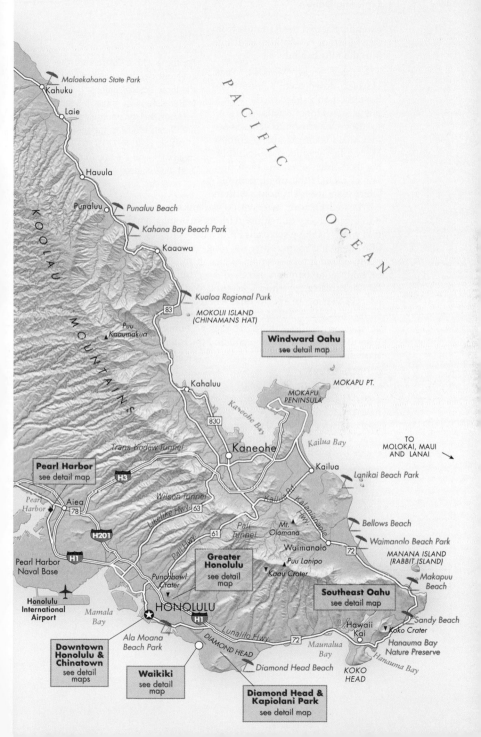

PACIFIC OCEAN

KOOLAU MOUNTAINS

Malaekahana State Park
Kahuku
Laie
Hauula
Punaluu · Punaluu Beach
Kahana Bay Beach Park
Kaaawa
Kualoa Regional Park
MOKOLII ISLAND
(CHINAMANS HAT)
83
Puu
Kaaumakua
Kahaluu

Windward Oahu
see detail map

MOKAPU PT.
MOKAPU
PENINSULA
Kaneohe Bay
830
Kaneohe
Kailua Bay
Kailua
Lanikai Beach Park

TO
MOLOKAI, MAUI
AND LANAI

Pearl Harbor
see detail map

H3
Trans-Kodaw Tunnel
Wilson Tunnel
Likelike Hwy
Aiea
78
Pearl
Harbor
H201
61
63
Kalii Rd
Kalanianaole Hwy
Mt.
Olomana
Pali
Tunnel
Bellows Beach
Waimanalo Beach Park
Waimanalo
72
MANANA ISLAND
(RABBIT ISLAND)
Puu Lanipo
Kaau Crater
H1
Pali Hwy
Pearl Harbor
Naval Base
Punchbowl
Crater

**Greater
Honolulu**
see detail map

Southeast Oahu
see detail map

Makapuu
Beach

Honolulu
International
Airport
Mamala
Bay
HONOLULU
H1
Ala Moana
Beach Park
Lunalilo Hwy
DIAMOND HEAD
72
Maunalua
Bay
Hawaii
Kai
Koko Crater
Sandy Beach
Hanauma Bay
Nature Preserve
Hanauma Bay
KOKO
HEAD

**Downtown
Honolulu &
Chinatown**
see detail
maps

Waikiki
see detail
map

Diamond Head Beach

**Diamond Head &
Kapiolani Park**
see detail map

extending across the flatlands from Pearl Harbor to Waikiki and high into the hills behind.

The main areas (Waikiki, Pearl Harbor, downtown, Chinatown) have the lion's share of the sights, but greater Honolulu also has a lot to offer. One reason to venture farther afield is the chance to glimpse Honolulu's residential neighborhoods. Species of classic Hawaiian homes include the tiny green-and-white plantation-era house with its

> ### CHEAP GAS
>
> For those with a Costco card, the cheapest gas on the island is at the three Costco stations. The one in Honolulu is on Arakawa Street, between Dillingham Boulevard and Nimitz Highway; the one in Waipio is at 94-1231 Ka Uka Boulevard, and the one in Kapolei is at 4589 Kapolei Parkway.

corrugated tin roof, two windows flanking a central door and small porch; the breezy bungalow with its swooping Thai-style roofline and two wings flanking screened French doors through which breezes blow into the living room. Note the tangled "Grandma-style" gardens and many *ohana* houses—small homes in the backyard of a larger home or built as apartments perched over the garage, allowing extended families to live together. Carports, which rarely house cars, are the island's version of rec rooms, where parties are held and neighbors sit to "talk story." Sometimes you see gallon jars on the flat roofs of garages or carports: these are pickled lemons fermenting in the sun. Also in the neighborhoods, you find the folksy restaurants and takeout spots favored by locals.

GUIDED TOURS

Guided tours are convenient; you don't have to worry about finding a parking spot or getting admission tickets. Most of the tour guides have taken special classes in Hawaiian history and lore, and many are certified by the state of Hawaii. On the other hand, you won't have the freedom to proceed at your own pace, nor will you have the ability to take a detour trip if something else catches your attention.

Polynesian Adventure. This company leads tours of Pearl Harbor and other Oahu sights and also offers a circle-island tour by motor coach, van, or mini-coach. ☎ *808/833–3000, 888/206–4531* ⊕ *www.polyad. com* ✉ *From $50.96.*

Discover Hawaii Tours. In addition to circle-island and other Oahu-based itineraries on motor and mini-coaches, this company can also get you from Waikiki to the lava flows of the Big Island or to Maui's Hana Highway and back in one day. ☎ *808/690–9050* ⊕ *www.discoverhawaiitours.com* ✉ *From $42.99.*

E Noa Tours. This outfitter's certified tour guides conduct circle-island, Pearl Harbor, and shopping tours. ☎ *808/591–2561, 800/824–8804* ⊕ *www.enoa.com* ✉ *From $29.*

WAIKIKI

Waikiki is approximately 3 miles east of downtown Honolulu.

A short drive from downtown Honolulu, Waikiki is Oahu's primary resort area. A mix of historic and modern hotels and condos front the sunny 2-mile stretch of beach, and many have clear views of Diamond Head. The area is home to much of the island's dining, nightlife, and shopping scene—from posh boutiques to hole-in-the-wall eateries to craft booths at the International Marketplace.

Waikiki was once a favorite retreat for Hawaiian royalty. In 1901 the Moana Hotel debuted, introducing Waikiki as an international travel destination. The region's fame continued to grow when Duke Kahanamoku helped popularize the sport of surfing, offering lessons to visitors at Waikiki. You can see Duke immortalized in a bronze statue, with a surfboard, on Kuhio Beach. Today there is a decidedly "urban resort" vibe here; streets are clean, gardens are manicured, and the sand feels softer than at beaches farther down the coast. There isn't much of a local culture—it's mainly tourist crowds—but you'll still find the relaxed surf-y vibe that has drawn people here for more than a century.

Kapiolani Park lies in the shadow of the Diamond Head crater, which is just beyond the easternmost limits of Waikiki. King David Kalakaua established the park in 1887, named it after his queen, and dedicated it "to the use and enjoyment of the people." Kapiolani Park is a 500-acre expanse where you can play all sorts of field sports, enjoy a picnic, see wild animals and tropical fish at the Honolulu Zoo and the Waikiki Aquarium, or hear live music at the Waikiki Shell or the Kapiolani Bandstand.

GETTING HERE AND AROUND

Bounded by the Ala Wai Canal on the north and west, the beach on the south, and the Honolulu Zoo to the east, Waikiki is compact and easy to walk around. TheBus runs multiple routes here from the airport and downtown Honolulu. By car, finding Waikiki from H1 can be tricky; look for the Punahou exit for the west end of Waikiki, and the King Street exit for the eastern end.

TOP ATTRACTIONS

FAMILY **Honolulu Zoo.** There are bigger and better zoos, but this one, though showing signs of neglect due to budget constraints, is a lush garden and has some great programs. To get a glimpse of the endangered *nene*, the Hawaii state bird, check out the zoo's Kipuka Nene Sanctuary. In fall 2017, the zoo welcomed new additions, with the birth of a baby sloth and seven critically endangered African wild dog puppies, and opened an ectotherm complex, which houses a Burmese python, elongated tortoises, and a giant African snail. Though many animals prefer to remain invisible—particularly the elusive big cats—the monkeys and elephants appear to enjoy being seen and are a hoot to watch. It's best to get to the zoo right when it opens, because the animals are livelier in the cool of the morning.

The Wildest Show in Town is a 10-week summer concert series. Or just head for the petting zoo, where kids can make friends with a llama or

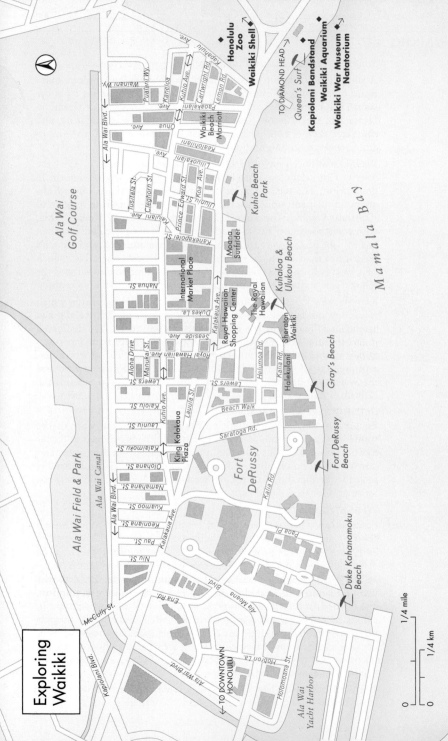

Exploring Waikiki

Honolulu Zoo
Waikiki Shell
Kapiolani Bandstand
Waikiki Aquarium
Waikiki War Museum Natatorium

Queen's Surf

TO DIAMOND HEAD

Mamala Bay

Kuhio Beach Park

Moana Surfrider

Kuhaloa & Ulukou Beach

The Royal Hawaiian

Sheraton Waikiki

Gray's Beach

Fort DeRussy Beach

Duke Kahanamoku Beach

Waikiki Beach Marriott

Royal Hawaiian Shopping Center

Halekulani

International Market Place

King Kalakaua Plaza

Fort DeRussy

Ala Wai Golf Course

Ala Wai Field & Park

Ala Wai Canal

Ala Wai Yacht Harbor

TO DOWNTOWN HONOLULU

Ala Wai Blvd.
Wainani Wy.
Pualani Wy.
Kaneloa
Kuhio Ave.
Cartwright Rd.
Lemon Rd.
Kapahulu Ave.
Ohua Ave.
Paokalani Ave.
Keaholani Ave.
Liliuokalani Ave.
Koa Ave.
Uluniu Ave.
Tusitala St.
Cleghorn St.
Prince Edward St.
Kaiulani Ave.
Kanekapolei St.
Nahua St.
Kalakaua Ave.
Dukes La.
Seaside Ave.
Aloha Drive
Manukai St.
Royal Hawaiian Ave.
Lewers St.
Lewers St.
Beach Walk
Saratoga Rd.
Kuhio Ave.
Kaiolu St.
Launiu St.
Lauula St.
Kalaimoku St.
Olohana St.
Namahana St.
Kuamoo St.
Keoniana St.
Pau St.
Niu St.
Kalakaua Ave.
Ala Wai Blvd.
Helumoa Rd.
Kalia Rd.
Kalia Rd.
Paoa Pl.
Ala Moana Blvd.
Ena Rd.
Hobron La.
Holomoana St.
McCully St.
Kapiolani Blvd.
Ala Wai Blvd.

1/4 mile
1/4 km
0
0

stand in the middle of a koi pond. There's an exceptionally good gift shop. On weekends, the Art on the Zoo Fence, on Monsarrat Avenue on the Diamond Head side outside the zoo, has affordable artwork by contemporary artists. Metered parking is available all along the *makai* (ocean) side of the park and in the lot next to the zoo—but it can fill up early. TheBus makes stops here along the way to and from Ala Moana Center and Sea Life Park (Routes 8 and 22). ⊠ *151 Kapahulu Ave., Waikiki* ☎ *808/971–7171* ⊕ *www.honoluluzoo.org* 🎟 *$19.*

FAMILY **Kapiolani Bandstand.** The Victorian-style Kapiolani Bandstand, which was originally built in the late 1890s, is Kapiolani Park's stage for community entertainment and concerts. Founded by King Kamehameha III in 1836, the Royal Hawaiian Band, today, the nation's only city-sponsored band, performs free concerts at the bandstand as well as at Iolani Palace and the center stage at Ala Moana Center. Visit the band's website for concert dates, and check event-listing websites and the *Honolulu Star-Advertiser*—Oahu's local newspaper—for event information at the bandstand. ⊠ *2805 Monsarrat Ave., Waikiki* ☎ *808/922–5331* ⊕ *www. rhb-music.com.*

FAMILY **Waikiki Aquarium.** This amazing little attraction harbors more than 3,500 organisms and 500 species of Hawaiian and South Pacific marine life, including endangered Hawaiian monk seals and sharks. *The Edge of the Reef* exhibit showcases five different types of reef environments found along Hawaii's shorelines. Check out exhibits on endangered green sea turtles, the Northwestern Hawaiian Islands (which explains the formation of the island chain), and jellyfish. A 60-foot exhibit houses sea horses, sea dragons, and pipefish. A self-guided audio tour is included with admission. The aquarium offers activities of interest to adults and children alike, including the Aquarium After Dark program, when visitors grab a flashlight and view fish going about their rarely observable nocturnal activities. ⊠ *2777 Kalakaua Ave., Waikiki* ☎ *808/923–9741* ⊕ *www.waikikiaquarium.org* 🎟 *$12.*

WORTH NOTING

Waikiki Shell. Grab one of the 6,000 "grass seats" (i.e., a spot on the lawn) for music under the stars (there are actual seats, as well). An eclectic array of musical acts put on concerts at this landmark venue throughout the summer and occasionally during the winter, weather permitting. Check local event-listing websites and newspaper entertainment sections to see who is performing. ⊠ *2805 Monsarrat Ave., Waikiki* ☎ *808/768–5400* ⊕ *www.blaisdellcenter.com/venues/waikiki-shell/.*

Waikiki War Memorial Natatorium. This Beaux-Arts-style, 1927 World War I monument, dedicated to the 101 Hawaiian servicemen who lost their lives in battle, stands proudly in Waikiki. The 100-meter saltwater swimming pool, the training spot for Olympians Johnny Weissmuller and Buster Crabbe and the U.S. Army during World War II, has been closed for decades, as the pool needs repair. Plans are under study to tear down the natatorium, though a nonprofit group continues fighting to save the facility. The site is closed to visitors, but you can stop by and look at it from the outside. ⊠ *2777 Kalakaua Ave., Waikiki* ⊕ *natatorium.org.*

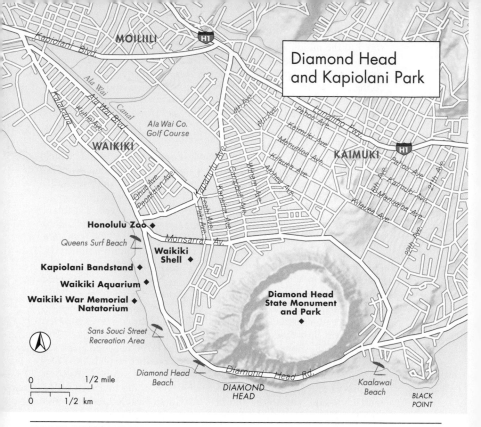

Ala Wai Co.
Golf Course

MOILILI

WAIKIKI

KAIMUKI

Honolulu Zoo ◆

Queens Surf Beach

Waikiki Shell ◆

Kapiolani Bandstand ◆

Waikiki Aquarium ◆

Waikiki War Memorial ◆
Natatorium

Sans Souci Street
Recreation Area

Monsarrat Av.

Diamond Head
State Monument
and Park
◆

Diamond Head Rd.

0 ___ 1/2 mile
0 ___ 1/2 km

Diamond Head
Beach

DIAMOND
HEAD

Kaalawai
Beach

BLACK
POINT

DIAMOND HEAD

Besides hiking Diamond Head, visitors will enjoy the eclectic shops and restaurants along Monsarrat Avenue like Diamond Head Market & Grill. Don't forget the amazing *poke* (seasoned raw fish) and other local goodies at Fort Ruger Market, and the Saturday farmers' market at Kapiolani Community College is arguably the best on the island.

Diamond Head State Monument and Park. Panoramas from this 760-foot extinct volcanic peak, once used as a military fortification, extend from Waikiki and Honolulu in one direction and out to Koko Head in the other, with surfers and windsurfers scattered like confetti on the cresting waves below. This 360-degree perspective is a great orientation for first-time visitors. On a clear day, look east past Koko Head to glimpse the outlines of the islands of Maui and Molokai.

To enter the park from Waikiki, take Kalakaua Avenue east, turn left at Monsarrat Avenue, head a mile up the hill, and look for a sign on the right. Drive through the tunnel to the inside of the crater. The ¾-mile trail to the top begins at the parking lot. Be aware that the hike to the crater is an upward ascent with numerous stairs to climb; if you aren't in the habit of getting occasional exercise, this might not be for you. At the top, you'll find a somewhat awkward scramble through a tunnel and bunker out into the open air, but the view is worth it.

Take bottled water with you to stay hydrated under the tropical sun. ■**TIP→ To beat the heat and the crowds, rise early and make the hike before 8 am.** As you walk, note the color of the vegetation; if the mountain is brown, Honolulu has been without significant rain for a while; but if the trees and undergrowth glow green, you'll know it's the wet season (winter) without looking at a calendar. This is when rare Hawaiian marsh plants revive on the floor of the crater. Keep an eye on your watch if you're here at day's end: the gates close promptly at 6 pm. ✉ *Diamond Head Rd. at 18th Ave., Diamond Head* ☎ *808/587–0300* ⊕ *dlnr.hawaii.gov/dsp/parks/oahu/diamond-head-state-monument* 🎫 *$1 per person, $5 per vehicle (cash only).*

PEARL HARBOR

Pearl Harbor is approximately 9 miles west of downtown Honolulu, beyond Honolulu International Airport.

December 7, 1941. Every American then alive recalls exactly what he or she was doing when the news broke that the Japanese had bombed Pearl Harbor, the catalyst that brought the United States into World War II. Those who are younger have learned about the events of the fateful day, when more than 2,000 people died, and a dozen ships were sunk. Here, in what is still a key Pacific naval base, the attack is remembered every day by thousands of visitors. In recent years, the memorial has been the site of reconciliation ceremonies involving Pearl Harbor veterans from both sides. There are five distinct sights in Pearl Harbor, but only two are part of World War II Valor in the Pacific National Monument. The others are privately operated. It's possible to make reservations for the national park sites at ⊕ *www.recreation.gov.*

Fodor's Choice ★ **Battleship Missouri Memorial.** Together with the *Arizona* Memorial, the USS *Missouri*'s presence in Pearl Harbor perfectly bookends America's World War II experience, which began December 7, 1941, and ended on the "Mighty Mo's" starboard deck with the signing of the Terms of Surrender. In 2017 the battleship underwent a $3.5-million renovation (now complete) to replace rusted steel and repaint its upper decks. It's the biggest preservation effort to the *Missouri* since it was drydocked in 2009 for a $15.5-million top-to-bottom paint job. To begin your visit, pick up tickets online or at the Pearl Harbor Visitor Center. Then board a shuttle bus for the eight-minute ride to Ford Island and the teak decks and towering superstructure of the last battleship ever built. Join a free, guided tour to learn more about the *Missouri*'s long and dramatic history. For history buffs, the Heart of the *Missouri* tour (for an additional $25) provides an up-close look into the battleship's engineering spaces, including access to its engine rooms, gun turret, damage control station, and aft battery plot room.

The *Missouri* is 887 feet long, 209 feet tall, with nine 116-ton guns, capable of firing up to 23 miles. Absorb these numbers during the tour, then stop to take advantage of the view from the decks. Near the entrance are a gift shop and a lunch wagon serving hamburgers and hot dogs. ✉ *Pearl Harbor, 63 Cowpens St., Pearl Harbor* ⚓ *You cannot drive directly to the USS Missouri; you must take a shuttle bus from the Pearl Harbor Visitor Center* ☎ *808/455–1600* ⊕ *www.ussmissouri.org* 🎫 *From $29.*

Pacific Aviation Museum. This museum opened on December 7, 2006, as a tribute to aviation in the Pacific. Located on Ford Island in Hangars 37 and 79, actual seaplane hangars that survived the Pearl Harbor attack, the museum is made up of a theater where a short film on Pearl Harbor kicks off the tour, an education center, a shop, and a restaurant. Exhibits—many of which are interactive and involve sound effects—include an authentic Japanese Zero in a diorama setting, vintage aircraft, and the chance to play the role of a World War II pilot using one of six flight simulators. Various aircraft are employed to narrate the great battles: the Doolittle Raid on Japan, the Battle of Midway, Guadalcanal, and so on. The actual Stearman N2S-3 in which President George H. W. Bush soloed is housed in Hangar 79. Purchase tickets at the Pearl Harbor Visitor Center or at the museum itself after you get off the shuttle bus. ⊠ *Ford Island, 319 Lexington Blvd., Pearl Harbor* ⊹ *You cannot drive directly to the museum; you must take a shuttle bus to Ford Island from the Pearl Harbor Visitor Center* ☎ *808/441–1000* ⊕ *www.pacificaviationmuseum.org* ⊠ *$25.*

FodorśChoice   **Pearl Harbor Visitor Center.** The Pearl Harbor Visitor Center reopened
★   after a $58-million renovation and is now the gateway to the World War II Valor in the Pacific National Monument and the starting point for visitors to this historic site. At the visitor center are interpretive exhibits in two separate galleries (*Road to War* and *Attack*) that feature photographs and personal memorabilia from World War II veterans. But there are other exhibits, a bookstore, and a Remembrance Circle, where you can learn about the people who lost their lives on December 7, 1941. Survivors are often on hand to give their personal accounts and answer questions. The visitor center is also where you start your tour of the USS *Arizona* Memorial if you have secured a walk-in or reserved a timed ticket (reserve at ⊕ *www.recreation.gov)* ⊠ *World War II Valor in the Pacific National Monument, 1 Arizona Memorial Pl., Pearl Harbor* ☎ *808/422–3399, 877/444–6777 Timed Ticket Reservations* ⊕ *www. nps.gov/valr* ⊠ *Free (timed-entry tickets $1.50).*

USS Arizona Memorial. Lined up tight in a row of seven battleships off Ford Island, the USS *Arizona* took a direct hit on December 7, 1941, exploded, and rests still on the shallow bottom where she settled. A visit to what is now known as the World War II Valor in the Pacific National Monument, begins prosaically—a line, a wait filled with shopping, visiting the museum, and strolling the grounds (though you can reserve timed tickets online at ⊕ *www.recreation.gov* and skip the wait). When your tour starts, you watch a short documentary film, then board the ferry to the memorial. The swooping, stark-white memorial, which straddles the wreck of the USS *Arizona,* was designed by Honolulu architect Alfred Preis to represent both the depths of the low-spirited, early days of the war, and the uplift of victory. A somber, contemplative mood descends upon visitors during the ferry ride; this is a place where 1,777 people died. Gaze at the names of the dead carved into the wall of white marble. Look at oil on the water's surface, still slowly escaping from the sunken ship. Scatter flowers (but no lei—the string is bad for the fish). Salute the flag. Remember Pearl Harbor. ⊠ *World War II Valor in the Pacific National Monument, Pearl Harbor* ☎ *808/422–3300,*

Continued on page 59

USS *West Virginia* (BB48), 7 December 1941

PEARL HARBOR

December 7, 1941. Every American then alive recalls exactly what he or she was doing when the news broke that the Japanese had bombed Pearl Harbor, the catalyst that brought the United States into World War II.

Although it was clear by late 1941 that war with Japan was inevitable, no one in authority seems to have expected the attack to come in just this way, at just this time. So when the Japanese bombers swept through a gap in Oahu's Koolau Mountains in the hazy light of morning, they found the bulk of America's Pacific fleet right where they hoped it would be: docked like giant stepping stones across the calm waters of the bay named for the pearl oysters that once prospered there. More than 2,000 people died that day, including 49 civilians. A dozen ships were sunk.

And on the nearby air bases, virtually every American military aircraft was destroyed or damaged. The attack was a stunning success, but it lit a fire under America, which went to war with "Remember Pearl Harbor" as its battle cry. Here, in what is still a key Pacific naval base, the attack is remembered every day by thousands of visitors, including many curious Japanese, who for years heard little World War II history in their own country. In recent years, the memorial has been the site of reconciliation ceremonies involving Pearl Harbor veterans from both sides.

GETTING AROUND

Pearl Harbor is both a working military base and the most-visited Oahu attraction. Four distinct destinations share a parking lot and are linked by footpath, shuttle, and ferry.

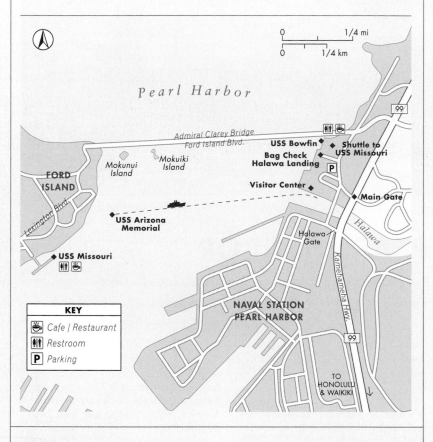

The visitor center is accessible from the parking lot. The USS *Arizona* Memorial itself is in the middle of the harbor; get tickets for the ferry ride at the visitor center. The USS *Bowfin* is also reachable from the parking lot.

The USS *Missouri* is docked at Ford Island, a restricted area of the naval base. Vehicular access is prohibited. To get there, take a shuttle bus from the station near the *Bowfin*.

ARIZONA MEMORIAL

Snugged up tight in a row of seven battleships off Ford Island, the USS *Arizona* took a direct hit that December morning, exploded, and rests still on the shallow bottom where she settled.

The swooping, stark-white memorial, which straddles the wreck of the USS *Arizona*, was designed to represent both the depths of the low-spirited, early days of the war, and the uplift of victory.

A visit here begins at the Pearl Harbor Visitor Center, which recently underwent a $58 million renovation. High definition projectors and interactive exhibits were installed, and the building was modernized. From the visitor center, a ferry takes you to the memorial itself, and a new shuttle hub now gives access to sites that were previously inaccessible, like the USS *Utah* and USS *Oklahoma*.

A somber, contemplative mood descends upon visitors during the ferry ride to the *Arizona*; this is a place where 1,177 crewmen lost their lives. Gaze at the names of the dead carved into the wall of white marble. Scatter flowers (but no lei—the string is bad for the fish). Salute the flag. Remember Pearl Harbor.

☎ *808/422–0561*
⊕ *www.nps.gov/valr*

USS *MISSOURI* (BB63)

Together with the *Arizona* Memorial, the *Missouri's* presence in Pearl Harbor perfectly bookends America's WWII experience that began December 7, 1941, and ended on the "Mighty Mo's" starboard deck with the signing of the Terms of Surrender.

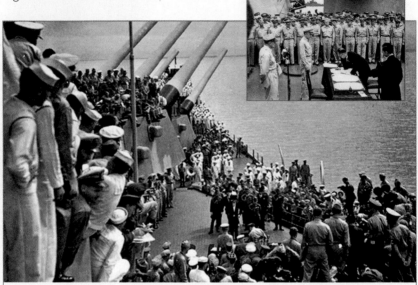

Surrender of Japan, USS *Missouri*, 2 September 1945

In the parking area behind the USS *Bowfin* Museum, board a shuttle for an eight-minute ride to Ford Island and the teak decks and towering superstructure of the *Missouri*. The last battleship ever built, the *Missouri* famously hosted the final act of WWII, the signing of the Terms of Surrender. The commission that governs this floating museum has surrounded her with buildings tricked out in WWII style with quonset huts serving as shaded eating areas for the nearby lunch wagon and a Victory Store housing a souvenir shop and covered with period mottos ("Don't be a blabateur").
■ **TIP→ Definitely hook up with a tour guide (no additional charge) or audio tour—these add a great deal to the experience.**

The *Missouri* is all about numbers: 209 feet tall, six 239,000-pound guns, capable of firing up to 23 miles away. Absorb these during the tour, then stop to take advantage of the view from the decks. The Mo is a work in progress, with only a handful of her hundreds of spaces open to view.
☎ *808/423–2263* or ☎ *888/877–6477*
⊕ *www.ussmissouri.com*

USS *BOWFIN* (SS287)

SUBMARINE MUSEUM & PARK

Launched one year to the day after the Pearl Harbor attack, the USS *Bowfin* sank 44 enemy ships during WWII and now serves as the centerpiece of a museum honoring all submariners.

Although the *Bowfin* no less than the *Arizona* Memorial commemorates the lost, the mood here is lighter. Perhaps it's the childlike scale of the boat, a metal tube just 16 feet in diameter, packed with ladders, hatches, and other obstacles, like the naval version of a jungle gym. Perhaps it's the World War II-era music that plays in the covered patio. Or it might be the museum's touching displays—the penciled sailor's journal, the Vargas girlie posters. Aboard the boat nicknamed "Pearl Harbor Avenger," compartments are fitted out as though "Sparky" was away from the radio room just for a moment, and "Cooky" might be right back to his pots and pans. The museum includes many artifacts to spark family conversations, among them a vintage dive suit that looks too big for Shaquille O'Neal. A caution: The *Bowfin* could be hazardous for very young children; no one under four allowed.

☎ *808/423-1341*
⊕ *www.bowfin.org*

PACIFIC AVIATION MUSEUM PEARL HARBOR

This museum opened on December 7, 2006, as as a tribute to aviation in the Pacific. Located on Ford Island in Hangars 37 and 79, actual seaplane hangars that survived the Pearl Harbor attack, the museum is made up of a theater where a short film on Pearl Harbor kicks off the tour, an education center, a shop, and a restaurant. Exhibits—many of which are interactive and involve sound effects—include an authentic Japanese Zero in a diorama setting, vintage aircraft, and the chance to play the role of a World War II pilot using one of six flight simulators. Various aircrafts are employed to narrate the great battles: the Doolittle Raid on Japan, the Battle of Midway, Guadalcanal, and so on. The actual Stearman N2S-3 in which President George H. W. Bush soloed is housed in Hangar 79. ☎ 808/441-1000 ⊕ www.pacificaviationmuseum.org ✉ $35; an aviator led tour is available for $10.

PLAN YOUR PEARL HARBOR DAY LIKE A MILITARY CAMPAIGN

DIRECTIONS

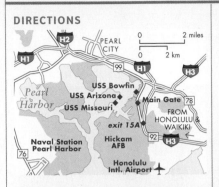

Take H–1 west from Waikiki to Exit 15A and follow signs. Or take The-Bus route 20 or 47 from Waikiki. Beware high-priced private shuttles. It's a 30-minute drive from Waikiki.

WHAT TO BRING

Picture ID is required during periods of high alert; bring it just in case.

You'll be standing, walking, and climbing all day. Wear something with lots of pockets and a pair of good walking shoes. Carry a light jacket, sunglasses, hat, and sunscreen.

No purses, packs, or bags are allowed. Take only what fits in your pockets. Cameras are okay but without the bags. A private bag storage booth is located in the parking lot near the visitors' center. Leave nothing in your car; theft is a problem despite bicycle security patrols.

HOURS

Hours are 7 am to 5 pm for the visitor center, though the attractions open at 8 am. The *Arizona* Memorial starts giving out tickets on a first-come, first-served basis at 7 am; the last tickets are given out at 3 pm. Spring break, summer, and holidays are busiest, and tickets sometimes run out by noon or earlier.

TICKETS

Arizona: Free. Add $7.50 for museum audio tours.

Aviation: $35 adults, $22 children. Add $10 for aviator's guided tour.

Missouri: $25 adults, $13 children. Add $25 for in-depth, behind-the-scenes tours.

Bowfin: $12 adults, $5 children. Children under 4 may go into the museum but not aboard the *Bowfin*.

KIDS

This might be the day to enroll younger kids in the hotel children's program. Preschoolers chafe at long waits, and attractions involve some hazards for toddlers. Older kids enjoy the *Bowfin* and *Missouri*, especially.

MAKING THE MOST OF YOUR TIME

Expect to spend at least half a day; a whole day is better if you're a military history buff.

At the *Arizona* Memorial, you'll get a ticket, be given a tour time, and then have to wait anywhere from 15 minutes to 3 hours. You must pick up your own ticket so you can't hold places. If the wait is long, skip over to the *Bowfin* to fill the time.

SUGGESTED READING

Pearl Harbor and the USS Arizona Memorial, by Richard Wisniewski. $5.95. 64-page magazine-size quick history.

Bowfin, by Edwin P. Hoyt. $14.95. Dramatic story of undersea adventure.

The Last Battleship, by Scott C. S. Stone. $11.95. Story of the Mighty Mo.

If you're a snorkeler, head straight for Hanauma Bay, the best and most popular place to snorkel on Oahu.

877/444–6777 Timed Ticket Reservations ⊕ www.nps.gov/valr ✉ Free (timed-entry tickets $1.50); museum audio tours $7.50. Arrive early for limited same-day tickets.

USS *Bowfin* Submarine Museum and Park. Launched one year to the day after the Pearl Harbor attack, the USS *Bowfin* claimed to have sunk 44 enemy ships during World War II and now serves as the centerpiece of a museum honoring all submariners. Although the *Bowfin* no less than the *Arizona* Memorial commemorates the lost, the mood here is lighter. Perhaps it's the childlike scale of the boat, a metal tube just 16 feet in diameter, packed with ladders, hatches, and other obstacles, like the naval version of a jungle gym. Perhaps it's the World War II–era music that plays in the covered patio, or it might be the museum's touching displays—the penciled sailor's journal, the Vargas girlie posters. Aboard the boat nicknamed "Pearl Harbor Avenger," compartments are fitted out as though "Sparky" was away from the radio room just for a moment, and "Cooky" might be right back to his pots and pans. The museum includes many artifacts to spark family conversations, among them a vintage dive suit that looks too big for Shaquille O'Neal. A guided audio tour is included with admission. The *Bowfin* could be hazardous for very young children; no one under four is allowed on the submarine, though children can visit the museum. ✉ *11 Arizona Memorial Place, Pearl Harbor ☎ 808/423–1341 ⊕ www.bowfin.org ✉ $15 to tour the submarine and museum; $6 to visit the museum only.*

World War II Valor in the Pacific National Monument. Two sights associated with the devastating Japanese attack on Pearl Harbor on December 7, 1941, are part of this national monument, which also tells the story of the internment of Japanese Americans, battles in the Aleutian Islands, and the occupation of Japan after World War II. The location, Pearl Harbor, is still a working military base as well as the most-visited sight in Oahu. Five distinct destinations are on the base: the visitor center and the USS *Arizona* Memorial, which are part of the national monument, as well as the USS *Bowfin,* the USS *Missouri,* and the Pacific Aviation Museum, all of which are privately operated. You can walk to the visitor center or the USS *Bowfin* from the parking lot, but the USS *Arizona* Memorial requires a ferry ride, and access to the USS *Missouri* and Pacific Aviation Museum require a shuttle bus. If you have not reserved tickets in advance (⊕ *www.recreation.gov*), all members of your party must be present; regardless, you'll need proper government-issued ID to gain access to the base. Timed-entry tickets (more than 1,300 daily) for the USS *Arizona* Memorial are available on a first-come-first-served basis starting at 7 am daily. No bags of any kind are allowed at any of the sights (except for the visitor center)—not even small purses—but cameras, cell phones, and wallets can be hand-carried. A bag check is available for $4 at the visitor center. Children under four are not allowed on the USS *Bowfin.* ⊠ *Pearl Harbor Visitor Center, 1 Arizona Memorial Place, Pearl Harbor* ☎ *808/422–3399, 877/444–6777 Timed Ticket Reservations* ⊕ *www.nps.gov/valr* ⊠ *Visitor center and USS Arizona Memorial free; advance tickets $1.50.*

DOWNTOWN HONOLULU

Honolulu's past and present play a delightful counterpoint throughout the downtown area, which is approximately 6 miles east of Honolulu International Airport. Postmodern glass-and-steel office buildings look down on the Aloha Tower, built in 1926 and, until the early 1960s, the tallest structure in Honolulu. Hawaii's history is told in the architecture of these few blocks: the cut-stone turn-of-the-20th-century storefronts of Merchant Street, the gracious white-columned American-Georgian manor that was the home of the Islands' last queen, the jewel-box palace occupied by the monarchy before it was overthrown, the Spanish-inspired stucco and tile-roofed Territorial Era government buildings, and the 21st-century glass pyramid of the First Hawaiian Bank Building.

GETTING HERE AND AROUND

To reach downtown Honolulu from Waikiki by car, take Ala Moana Boulevard to Alakea Street and turn right; three blocks up on the right, between South King and Hotel streets, there's a municipal parking lot in Alii Place on the right. There are also public parking lots in buildings along Alakea, Smith, Beretania, and Bethel streets (Chinatown Gateway on Bethel Street is a good choice). The best parking downtown, however, is metered street parking along Punchbowl Street—when you can find it.

Another option is to take Route 20 or 42 of highly popular and convenient TheBus to the Aloha Tower Marketplace, or take a trolley from Waikiki.

Take a guided tour of Iolani Palace, America's only royal residence, built in 1882.

TOURS

American Institute of Architects (AIA) Honolulu Walking Tour. Join an AIA tour to see downtown Honolulu from an architectural perspective, including the restored Hawaii Theatre, city seat Honolulu Hale, Iolani Palace, Kawaiahao Church, and the open-air state capitol. Tours are led by AIA Honolulu members and architects and are offered on the second and fourth Saturday of each month. Advance reservations are required. AIA also offers a companion tour booklet for an additional $5 with the tour, $10 without. ⊠ *Honolulu* ☎ *808/628–7243* ⊕ *www. aiahonolulu.org* ✉ *$15.*

TOP ATTRACTIONS

Fodor's Choice
★

Iolani Palace. America's only official royal residence was built in 1882 on the site of an earlier palace. It contains the thrones of King Kalakaua and his successor (and sister) Queen Liliuokalani. Bucking the stereotype of simple island life, the palace had electric lights even before the White House. Downstairs galleries showcase the royal jewelry, and a kitchen and offices restored to the glory of the monarchy. The palace is open for guided tours or self-guided audio tours, and reservations are recommended. ■ **TIP→ If you're set on taking a guided tour, call or book online for reservations a few days in advance.** Tours are available only in the mornings and are limited. The palace gift shop and ticket office was formerly the Iolani Barracks, built to house the Royal Guard. ⊠ *364 South King St., Downtown* ☎ *808/522–0832* ⊕ *www. iolanipalace.org* ✉ *$21.75 guided tour, $14.75 audio tour, $5 downstairs galleries only* ☉ *Closed Sun. (except for monthly Kamaaina Sun.).*

Kamehameha I Statue. Paying tribute to the Big Island chieftain who united all the warring Hawaiian Islands into one kingdom at the turn of the 18th century, this statue, which stands with one arm outstretched in welcome, is one of three originally cast in Paris by American sculptor T. R. Gould. The original statue, lost at sea and replaced by this one, was eventually salvaged and is now in Kapaau, on the Big Island, near the king's birthplace. Each year on the king's birthday (June 11), the more famous copy is draped in fresh lei that reach lengths of 18 feet and longer. A parade proceeds past the statue, and Hawaiian civic clubs, women in hats and impressive long *holoku* dresses, and men in sashes and cummerbunds, pay honor to the leader whose name means "The One Set Apart." ⊠ *417 S. King St., outside Aliiolani Hale, Downtown.*

Kawaiahao Church. Fancifully called Hawaii's Westminster Abbey, this historic house of worship witnessed the coronations, weddings, and funerals of generations of Hawaiian royalty. Each of the building's 14,000 coral blocks was quarried from reefs offshore at depths of more than 20 feet and transported to this site. Interior woodwork was created from the forests of the Koolau Mountains. The upper gallery has an exhibit of paintings of the royal families. The graves of missionaries and of King Lunalilo are adjacent. Services in English, with songs and prayers in Hawaiian, are held each Sunday, and the church members are exceptionally welcoming, greeting newcomers with lei; their affiliation is United Church of Christ. Although there are no guided tours, you can look around the church at no cost. ⊠ *957 Punchbowl St., at King St., Downtown* ☎ *808/469–3000* ⊕ *www.kawaiahao.org* ☜ *Free.*

WORTH NOTING

Aloha Tower Marketplace. In fall 2015, the 89-year-old Aloha Tower, opened in 1926, became the new home to Hawaii Pacific University students. The Aloha Tower Marketplace now houses students in the Waterfront Loft residences on the second floor, as well as learning facilities. Most marketplace businesses that are open or slated to open are geared for the university crowd. But you can still get a bird's-eye view of this working harbor by taking a free ride up to the observation deck of Aloha Tower. In its day, the tower lighthouse could be seen from 15 miles at sea. Cruise ships usually dock at Piers 10 and 11 alongside the marketplace. ⊠ *1 Aloha Tower Dr., Downtown* ✛ *At Piers 10 and 11* ⊕ *www.alohatower.com.*

■ QUICK BITES

Murphy's Bar & Grill. In a vintage brick building at the corner of Nuuanu Street and Merchant, Murphy's Bar & Grill is an old-fashioned Irish pub, sports bar, and *kamaaina*-style (i.e., local) family restaurant. Comfort food is the order of the day, and the friendly bartenders happily handle the weekend bar crowd. ⊠ *2 Merchant St., Downtown* ☎ *808/531–0422* ⊕ *www.murphyshawaii.com.*

Hawaiian Mission Houses Historic Site and Archives. The determined Hawaii missionaries arrived in 1820, gaining royal favor and influencing a wide array of island life. Their descendants became leaders in government, business, and education. At Hawaiian Mission Houses Historic Site and Archives (previously Mission Houses Museum), you can

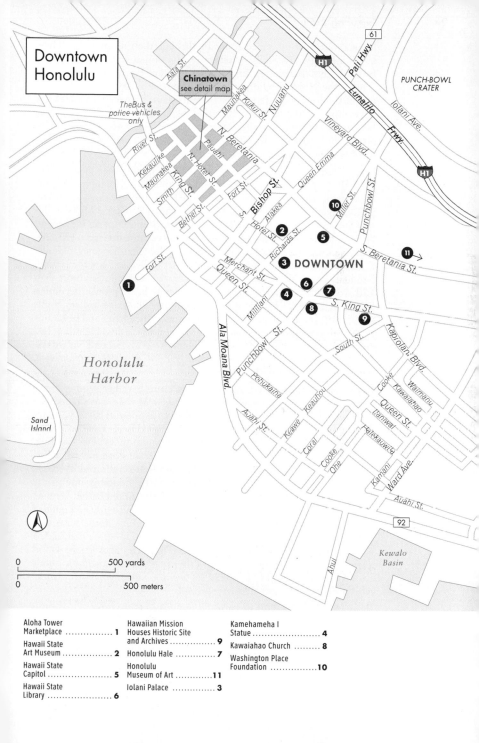

Downtown Honolulu

Chinatown
see detail map

PUNCH-BOWL CRATER

61

H1

Pali Hwy.

Lunalilo Hwy.

Iolani Ave.

H1

Aala St.

TheBus & police vehicles only

Maunakea

Kukui St.

Nuuanu

Vineyard Blvd.

River St.

N. Beretania

Pauahi

Queen Emma

Kekaulike

N. Hotel St.

Maunakea

King St.

Smith

Fort St.

Bethel St.

Fort St.

Bishop St.

Alakea

Miller St.

Punchbowl St.

Hotel St.

Richards St.

S. Beretania St.

Fort St.

❷

❺

❿

⓫

Merchant St.

Queen St.

❸ **DOWNTOWN**

❻

❼

Ala Moana Blvd.

Mililani

❹

❽

S. King St.

❾

Honolulu Harbor

Punchbowl St.

South St.

Kapiolani Blvd.

Waimanu

Pohukaina

Keauhou

Cooke

Kawaiahao

Sand Island

Auahi St.

Kawe

Coral

Kamani

Queen St.

Ilaniwai

Honokauwila

Ward Ave.

Cooke

One

Ahui

Auahi St.

92

Kewalo Basin

0 ⟶ 500 yards

0 ⟶ 500 meters

learn about their influence and walk through their original dwellings, including Hawaii's oldest Western-style wooden structure, a white-frame house that was prefabricated in New England and shipped around the Horn. Certain areas of the museum may be seen only on one of the hourly guided tours. Docents paint an excellent picture of what mission life was like. Rotating displays showcase such arts as Hawaiian quilting, portraits, even toys, and a rich archival library is also open to the public. ⊠ *553 S. King St., Downtown* ☎ *808/447–3910* ⊕ *www.missionhouses.org* ⊠ *$10.*

Hawaii State Art Museum. Hawaii was the first state in the nation to legislate that a portion of the taxes paid on commercial building projects be set aside for the purchase of artwork. The state purchased an ornate period-style building (that once was the Armed Services YMCA Building) and in 2002 opened a 12,000-square-foot museum on the second floor dedicated to the art of Hawaii in all its ethnic diversity. HiSAM, as it's nicknamed, has a **Diamond Head Gallery** featuring new acquisitions and thematic shows from the State Art Collection and the Hawaii Foundation on Culture and the Arts. The **Ewa Gallery** houses more than 150 works documenting Hawaii's visual-arts history since becoming a state in 1959. Also included are an outdoor sculpture gallery, a gift shop, a café, and educational meeting rooms. All galleries and programs at the museum are free. Check for free monthly events including live entertainment on First Fridays, and family-friendly Second Saturdays. ⊠ *250 S. Hotel St., 2nd fl., Downtown* ☎ *808/586–0300* ⊕ *www.sfca. hawaii.gov* ⊠ *Free* ☉ *Closed Sun.–Mon.*

Hawaii State Capitol. The capitol's architecture is richly symbolic: the columns resemble palm trees, the legislative chambers are shaped like volcanic cinder cones, and the central court is open to the sky, representing Hawaii's open society. Replicas of the Hawaii state seal, each weighing 7,500 pounds, hang above both its entrances. The building, which in 1969 replaced Iolani Palace as the seat of government, is surrounded by reflecting pools, just as the Islands are embraced by water. A pair of statues, often draped in lei, flank the building: one of the beloved Queen Liliuokalani and the other of the sainted Father Damien de Veuster, famous for helping Molokai leprosy patients. Free guided tours are offered every Wednesday from May to June. Otherwise, self-guided tours are available year-round when the building is open. ⊠ *415 S. Beretania St., Downtown* ⚜ *For guided tours, meet at Room 415 at 1 pm on the fourth floor. Self-guided tour booklets are available online or at Room 415.* ☎ *808/586–0221* ⊕ *governor.hawaii.gov/hawaii-state-capitol-tours* ⊠ *Free* ☉ *Closed weekends.*

Hawaii State Library. This beautifully renovated main library was built in 1913. Its Samuel Manaiakalani Kamakau Room, on the first floor in the *mauka* (Hawaiian for "mountain") courtyard, houses an extensive Hawaii and Pacific book collection and pays tribute to Kamakau, a missionary student whose 19th-century writings in English offer rare and vital insight into traditional Hawaiian culture. ⊠ *478 S. King St., Downtown* ☎ *808/586–3500* ⊕ *www.librarieshawaii.org* ⊠ *Free* ☉ *Closed Sun.*

Shangri La

The marriage of heiress Doris Duke to a much older man when she was 23 didn't last. But their around-the-world honeymoon did leave her with two lasting loves: Islamic art and architecture, which she first encountered on that journey; and Hawaii, where the honeymooners made an extended stay while Doris learned to surf and befriended islanders unimpressed by her wealth.

Today visitors to her beloved Oahu home—where she spent most winters—can share both loves by touring her estate. The sought-after tours, which are coordinated by and begin at the Honolulu Museum of Art in downtown Honolulu, start with a visit to the Arts of the Islamic World Gallery. A short van ride then takes small groups on to the house itself, on the far side of Diamond Head. *For more information, see the listing in Southeast Oahu.*

Honolulu Hale. This Mediterranean Renaissance–style building was constructed in 1929 and serves as the center of government for the City and County of Honolulu. Stroll through the shady, open-ceiling lobby with exhibits of local artists. During the winter holiday season, the Hale becomes the focal point for the annual Honolulu City Lights, a display of lighting and playful holiday scenes spread around the campus, including the famous, gigantic Shaka Santa and Tute Mele. The mayor's office keeps a calendar of upcoming events. ⊠ *530 S. King St., Downtown* ☎ *808/768–4385 for general city info* ⊕ *www.honolulu. gov/visitors* ⊠ *Free* ⊘ *Closed weekends.*

Fodor's Choice
★

Honolulu Museum of Art. Originally built around the collection of a Honolulu matron who donated much of her estate to the museum, the academy is housed in a maze of courtyards, cloistered walkways, and quiet, low-ceiling spaces. There's an impressive permanent collection that includes the third-largest collection of Hiroshige's *ukiyo-e* Japanese prints in the country (donated by James Michener); Italian Renaissance paintings; and American and European art by Monet, van Gogh, and Whistler, among many others. The newer Luce Pavilion complex, nicely incorporated into the more traditional architecture of the place, has a traveling-exhibit gallery, a Hawaiian gallery, an excellent café, and a gift shop. The Doris Duke Theatre screens art films. This is also the jumping-off point for tours of Doris Duke's estate, Shangri La. Admission here includes same-day entry to Spalding House, formerly the Contemporary Museum. ⊠ *900 S. Beretania St., Downtown* ☎ *808/532–8700* ⊕ *www.honolulumuseum.org* ⊠ *$20 (free 1st Wed. and 3rd Sun. of the month)* ⊘ *Closed Mon.*

Washington Place Foundation. For many years the home of Hawaii's governors, this white-column mansion was built by sea captain John Dominis, whose son married Liliuokalani, the woman who became the Islands' last queen. Deposed by American-backed forces, the queen returned to the home—which is in sight of the royal palace—and lived there until her death. It was then home to Hawaii's sitting governors from 1922 to 2002. The nonprofit Washington Place Foundation now operates the gracious estate. In 2013 it underwent a major renovation to repair the building's roof and its lanai. It is now open for public tours on Thursday only (required reservations can be made by phone or online). ✉ *320 S. Beretania St., Downtown* ☎ *808/586–0248 for tour reservations* ⊕ *www.washingtonplacefoundation.org* ✉ *Donations accepted* ◎ *Closed Fri.–Wed.*

CHINATOWN

Chinatown's original business district was made up of dry-goods and produce merchants, tailors and dressmakers, barbers, herbalists, and dozens of restaurants. The meat, fish, and produce stalls remain, but the mix is heavier now on gift and curio stores, lei stands, jewelry shops, and bakeries, with a smattering of noodle makers, travel agents, Asian-language video stores, and dozens of restaurants.

The name "Chinatown" here has always been a misnomer. Though three-quarters of Oahu's Chinese lived closely packed in these 25 acres in the late 1800s, even then the neighborhood was half Japanese. Today you hear Vietnamese and Tagalog as often as Mandarin and Cantonese, and there are voices of Japan, Singapore, Malaysia, Korea, Thailand, Samoa, and the Marshall Islands, as well.

Perhaps a more accurate name is the one used by early Chinese: *Wah Fau* (Chinese port), signifying a landing and jumping-off place. Chinese laborers, as soon as they completed their plantation contracts, hurried into the city to start businesses here. It's a launching point for today's immigrants, too: Southeast Asian shops almost outnumber Chinese; stalls carry Filipino specialties like winged beans and goat meat; and in one tiny space, knife-wielding Samoans skin coconuts to order.

In the half century after the first Chinese laborers arrived in Hawaii in 1851, Chinatown was a link to home for the all-male cadre of workers who planned to return to China rich and respected. Merchants not only sold supplies, they held mail, loaned money, wrote letters, translated documents, sent remittances to families, served meals, offered rough bunkhouse accommodations, and were the center for news, gossip, and socializing.

Although much happened to Chinatown in the 20th century—beginning in January 1900, when almost the entire neighborhood was burned to the ground to halt the spread of bubonic plague—it remains a bustling, crowded, noisy, and odiferous place bent primarily on buying and selling, and sublimely oblivious to its status as a National Historic District or the encroaching gentrification on nearby Nuuanu Avenue.

GETTING HERE AND AROUND

Chinatown occupies 15 blocks immediately north of downtown Honolulu—it's flat, compact, and very walkable.

GUIDED TOURS

Hawaii Food Tours. Come hungry for food writer Matthew Gray's culinary Hole-in-the-Wall Tour through Honolulu, which includes discussion of Hawaiian culinary history and the diversity of the Islands' food

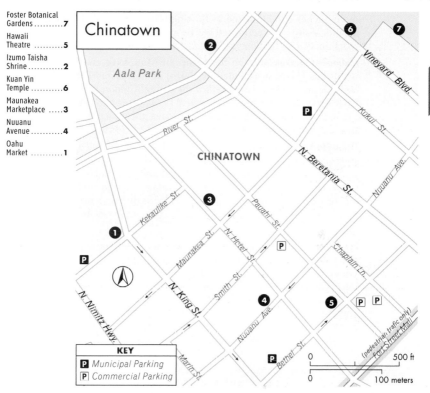

culture, along with 15- to 20-plus samples of local favorites as you walk to a variety of ethnic restaurants, markets, and bakeries, including two hours in Chinatown. It's a great way to get a delicious taste of Hawaii's culture. The tour begins at 9 am. Gray also has a North Shore Food Tour, which includes transportation from Waikiki. ☎ 808/926–3663 ⊕ www.hawaiifoodtours.com ☜ From $139.

TOP ATTRACTIONS

Izumo Taisha Shrine. From Chinatown Cultural Plaza, cross a stone bridge to the Izumo Taishakyo Mission of Hawaii to visit this shrine established in 1906. It honors Okuninushi-no-Mikoto, a *kami* (god) who is believed in Shinto tradition to bring good fortune if properly courted (and thanked afterward). ⊠ 215 N. Kukui St., Chinatown ✛ At the canal ☎ 808/538–7778.

Kuan Yin Temple. A couple of blocks *mauka* (toward the mountains) from Chinatown is the oldest Buddhist temple in the Islands. Mistakenly called a goddess by some, Kuan Yin, also known as Kannon, is a *bodhisattva*—one who chose to remain on Earth doing good even after achieving enlightenment. Transformed from a male into a female figure centuries ago, she is credited with a particular sympathy for women. You will see representations of her all over the Islands: holding a lotus flower (beauty from the mud of human frailty), as at the temple; pouring out a pitcher of oil (like mercy flowing); or as a sort of Madonna with a child. Visitors are permitted but be aware this is a practicing place of worship. ⊠ *170 N. Vineyard Blvd., Chinatown.*

Maunakea Marketplace. On the corner of Maunakea and Hotel streets is this busy plaza surrounded by shops, an indoor market, and a food court. It gets packed every year for the annual Chinese Lunar New Year. ■ **TIP→ If you appreciate fine tea, visit the unpretentious tea counter in the Tea Hut, a curio shop filled with Chinese gifts and good luck charms.** ⊠ *1120 Maunakea St., Chinatown* ☎ *808/524–3409.*

Oahu Market. In this market founded in 1904, you'll find a taste of old-style Chinatown, where you might be hustled aside as a whole pig (dead, of course) is wrestled through the crowd and where glassy-eyed fish of every size and hue lie stacked forlornly on ice. Try the bubble tea (juices and flavored teas with tapioca balls inside) or pick up a bizarre magenta dragonfruit for breakfast. ⊠ *N. King St., Chinatown* ✛ *At Kekaulike St.*

WORTH NOTING

Foster Botanical Gardens. Some of the trees in this botanical garden, which opened in 1931, date back to 1853, when Queen Kalama allowed a young German doctor to lease a portion of her land. Over 150 years later, you can see these trees and countless others along with bromeliads, orchids, and other tropical plants, some of which are rare or endangered. Look out in particular for the cannonball tree and the redwood-size Quipo tree. A docent-led tour is available every day at 10:30 am (call for reservations). ⊠ *50 N. Vineyard Blvd., Chinatown* ☎ *808/522–7060* ⊕ *www.honolulu.gov/parks/hbg.html* ▧ *$5.*

Hawaii Theatre. Opened in 1922, this theater earned rave reviews for its neoclassical design, with Corinthian columns, marble statues, and plush carpeting and drapery. Nicknamed the "Pride of the Pacific," the facility was rescued from demolition in the early 1980s and underwent a $30-million renovation. Listed on both the State and National Register of Historic Places, it has become the centerpiece of revitalization efforts of Honolulu's downtown area. The 1,400-seat venue hosts concerts, theatrical productions, dance performances, and film screenings. Guided tours of the theater end with a mini-concert on the historic orchestral pipe organ and can be booked through the box office. If interested one of the weekly tours on Tuesdays at 11 am, call a few days ahead to reserve. ⊠ *1130 Bethel St., Chinatown* ☎ *808/528–0506* ⊕ *www.hawaiitheatre.com* ▧ *$10* ☉ *Closed Wed.–Mon.*

Nuuanu Avenue. Here on Chinatown's main *mauka–makai* drag and on Bethel Street, which runs parallel, are clustered art galleries, restaurants, a wineshop, an antiques auctioneer, a dress shop or two, one small theater/exhibition space (the Arts at Mark's Garage), and one historic stage (the Hawaii Theatre). **First Friday** art nights, when galleries stay open until 9 pm, draw crowds. Many stay later and crowd Chinatown's bars. If you like art and people-watching and are fortunate enough to be on Oahu the first Friday of the month, this event shouldn't be missed. ⊠ *Nuuanu Ave., Chinatown.*

KAKAAKO

This 600-acre section of Honolulu between Ala Moana Center and downtown is in the middle of a decade-long redevelopment plan that began in 2012; it remains a neighborhood in transition. Now home to everything from ramshackle mechanic shops to the University of Hawaii's medical school, Kakaako's old warehouses and mom-and-pop storefronts are being replaced by gleaming luxury condos, shops, and restaurants. The neighborhood is bustling with construction crews and swaying cranes. Many new condo buildings have already been finished, and others grow taller by the day or are about to break ground. It's also home to new big-box stores including T.J. Maxx, as well as smaller local boutiques. Every month seems to bring new happenings such as the Honolulu Night Market, a pop-up shopping event.

Hawaii Pirate Ship Adventures. The *Treasure Seeker*, an 83-foot black galleon, sailed from San Diego to Hawaii in 2013 to bring swashbuckling fun to Waikiki waters. Daytime excursions include costumed actors leading kids of all ages in a pirate adventure complete with props. At night, the ship brightens up with flashing lights and music for an adults-only evening cruise, a BYOB party on the high seas. Check the website for the specific sailing days, and arrive at least 30 minutes prior to departure time. ■TIP→ Time your evening cruise for a Friday night to get a great water view of the Hilton Hawaiian Village fireworks. ✉ *Kewalo Basin Harbor, 1085 Ala Moana Blvd., Slip A, Kakaako* ☎ *808/201–7382* ⊕ *www.hawaiipirateship.com* ✂ *$64.*

ALA MOANA

Ala Moana abuts Waikiki to the east (stopping at the Ala Wai Canal) and King Street to the north. Kakaako, Kewalo Basin Harbor, and the Blaisdell Center complex roughly mark its western edge. Probably its most notable attraction is the sprawling Ala Moana Center, jam-packed with almost any store you could wish for.

IWILEI

Before the arrival of Captain Cook, Iwilei was a network of fishponds. After his arrival it became home to a prison, railway depot, and houses of ill repute. (When the red-light district was shut down in 1916, one prostitute hopped a ship to Pago Pago. Also on the ship was Somerset Maugham, who immortalized her as Sadie Thompson in his short story "Rain.") Today it is an industrial zone offering a few reasons to visit—the Dole Cannery shopping complex with a multiplex (home to the Hawaii International Film Festival each fall) being the primary one. The shopping center really was a pineapple cannery before its conversion; almost any local of a certain age has tales of summer jobs there.

MAKIKI HEIGHTS

Makiki includes the more unassuming neighborhood where President Barack Obama grew up. Other highlights include the exclusive Punahou School he attended and the notable Central Union Church, as well as the Tantalus area overlook.

Spalding House. In the exclusive Makiki Heights neighborhood, just minutes from downtown Honolulu, the Spalding House features an array of artwork with a large contemporary art collection. A new, school curriculum–themed gallery comprising works from the permanent collection as well as commissioned installations by local and internationally known artists, rotates every six months with topics like art, math, science, and music, making it accessible for kids and interesting for adults. Situated in the 3½-acre Alice Cooke Spalding home and estate (built in 1925), the museum offers changing exhibitions as well as a peaceful sculpture garden with breathtaking views of Diamond Head and Waikiki and a gift shop. On permanent view is David Hockney's opera set for *L'enfant et les sortilèges*. Previously known as the Contemporary Museum, Spalding House became part of the Honolulu Museum of Art organization, so a single admission gets you into both museums on the same day. ⊠ *2411 Makiki Heights Dr., Makiki Heights* ☎ *808/526–1322* ⊕ *www.honolulumuseum.org* ⊒ *$20, includes Honolulu Museum of Art* ⊙ *Closed Mon.*

Tantalus and Round Top Scenic Drive. A few minutes and a world away from Waikiki and Honolulu, this scenic drive shaded by vine-draped trees has frequent pullouts with views of Diamond Head and the Ewa side of Honolulu. It's a nice change of pace from urban life below. At Puu Ualakaa Park, stop to see the sweeping view from Manoa Valley to Honolulu. To start the drive, go to Punchbowl Memorial Cemetery and follow Tantalus Drive as it climbs uphill. ⊠ *3200 Round Top Dr., Makiki Heights.*

KALIHI

North of downtown Honolulu, just off H1, is the tightly packed neighborhood of Kalihi. It's home to large industrial pockets but also the stellar Bishop Museum, Lion Coffee headquarters, and great local eateries like Young's Fish Market, Helena's Hawaiian Food, Mitsu-Ken (plus Liliha Bakery in neighboring Liliha that's not to be missed for its *ono coco* puffs).

Fodor'sChoice **Bishop Museum.** Founded in 1889 by Charles R. Bishop as a memorial
★   to his wife, Princess Bernice Pauahi Bishop, the museum began as a repository for the royal possessions of this last direct descendant of King Kamehameha the Great. Today it's the state's designated history and culture museum. Its five exhibit halls house almost 25 million items that tell the history of the Hawaiian Islands and their Pacific neighbors. The complex also features a 16,500-square-foot natural-science wing with a three-story simulated volcano at its center, where twice-daily "lava melt" shows take place, much to the enjoyment of younger patrons.

The renovated Pacific Hall (formerly Polynesian Hall) now focuses on the history of the entire Pacific region.

The Hawaiian Hall, with state-of-the art and often interactive displays, teaches about the Hawaiian culture. Spectacular Hawaiian artifacts—lustrous feather capes, bone fishhooks, the skeleton of a giant sperm whale, photography and crafts displays, and an authentic, well-preserved grass house—are displayed inside a three-story 19th-century Victorian-style gallery. The building alone, with its huge Victorian turrets and immense stone walls, is worth seeing. Also check out the planetarium, daily tours, *lauhala*-weaving and science demonstrations, special exhibits, the Shop Pacifica, and the Bishop Museum Café, which serves *ono* (delicious) Hawaiian food by local restaurant Highway Inn. ⊠ *1525 Bernice St., Kalihi* ☎ *808/847–3511* ⊕ *www.bishopmuseum.org* ⊠ *$24.95 (parking $5).*

NUUANU

Immediately *mauka* of Kalihi, off Pali Highway, are a renowned resting place and a carefully preserved home where royal families retreated during the doldrums of summer. Nuuanu Pali was the sight of a famous battle that was key to King Kamehameha I's success in uniting all the Hawaiian Islands under his rule and becoming the Islands' first monarch. Nuuanu Valley is known for its lush, quiet beauty and has several notable cemeteries, churches, and embassies.

National Memorial Cemetery of the Pacific. Nestled in the bowl of Puowaina, or Punchbowl Crater, this 112-acre cemetery is the final resting place for more than 50,000 U.S. war veterans and family members and is a solemn reminder of their sacrifice. Among those buried here is Ernie Pyle, the famed World War II correspondent who was killed by a Japanese sniper on Ie Shima, an island off the northwest coast of Okinawa. There are intricate stone maps providing a visual military-history lesson. Puowaina, formed 75,000–100,000 years ago during a period of secondary volcanic activity, translates as "Hill of Sacrifice." Historians believe this site once served as an altar where ancient Hawaiians offered sacrifices to their gods. ■ TIP→ The entrance to the cemetery has unfettered views of Waikiki and Honolulu—perhaps the finest on Oahu. ⊠ *2177 Puowaina Dr., Nuuanu* ☎ *808/532–3720* ⊕ *www.cem. va.gov/cem/cems/nchp/nmcp.asp* ⊠ *Free.*

Queen Emma Summer Palace. Queen Emma, King Kamehameha IV's wife, used this stately white home, built in 1848, as a retreat from the rigors of court life in hot and dusty Honolulu during the mid-1800s. It has an eclectic mix of European, Victorian, and Hawaiian furnishings and has excellent examples of Hawaiian quilts and koa-wood furniture. ⊠ *2913 Pali Hwy., Nuuanu* ☎ *808/595–3167* ⊕ *www.daughtersofhawaii.org* ⊠ *$10.*

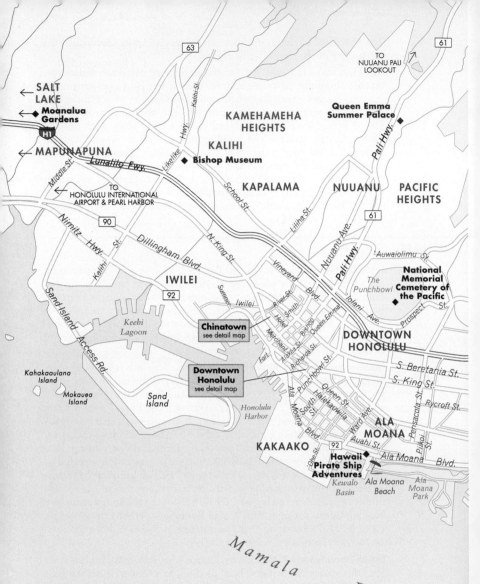

SALT
LAKE

Moanalua
Gardens

H1

MAPUNAPUNA

TO
HONOLULU INTERNATIONAL
AIRPORT & PEARL HARBOR

Lunalilo Fwy.

Middle St.

Nimitz Hwy.

90

Kalihi St.

Dillingham Blvd.

Likelike Hwy.

63

KAMEHAMEHA
HEIGHTS

KALIHI

Bishop Museum

KAPALAMA

School St.

Liliha St.

N. King St.

IWILEI

92

Keehi
Lagoon

Sand Island Access Rd.

Kahakaulana
Island

Mokauea
Island

Sand
Island

Summer St.

Vineyard Blvd.

Iwilei

River St.

Smith

Hotel

Chinatown
see detail map

Maunakea St.

Fort

Nuuanu Ave.

Pali Hwy.

Beretania

Queen Emma
Summer Palace

TO
NUUANU PALI
LOOKOUT

61

NUUANU

PACIFIC
HEIGHTS

61

Auwaiolimu St.

The
Punchbowl

National
Memorial
Cemetery of
the Pacific

Prospect St.

Iolani Ave.

DOWNTOWN
HONOLULU

Downtown
Honolulu
see detail map

Honolulu Harbor

Bishop

Alakea St.

Richards St.

Queen Emma

Punchbowl St.

Queen St.

Halekauwila

King St.

South St.

Ala Moana Blvd.

Ohe St.

Ward Ave.

KAKAAKO

92

Hawaii
Pirate Ship
Adventures

Kewalo
Basin

Auahi St.

Ala Moana Beach

ALA
MOANA

S. Beretania St.

S. King St.

Rycroft St.

Pensacola St.

Piikoi St.

Ala Moana Blvd.

Ala
Moana
Park

Honolulu Harbor

M a m a l a   B a y

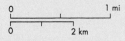

0   1 mi

0   2 km

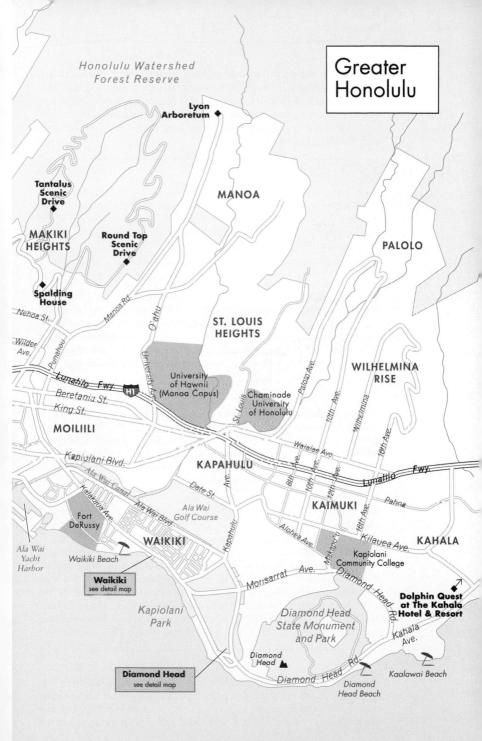

MOILIILI

Packed into the neighborhood of Moiliili are flower and lei shops, restaurants (Dagon, Fukuya Delicatessen, Sweet Home Café), and little stores such as Kuni Island Fabrics, a great source for Hawaiian quilting and other crafting materials; and Siam Imports, for goodies from Thailand. Most places of interest are along King Street, between Isenberg and Waialae avenues.

KAPAHULU

Walk just a few minutes from the eastern end of Waikiki, and you'll find yourself in this very local main drag of restaurants, antiques shops (Bailey's Antiques and Aloha Shirts [⊠ *517 Kapahulu Ave.*] is the place for rare, $5,000 wearable collectibles), and sports rental outfits (kayaking, surfing, diving, biking).

KAIMUKI

Ten minutes beyond Kapahulu is this commercial thoroughfare that runs through an old neighborhood filled with cool old Craftsman bungalows (that are slowly being knocked down to make room for ticky-tacky boxes). It may have the highest and most diverse concentration of eateries on the island, from a Jamaican restaurant and a shabu-shabu house to a chic, contemporary bistro and a nougat manufacturer.

MANOA

Manoa is probably best known as the home to the University of Hawaii's main campus. The surrounding area is chock-full of interesting coffee shops, restaurants, and stores fed by the collegiate and professorial crowd. History and beauty linger around verdant Manoa Valley at places like the Manoa Chinese Cemetery, and Lyon Arboretum. Manoa Valley Theatre puts on top-notch community theater productions year-round.

Lyon Arboretum. Tucked all the way back in Manoa Valley, this is a gem of an arboretum operated by the University of Hawaii. Hike to a waterfall or sit and enjoy beautiful views of the valley. You'll also see an ethnobotanical garden, a Hawaiian hale and garden, and one of the largest palm collections anywhere—all within a parklike setting. Its educational mission means there are regular talks and walks with university faculty. Docents give 60-minute tours weekdays at 10 am (call ahead to reserve a spot). There are also self-guided tours. ⊠ *3860 Manoa Rd., Manoa* ☎ *808/988–0461* ⊕ *www.hawaii.edu/lyonarboretum* ⊠ *$5 (suggested donation); guided tour $10* ☉ *Closed Sun.*

KAHALA

Oahu's wealthiest neighborhood has streets lined with multimillion-dollar homes. At intervals along tree-lined Kahala Avenue are narrow lanes that provide public access to Kahala's quiet, narrow coastal beaches offering views of Koko Head. Kahala Mall includes restaurants, a movie

Waikiki and Honolulu, looking west to Diamond Head, as seen from above.

theater, and a Whole Foods grocery store. Kahala is also the home of the private Waialae Country Club and golf course, site of the annual Sony Open PGA golf tournament in January.

Dolphin Quest at The Kahala Hotel & Resort. This worldwide dolphin-encounter group has an Oahu location in the Kahala Hotel & Resort, where trained Atlantic bottlenose dolphins hold court in an enclosed lagoon at the center of the hotel. The Kid's Aquatic Adventure is a 90-minute session of feeding and interacting with sting rays and dolphins. For the adults, there is more variety starting with a 15-minute encounter and going up to the "Trainer for a Week" experience. ✉ *The Kahala Hotel & Resort, 5000 Kahala Ave., Kahala* ☎ *808/739–8918* ⊕ *www.kahalaresort.com/Experiences/Dolphin-Quest* 💳 *From $189 for a 15-min encounter.*

MAPUNAPUNA

Mapunapuna is an area filled with factories and offices surrounding the airport. Tucked amid car dealerships, a Kaiser Permanente medical center, and the island's Harley Davidson outlet are fast-food joints, a Chinese restaurant, local plate-lunch places, and Mitch's, a somewhat undiscovered gem of a sushi spot.

KAPALAMA

This sliver of land that runs from ocean to mountain (known as an *ahupuaa* in Hawaiian) is presided over by famed Kamehameha Schools, which from its hillside perch looks down on this warren of modest homes and shops—and the Bishop Museum.

SALT LAKE

There's no longer a lake, salty or not, in this suburb of Honolulu. Instead you'll find a largely residential neighborhood with a commercial core at Salt Lake Shopping Center plus the oasis of Moanalua Gardens.

Moanalua Gardens. This lovely park is a great place to bring a picnic, spread out a blanket, and take a snooze, fly a kite, or simply idle an afternoon away. It's also the location of the internationally acclaimed Prince Lot Hula Festival in July. You'll often see Japanese visitors taking pictures by a sprawling monkeypod tree nicknamed the Hitachi Tree and famous for advertising the Hitachi brand in Japan. Call the Moanalua Gardens Foundation to see about park booklets and occasional hikes. To reach Moanalua Gardens, take the Moanalua Freeway (78) westbound. Take the Tripler exit, then take a right on Jarrett White Road. Turn left at the first cross street onto Mahiole Street. The gardens are on the left. ⊠ *2850 Moanalua Rd., Salt Lake* ☎ *808/729–6322* ⊕ *www.moanaluagardens.com* ✉ *$3.*

SOUTHEAST OAHU

Approximately 10 miles southeast of Waikiki.

Driving southeast from Waikiki on busy four-lane Kalanianaole Highway, you'll pass a dozen bedroom communities tucked into the valleys at the foot of the Koolau Range, with fleeting glimpses of the ocean from a couple of pocket parks. Suddenly civilization falls away, and the road narrows to two lanes, and you enter the rugged coastline of Koko Head and Ka Iwi.

This is a cruel coastline: dry, windswept, and rocky shores, with untamed waves that are notoriously treacherous. While walking its beaches, do not turn your back on the ocean, don't venture close to wet areas where high waves occasionally reach, and be sure to heed warning signs.

At this point, you're passing through Koko Head Regional Park. On your right is the bulging remnant of a pair of volcanic craters that the Hawaiians called Kawaihoa, known today as Koko Head. To the left is Koko Crater and an area of the park that includes a hiking trail, a dryland botanical garden, a firing range, and a riding stable. Ahead is a sinuous shoreline with scenic pullouts and beaches to explore. Named the Ka Iwi Coast (*iwi*, "ee-vee," are bones—sacred to Hawaiians and full of symbolism) for the channel just offshore, this area was once home to a ranch and small fishing enclave that were destroyed by a tidal wave in the 1940s.

GETTING HERE AND AROUND

Driving straight from Waikiki to Makapuu Point takes from a half to a full hour, depending on traffic. There aren't a huge number of sights per se in this corner of Oahu, so a couple of hours should be plenty of exploring time, unless you make a lengthy stop at a particular point.

Halona Blowhole. Below a scenic turnout along the Koko Head shoreline, this oft-photographed lava tube sucks the ocean in and spits it out. Don't get too close, as conditions can get dangerous. ■TIP→ Look to your right to see the tiny beach below that was used to film the wave-washed love scene in *From Here to Eternity.* In winter this is a good spot to watch whales at play. Offshore, the island of Molokai calls like a distant siren, and every once in a while Lanai is visible in blue silhouette. Take your valuables with you and lock your car, because this scenic location is overrun with tourists and therefore a hot spot for petty thieves. ✉ *Kalanianaole Hwy., Hawaii Kai ✛ 1 mile east of Hanauma Bay.*

Koko Crater Botanical Gardens. If you've visited any of Oahu's other botanical gardens, this one will be in stark contrast. Inside the tallest tuff cone on Oahu, in one of the hottest and driest areas on the island, Koko Crater Botanical Garden allows visitors the opportunity to see dryland species of plants including baobab trees, cacti, plumeria, and bougainvillea. ✉ *Entrance at end of Kokonani St., near Hawaii Kai Dr., Hawaii Kai* ☎ *808/522–7066* ⊕ *www.honolulu. gov/parks/hbg.html* 🔖 *Free.*

Kokonuts Shave Ice and Snacks. Stop for shave ice on the South Shore? President Barack Obama did while visiting the island after the 2008 election. ✉ *7192 Kalanianaole Hwy., Hawaii Kai* ☎ *808/396–8809.*

Lanai Lookout. A little over half a mile past Hanauma Bay as you head toward Makapuu Point, you'll see a turnout on the ocean side with some fine views of the coastline. In winter you'll have an opportunity to see storm-generated waves crashing against lava cliffs. This is also a popular place for winter whale-watching, so bring your binoculars, some sunscreen, and a picnic lunch and join the small crowd scanning for telltale white spouts of water only a few hundred yards away. On clear days you should be able to see the islands of Molokai and Lanai off in the distance, hence the name. ✉ *Kalanianaole Hwy., Hawaii Kai* ✛ *Just past Hanauma Bay.*

Makapuu Point. This spot has breathtaking views of the ocean, mountains, and the windward Islands. The point of land jutting out in the distance is Mokapu Peninsula, site of a U.S. Marine base. The spired mountain peak is Mt. Olomana. On the long pier is part of the Makai Undersea Test Range, a research facility that's closed to the public. Offshore is Manana Island (Rabbit Island), a picturesque cay said to resemble a swimming bunny with its ears pulled back. Ironically enough, Manana Island was once overrun with rabbits, thanks to a rancher who let a few hares run wild on the land. They were eradicated in 1994 by biologists who grew concerned that the rabbits were destroying the island's native plants.

Nestled in the cliff face is the **Makapuu Lighthouse,** which became operational in 1909 and has the largest lighthouse lens in America. The lighthouse is closed to the public, but near the Makapuu Point turnout you can find the start of a paved mile-long road (it's closed to vehicular traffic). Hike up to the top of the 647-foot bluff for a closer view of the lighthouse and, in winter, a great whale-watching vantage point. For the more adventurous, at the whale-watching sign on the main path, head down a switchback trail to the Makapuu tide pools below. ✉ *Ka Iwi State Scenic Shoreline, Kalanianaole Hwy., Kaneohe* ✛ *At Makapuu Beach* ⊕ *dlnr.hawaii.gov/dsp/hiking/oahu/ makapuu-point-lighthouse-trail.*

Fodor's Choice
★

Shangri La. In 1936 heiress Doris Duke bought 5 acres at Black Point, down the coast from Waikiki, and began to build and furnish the first home that would be all her own. She called it Shangri La. For more than 50 years, the home was a work in progress as Duke traveled the world, buying art and furnishings, picking up ideas for her Mughal Garden, for the Playhouse in the style of a 17th-century Irani pavilion, and for the water terraces and tropical gardens. When she died in 1993, Duke left instructions that her home was to become a public center for the study of Islamic art.

To walk through the house and its gardens—which have remained much as Duke left them with only some minor conservation-oriented changes—is to experience the personal style of someone who saw everything as raw material for her art. (The courtyard and pool underwent extensive renovations starting in 2017.) With her trusted houseman, Jin de Silva, she helped build the elaborate Turkish Room, trimming tiles and painted panels to retrofit the existing space (including raising the ceiling and lowering the floor) and building a fountain of her own design. Among many aspects of the home inspired by the Muslim tradition is the entry: an anonymous gate, a blank white wall, and a wooden door that bids you, "Enter herein in peace and security" in Arabic script. Inside, tiles glow, fountains tinkle, and shafts of light illuminate artworks through arches and high windows. In 2014, after years of renovation, Duke's bedroom (the Mughal Suite) opened to the public. This was her private world, entered only by trusted friends.

The house is open by guided tour only and reservations are required. Book your tour as early as possible, as tours fill up very quickly. Tours take 2½ hours including transportation from the Honolulu Museum of Art (*900 S. Beretania St., downtown Honolulu*), where all tours begin. Children under eight are not admitted. ⊠ *Hawaii Kai* ☎ *808/532–3853 for Honolulu Museum of Art* ⊕ *www.shangrilahawaii.org or honolulumuseum.org/385-about_shangri_la* ⊠ *Tour $25 ($1.50 fee for online reservations, $2 for phone reservations)* ⊗ *Closed Sun.–Tues. and Sept.*

WINDWARD OAHU

Approximately 15 miles northeast of downtown Honolulu (20–25 minutes by car), approximately 25 miles southeast of downtown Honolulu via Ka Iwi and Waimanalo (35–45 minutes by car).

Looking at Honolulu's topsy-turvy urban sprawl, you would never suspect the windward side existed. It's a secret Oahuans like to keep, so they can watch the awe on the faces of their guests when the car emerges from the tunnels through the mountains and they gaze for the first time on the panorama of turquoise bays and emerald valleys watched over by the knife-edged Koolau ridges. Jaws literally drop. Every time. And this just a 15-minute drive from downtown.

It's on this side of the island where many Native Hawaiians live. Evidence of traditional lifestyles is abundant in crumbling fishponds, rock platforms that once were altars, taro patches still being worked, and throw-net fishermen posed stock-still above the water (though today, they're invariably wearing polarized sunglasses, the better to spot the fish).

Here the pace is slower, more oriented toward nature. Beachgoing, hiking, diving, surfing, and boating are the draws, along with a visit to the Polynesian Cultural Center, and poking through little shops and wayside stores.

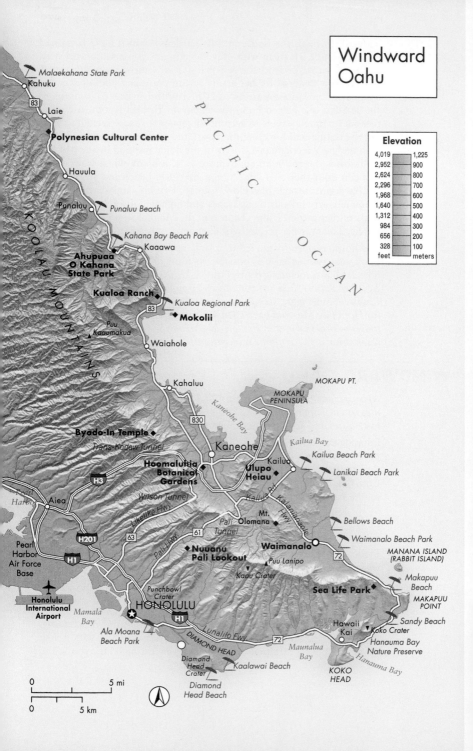

Windward Oahu

Malaekahana State Park
Kahuku
83
Laie
Polynesian Cultural Center
Hauula
Punaluu   Punaluu Beach
Kahana Bay Beach Park
Kaaawa
**Ahupuaa
O Kahana
State Park**
Kualoa Ranch   Kualoa Regional Park
83   **Mokolii**
Puu
Kaaumakua
Waiahole
Kahaluu
Byodo-In Temple
Trans-Koolau Tunnel
830   **Kaneohe**
**Hoomaluhia
Botanical
Gardens**
H3
Wilson Tunnel
Aiea
H201
Pearl
Harbor
Pali
Harbor
Punchbowl
Crater
Pearl
Harbor
Air Force
Base
Honolulu
International
Airport
Mamala
Bay
Ala Moana
Beach Park
HONOLULU
H1
Likelike Hwy.
Pali Lnwy.
63   61
Pali
Tunnel
**Nuuanu
Pali Lookout**
Kaau Crater
Puu Lanipo
Mt.
Olomana
**Ulupo
Heiau**
Kailua   Kailua Bay
Kailua Beach Park
Lanikai Beach Park
Kailua Rd.
Kalanianaole Hwy.
Waimanalo
Bellows Beach
72   Waimanalo Beach Park
MANANA ISLAND
(RABBIT ISLAND)
Makapuu
Beach
MAKAPUU
POINT
Sea Life Park
Hawaii
Kai
Koko Crater   Sandy Beach
Hanauma Bay
Nature Preserve
KOKO
HEAD
Hanauma Bay
Maunalua
Bay
Lunalilo Fwy.
DIAMOND HEAD
72
Diamond
Head
Crater   Kaalawai Beach
Diamond
Head Beach

KOOLAU MOUNTAINS

MOKAPU
PENINSULA
MOKAPU PT.

PACIFIC OCEAN

Elevation

feet	meters
4,019	1,225
2,952	900
2,624	800
2,296	700
1,968	600
1,640	500
1,312	400
984	300
656	200
328	100
feet	meters

0   5 mi
0   5 km

CLOSE UP

Windward Oahu Villlages

Tiny villages—generally consisting of a sign, store, a beach park, possibly a post office, and not much more—are strung along Kamehameha Highway on the windward side. Each has something to offer. In **Waiahole**, look for fruit stands and an ancient grocery store. In **Kaaawa**, there's a lunch spot and convenience store–gas station. In **Punaluu**, get a plate lunch at Keneke's, or visit venerable Ching General Store. Kim Taylor Reece's photo studio, featuring haunting portraits of hula dancers, is between Punaluu and Hauula. **Hauula** has the gallery of fanciful landscape artist Lance Fairly; the Shrimp Shack; Hauula Gift Shop & Art Gallery, formerly yet another Ching Store, now a clothing shop where sarongs wave like banners; and, at Hauula Kai Shopping Center, Tamura's Market, with excellent seafood and the last liquor before Mormon-dominated Laie.

GETTING HERE AND AROUND

For a driving experience you won't soon forget, take the H3 freeway over to the windward side. As you pass through the tunnels, be prepared for one of the most breathtaking stretches of road anywhere.

TOP ATTRACTIONS

Fodor's Choice

★

Byodo-In Temple. Tucked away in the back of the Valley of the Temples cemetery is a replica of the 11th-century Temple at Uji in Japan. A 2-ton carved wooden statue of the Buddha presides inside the main temple building. Next to the temple building are a meditation pavilion and gardens set dramatically against the sheer, green cliffs of the Koolau Mountains. You can ring the 5-foot, 3-ton brass bell for good luck and feed some of the hundreds of koi, ducks, and swans that inhabit the garden's 2-acre pond. Or, you can enjoy the peaceful surroundings and just relax. ⊠ *47-200 Kahekili Hwy., Kaneohe* ☎ *808/239–8811* ⊕ *www.byodo-in.com* ✉ *$5 (cash only)*.

NEED A BREAK

✕ **Kalapawai Market.** Generations of children have purchased their beach snacks and sodas at Kalapawai Market, near Kailua Beach. A Windward Oahu landmark since 1932, the green-and-white market has distinctive charm. ⊠ **306 S. Kalaheo Ave., Kailua** ☎ **808/262–4359** ⊕ **www.kalapawai-market.com.**

Nuuanu Pali Lookout. This panoramic perch looks out to expansive views of Windward Oahu. It was in this region that King Kamehameha I drove defending forces over the edges of the 1,200-foot-high cliffs, thus winning the decisive battle for control of Oahu. ■TIP→ From here, views stretch from Kaneohe Bay to Mokolii ("little lizard," also called Chinaman's Hat), a small island off the coast, and beyond. Temperatures at the summit are several degrees cooler than in warm Waikiki, so bring a jacket along. Hang on tight to any loose possessions and consider wearing pants; it gets extremely windy at the lookout, which is part of the fun. Lock your car in the pay-to-park lot; break-ins have occurred here (this wayside is in the most trafficked state park in Hawaii). ⊠ *Kaneohe* ⊹ *Top of Pali Hwy.* ⊕ *dlnr.hawaii.gov/dsp/parks/ oahu/nuuanu-pali-state-wayside* 🎫 *Free* ☞ *Parking $3 per car.*

NEED A BREAK

✕ **Island Snow.** Long a favorite of Windward Oahu residents for its shave ice counter within the clothing store, Island Snow has more recently become known as the place where President Obama and his daughters have gone for the sweet treat when they vacation in Hawaii. Extra fluffy shave ice topped off with local syrup flavors and a milky "snow cap" make this one of the best shave ice stops on the island. ⊠ *130 Kailua Rd., Kailua* ⊹ *Separate entrance from clothing shop* 🖀 *808/263–6339.*

EN ROUTE

Mokolii. As you drive the Windward and North shores along Kamehameha Highway, you'll note a number of interesting geological features. At Kualoa look to the ocean and gaze at the uniquely shaped little island of Mokolii ("little lizard"), a 206-foot-high sea stack also known as Chinaman's Hat. According to Hawaiian legend, the goddess Hiiaka, sister of Pele, slew the dragon Mokolii and flung its tail into the sea, forming the distinct islet. Other dragon body parts—in the form of rocks, of course—were scattered along the base of nearby Kualoa Ridge. ■ TIP➔ In Laie, if you turn right on Anemoku Street, and right again on Naupaka, you come to a scenic lookout where you can see a group of islets, dramatically washed by the waves. ⊠ *49-479 Kamehameha Hwy., Kaneohe.*

FAMILY **Polynesian Cultural Center.** Re-created individual villages showcase the lifestyles and traditions of Hawaii, Tahiti, Samoa, Fiji, the Marquesas Islands, New Zealand, and Tonga. Focusing on individual islands within its 42-acre center, 35 miles from Waikiki, the Polynesian Cultural Center was founded in 1963 by the Church of Jesus Christ of Latter-day Saints. It houses restaurants, hosts luau, and demonstrates cultural traditions such as hula, fire dancing, and ancient customs and ceremonies. The Hukilau Marketplace carries Polynesian handicrafts. There are multiple packages available, from basic admission to an all-inclusive deal. Every May the PCC hosts the World Fireknife Dance Competition, an event that draws the top fire-knife dance performers from around the world. Get tickets for that event in advance. ■ TIP➔ If you're staying in Honolulu, see the center as part of a van tour so you won't have to drive home late at night after the two-hour evening show. ⊠ *55-370 Kamehameha Hwy., Laie* 🖀 *800/367–7060* ⊕ *www.polynesia.com* 🎫 *From $64.95* ⊘ *Closed Sun.*

WORTH NOTING

Ahupuaa O Kahana State Park. This park offers the true Hawaiian experience: a beautiful windward bay sits a short walk away from the Huilua Fishpond, a national historic landmark. The fishpond is undergoing restoration to reinforce the rock walls. There are rain-forest hikes chock-full of local fruit trees, a hunting area for pigs, and a coconut grove for picnicking. The water is suitable for swimming and bodysurfing, though it's a little cloudy for snorkeling. ⊠ *52-222 Kamehameha*

*Hwy., near Kahana Bay, Kaaawa ⊕ dlnr.hawaii.gov/dsp/parks/oahu/
ahupuaa-o-kahana-state-park.*

Hoomaluhia Botanical Gardens. The name, which means "a peaceful refuge," describes the serenity and feeling of endless space you find in
this verdant garden framed by the stunning Koolau mountain range.
Inside its 400 acres are plant collections from such tropical areas as the
Americas, Africa, Melanesia, the Philippines, and Hawaii. Not just for
the botanist, Hoomaluhia also has a 32-acre lake and open lawns ideal
for picnicking and camping by permit. Families can also take advantage
of the park's catch-and-release tilapia fishing program; staff provides
free bamboo poles at the visitor center. ⊠ *45-680 Luluku Rd., Kaneohe*
☎ *808/233–7323* ⊕ *www.honolulu.gov/parks/hbg.html* 🕾 *Free.*

Kualoa Ranch. Encompassing 4,000 acres, about 45 minutes by car from
Waikiki, this working ranch offers a wide range of activities—from ATV
and horseback tours to ziplining or expeditions into the valley on an
electric bike. The mountains, which serve as the backdrop of this scenic
ranch, may seem familiar, as the ranch has served as the set for movies
such as *Jurassic Park* and *Wind Talkers,* and TV shows like *Magnum,
P.I.* and *Lost* (and you can take a movie sites tour). From the grounds,
you'll have a wonderful view of the ocean and Chinaman's Hat. You
can drop by the visitor center anytime, but it's best to book activities
and tours two or three days in advance. ⊠ *49-560 Kamehameha Hwy.,
Kaaawa* ☎ *808/237–7321* ⊕ *www.kualoa.com* 🕾 *From $45.95.*

FAMILY **Sea Life Park.** Dolphins leap and spin and penguins frolic at this marine-
life attraction 15 miles from Waikiki at scenic Makapuu Point. The
park has a 300,000-gallon Hawaiian reef aquarium, a breeding sanctuary for Hawaii's endangered *honu* sea turtles, penguin and Hawaiian
monk seal habitats, an aviary, a seabird sanctuary, and many more
marine attractions. Sign up for a dolphin, sea lion, or shark encounter
and get up close and personal in the water with these sea creatures.
⊠ *41-202 Kalanianaole Hwy., Waimanalo* ☎ *808/259–2500* ⊕ *www.
sealifeparkhawaii.com* 🕾 *$39.99 (parking $5).*

Ulupo Heiau. Although they may look like piles of rocks to the uninti-
ated, *heiau* are sacred stone platforms for the worship of the gods and
date from ancient times. *Ulupo* means "night inspiration," referring to
the legendary Menehune, a mythical race of diminutive people who are
said to have built the heiau under the cloak of darkness. Find this spot,
with signs near the heiau also explaining Kailua's early history, tucked
next to the Windward YMCA. ⊠ *Kalanianaole Hwy. and Kailua Rd.,
Kailua* ✛ *Behind the Windward YMCA* ⊕ *dlnr.hawaii.gov/dsp/parks/
oahu/ulupo-heiau-state-historic-site.*

Waimanalo. This modest little seaside town flanked by chiseled cliffs
is worth a visit. Home to more Native Hawaiian families than Kailua
to the north or Hawaii Kai to the south, Waimanalo's biggest draws
are its beautiful beaches, offering glorious views to the windward side.
Bellows Beach is great for swimming, bodysurfing, and camping, and
Waimanalo Beach Park is also safe for swimming. Down the side roads,
as you head *mauka* (toward the mountains), are little farms that grow
a variety of fruits and flowers. Toward the back of the valley are small

Stroll along Kailua Beach, which many consider to be Oahu's best beach, as well as the hottest place to windsurf on the island.

ranches with grazing horses. ■TIP➜ If you see any trucks selling corn and you're staying at a place where you can cook it, be sure to get some in Waimanalo. It may be the sweetest you'll ever eat, and the price is the lowest on Oahu. ⊠ *Kalanianaole Hwy., Waimanalo.*

THE NORTH SHORE

Approximately 35 miles (one hour by car) north of downtown Honolulu, approximately 25 miles (one hour by car) from Kualoa Regional Park (Chinaman's Hat) in Windward Oahu.

An hour from town and a world away in atmosphere, Oahu's North Shore, roughly from Kahuku Point to Kaena Point, is about small farms and big waves, tourist traps, and otherworldly landscapes. Parks and beaches, roadside fruit stands and shrimp shacks, a bird sanctuary, and a valley preserve offer a dozen reasons to stop between the onetime plantation town of Kahuku and the surf mecca of Haleiwa.

Haleiwa has had many lives, from resort getaway in the 1900s to plantation town through the 20th century to its life today as a surf and tourist magnet. Beyond Haleiwa is the tiny village of Waialua, a string of beach parks, an airfield where gliders, hang gliders, and parachutists play, and, at the end of the road, Kaena Point State Recreation Area, which offers a brisk hike, striking views, and whale-watching in season.

Pack wisely for a day's North Shore excursion: swim and snorkel gear, light jacket and hat (the weather is mercurial, especially in winter), sunscreen and sunglasses, bottled water and snacks, towels and

2

a picnic blanket, and both sandals and closed-toe shoes for hiking. A small cooler is nice; you may want to pick up some fruit or fresh corn. As always, leave valuables in the hotel safe and lock the car whenever you park.

GETTING HERE AND AROUND

From Waikiki, the quickest route to the North Shore is H1 east to H2 north, and then the Kamehameha Highway past Wahiawa; you'll hit Haleiwa in just under an hour. The windward route (H1 east, H3, Like-like or Pali Highway, through the mountains, or Kamehameha Highway north) takes at least 90 minutes to Haleiwa, but the drive is far prettier.

Haleiwa. Today Haleiwa is a fun mix of old and new, with charming general stores and contemporary boutiques, galleries, and eateries. During the 1920s this seaside hamlet boasted a posh hotel at the end of a railroad line (both long gone), while the 1960s saw hippies gathered here, followed by surfers from around the world. Be sure to stop in at **Liliuokalani Protestant Church**, founded by missionaries in the 1830s. It's fronted by a large, stone archway built in 1910 and covered with night-blooming cereus. ⊠ *Haleiwa ✛ Follow H1 west from Honolulu to H2 north, exit at Wahiawa, follow Kamehameha Hwy. 6 miles, turn left at signaled intersection, then right into Haleiwa.*

NEED A BREAK

✕ **Matsumoto Shave Ice.** For a real slice of Haleiwa life, stop at Matsumoto Shave Ice, a family-run business in a building dating to 1910, for shave ice in every flavor imaginable. For something different, order a shave ice with adzuki beans—the red beans are boiled until soft, mixed with sugar, and then placed in the cone with the ice on top. ⊠ *66-111 Kamehameha Hwy., Suite 605, Haleiwa* ☎ *808/637-4827* ⊕ *www.matsumotoshaveice.com.*

Kaena Point State Recreation Area. The name means "the heat" and, indeed, this windy barren coast lacks both shade and freshwater (or any man-made amenities). Pack water, wear sturdy closed-toe shoes, don sunscreen and a hat, and lock the car. The hike is along a rutted dirt road, mostly flat and nearly 3 miles long, (one way) ending in a rocky, sandy headland. It is here that Hawaiians believed the souls of the dead met with their family gods, and, if judged worthy to enter the afterlife, leapt off into eternal darkness at Leinaakauane, just south of the point. In summer and at low tide, the small coves offer bountiful shelling; in winter, don't venture near the water. Rare native plants dot the landscape and seabirds like the Laysan albatross nest here. If you're lucky, you might spot seals sunbathing on the rocks. From November through March, watch for humpbacks, spouting and breaching. Binoculars and a camera are highly recommended. ⊠ *69-385 Farrington Hwy., Waialua* ⊕ *dlnr.hawaii.gov/dsp/parks/oahu/kaena-point-state-park.*

Puu o Mahuka Heiau. Worth a stop for its spectacular views from a bluff high above the ocean overlooking Waimea Bay, this sacred spot is the largest heiau on the island and spans nearly 2 acres. At one time it was used as a *heiau luakini,* or a temple for human sacrifices. It's now on the National Register of Historic Places. Turn up the road at the Pupukea Foodland and follow the road up to the heiau. ⊠ *Pupukea Rd., ½ mile north of Waimea Bay, Haleiwa ✛ From Rte. 83, turn right* *on Pupukea Rd. and drive 1 mile uphill* ⊕ *dlnr.hawaii.gov/dsp/parks/ oahu/puu-o-mahuka-heiau-state-historic-site.*

FAMILY

Fodor's Choice

★

Waimea Valley. Waimea may get lots of press for the giant winter waves in the bay, but the valley itself is a newsmaker and an ecological treasure in its own right. The local nonprofit is working to conserve and restore the natural habitat. Follow the Kamananui Stream up the valley through the 1,875 acres of gardens. The botanical collections here include more than 5,000 species of tropical flora, including a superb gathering of Polynesian plants. It's the best place on the island to see native species, such as the endangered Hawaiian moorhen. You can also see the restored Hale o Lono *heiau* (shrine) along with other ancient archaeological sites; evidence suggests that the area was an important spiritual center. Daily activities include botanical walking tours and cultural tours. At the back of the valley, Waihi Falls plunges 45 feet into a swimming pond. ■TIP→ Bring your board shorts—a swim is the perfect way to end your hike. Be sure to bring mosquito repellent, too; it can get buggy. ✉ *59-864 Kamehameha Hwy., Haleiwa* ☎ *808/638–7766* ⊕ *www.waimeavalley.net* ☜ *$16.*

QUICK
BITES

Ted's Bakery. The chocolate *haupia* (coconut pudding) pie at Ted's Bakery is legendary. Stop in for a take-out pie or for a quick plate lunch or sandwich. ✉ **59-024 Kamehameha Hwy., Haleiwa** ✦ **Near Sunset Beach** ☎ **808/638–8207** ⊕ **www.tedsbakery.com.**

CENTRAL OAHU

Wahiawa is approximately 20 miles (30–35 minutes by car) north of downtown Honolulu, 15 miles (20–30 minutes by car) south of the North Shore.

Oahu's central plain is a patchwork of old towns and new residential developments, military bases, farms, ranches, and shopping malls, with a few visit-worthy attractions and historic sites scattered about. Central Oahu encompasses the Moanalua Valley, residential Pearl City and Mililani, and the old plantation town of Wahiawa, on the uplands halfway to the North Shore.

GETTING HERE AND AROUND
For Central Oahu, all sights are most easily reached by either the H1 or H2 freeway.

FAMILY

Dole Plantation. Pineapple plantation days are nearly defunct in Hawaii, but you can still celebrate Hawaii's famous golden fruit at this promotional center with exhibits, a huge gift shop, a snack concession, educational displays, and the world's second-largest maze. Take the self-guided Garden Tour, or hop aboard the Pineapple Express for a 20-minute train tour to learn a bit about life on a pineapple plantation. Kids love the more than 3-acre Pineapple Garden Maze, made up of 14,000 tropical plants and trees. If you do nothing else, stop by the cafeteria in the back for a delicious pineapple soft-serve Dole Whip. This is about a 40-minute drive from Waikiki, a suitable stop on the way to or from the North Shore. ✉ *64-1550 Kamehameha Hwy.,*

DID YOU KNOW?

Waikiki Beach stretches from Hilton Hawaiian Village to Kapiolani Park and Diamond Head, and if you surf here you'll be hanging 10 with the best of 'em.

Wahiawa ☎ *808/621–8408* ⊕ *www.doleplantation.com* 🖵 *Plantation free, Pineapple Express $10.50, maze $8, garden tour $7.*

Kukaniloko Birthstone State Monument. In the cool uplands of Wahiawa is haunting Kukaniloko, where noble chieftesses went to give birth to high-ranking children. One of the most significant cultural sites on the island, the lava-rock stones here were believed to possess the power to ease the labor pains of childbirth. The site is marked by approximately 180 stones covering about a half acre. It's a 40- to 45-minute drive from Waikiki. ⊠ *Kamehameha Hwy. and Whitmore Ave., Wahiawa* ✛ *The north side of Wahiawa town.*

WEST (LEEWARD) OAHU

Kapolei is approximately 20 miles (30 minutes by car) west of downtown Honolulu, and 12 miles (20 minutes by car) from Mililani; traffic can double or triple the driving time.

West (or Leeward) Oahu has the island's "second city"—the planned community of Kapolei, where for years the government has been trying to attract enough jobs to lighten inbound traffic to downtown Honolulu—then continues on past far-flung resorts to the Hawaiian communities of Nanakuli and Waianae, to the beach and the end of the road at Keaweula, aka Yokohama Bay.

A couple of cautions as you head to the leeward side: Highway 93 is a narrow, winding two-lane road, notorious for accidents. There's an abrupt transition from freeway to highway at Kapolei, and by the time you reach Nanakuli, it's a country road, so *slow down.* ■TIP→ Car break-ins and beach thefts are common here.

GETTING HERE AND AROUND
West Oahu begins at folksy Waipahu and continues past Makakilo and Kapolei on H1 and Highway 93, Farrington Highway.

Hawaii's Plantation Village. Starting in the 1800s, immigrants seeking work on the sugar plantations came to these Islands like so many waves against the shore. At this living museum 30 minutes from downtown Honolulu (without traffic), visit authentically furnished buildings, original and replicated, that re-create and pay tribute to the plantation era. See a Chinese social hall; a Japanese shrine, sumo ring, and saimin stand; a dental office; and historic homes. The village is open for guided tours only. ⊠ *Waipahu Cultural Gardens Park, 94-695 Waipahu St., Waipahu* ☎ *808/677–0110* ⊕ *www.hawaiiplantationvillage.org* 🖵 *$15.*

FAMILY **Wet'n'Wild Hawaii.** This 29-acre family attraction has waterslides, water cannons, and waterfalls. ⊠ *400 Farrington Hwy., Kapolei* ✛ *Off H1 at Exit 1* ☎ *808/674–9283* ⊕ *www.wetnwildhawaii.com* 🖵 *$49.99* ☞ *$8 per car.*

BEACHES

Updated by
Trina Kudlacek

Tropical sun mixed with cooling trade winds and pristine waters make Oahu's shores a literal heaven on earth. But contrary to many assumptions, the island is not one big beach. There are miles and miles of coastline without a grain of sand, so you need to know where you're going to fully enjoy the Hawaiian experience.

Much of the island's southern and eastern coasts is protected by inner reefs. The reefs provide still coastline water but not much as far as sand is concerned. Nevertheless, where there are beaches on the south and east shores, they are mind-blowing. In West Oahu and on the North Shore, you can find the wide expanses of sand you would expect for enjoying the sunset. Sandy bottoms and protective reefs make the water an adventure in the winter months. Most visitors assume the seasons don't change a bit in the Islands, and they would be mostly right—except for the waves, which are big on the south shore in summer and placid in winter. It's exactly the opposite on the north side, where winter storms bring in huge waves, but the ocean becomes glasslike come May and June.

HONOLULU

WAIKIKI

The 2-mile strand called Waikiki Beach extends from Hilton Hawaiian Village on one end to Kapiolani Park and Diamond Head on the other. Although it's one contiguous piece of beach, it's as varied as the people that inhabit the Islands. Whether you're an old-timer looking to enjoy the action from the shade or a sports nut wanting to do it all, you can find every beach activity here without ever jumping in the rental car.

Plenty of parking exists on the west end at the Ala Wai Marina, where you can park in metered stalls around the harbor for $1 an hour. For parking on the east end, Kapiolani Park and the Honolulu Zoo also have metered parking for $1 an hour—more affordable than the $10

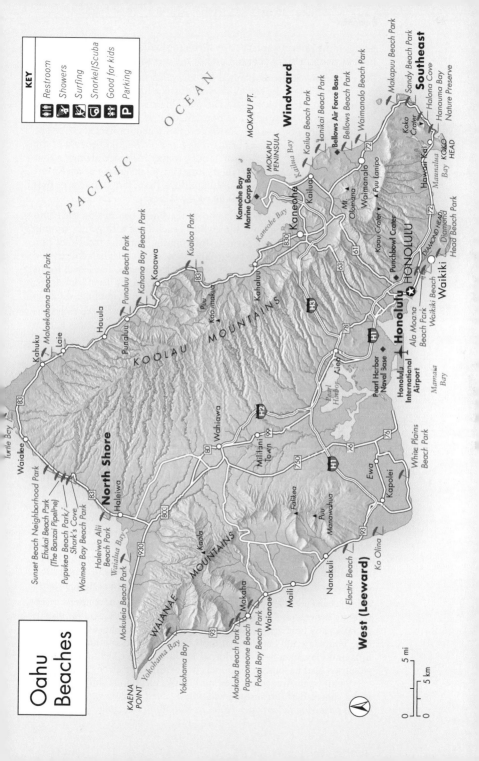

Oahu
Beaches

KEY

Restroom
Showers
Surfing
Snorkel/Scuba
Good for kids
P Parking

PACIFIC

OCEAN

MOKAPU PT.

Windward

Makapuu Beach Park

Southeast

Sandy Beach Park

Koko
Crater

Halona Cove

Hanauma Bay
Nature Preserve

Makapuu Beach Park

Bellows Beach Park

Waimanalo Beach Park

Kailua Beach Park

Lanikai Beach Park

MOKAPU
PENINSULA

Kailua Bay

Kaneohe Bay
Marine Corps Base

Kaneohe Bay

Kaneohe

Kailua

Waimanalo

Mt.
Olomana

Puu lanipo

Kaau Crater

DIAMOND HEAD

Diamond
Head Beach Park

KOKO
HEAD

Hawaii Kai

Maunalua
Bay

72

72

Punchbowl Crater

H1

Honolulu
International
Airport

Pearl Harbor
Naval Base

Pearl Harbor

Aiea

78

H3

61

63

Kaneohe Bay

830

Kahaluu

Kualoa Park

Kaaawa

Kahana Bay Beach Park

Punaluu Beach Park

Malaekahana Beach Park

Puu
Kaaikukua

83

Punaluu

Hauula

Laie

Kahuku

KOOLAU MOUNTAINS

HONOLULU

Ala Moana
Beach Park

Waikiki Beach

Waikiki

Mamala
Bay

76

White Plains
Beach Park

Ewa

Kapolei

750

H1

Waipahu

Mililani
Town

99

Wahiawa

80

H2

83

930

North Shore

Haleiwa

Waialua Bay

Waialee

Turtle Bay

83

Sunset Beach Neighborhood Park
Ehukai Beach Park
(The Banzai Pipeline)
Pupukea Beach Park/
Shark's Cove
Waimea Bay Beach Park

Haleiwa Alii
Beach Park

Mokuleia Beach Park

KAENA
POINT

Yokohama Bay

Yokohama Bay

93

Ko Olina

West (Leeward)

Electric Beach

Nanakuli

Maili

Waianae

Makaha

Makaha Beach Park
Papaoneone Beach
Pokai Bay Beach Park

WAIANAE
MOUNTAINS

Kaala

Puu
Manawahua

Poliikea

Ewa

Kapolei

N

0 ___ 5 mi

0 ___ 5 km

per hour the resorts want. ■ TIP→ If you're staying outside the area, our best advice is to park at either end of the beach and walk in.

FAMILY **Duke Kahanamoku Beach.** Named for Hawaii's famous Olympic swimming champion, Duke Kahanamoku, this is a hard-packed beach with the only shade trees on the sand in Waikiki. It's great for families with young children because it has both shade and the calmest waters in Waikiki, thanks to a rock wall that creates a semiprotected cove. The ocean clarity here is not as brilliant as most of Waikiki because of the stillness of the surf, but it's a small price to pay for peace of mind about youngsters. The beach fronts the Hilton Hawaiian Village Beach Resort and Spa. **Amenities:** food and drink; parking (fee); showers; toilets. **Best for:** sunset; walking. ⊠ *2005 Kalia Rd., Waikiki.*

FAMILY **Fort DeRussy Beach Park.** This is one of the finest beaches on the south
Fodor's Choice side of Oahu. A wide, soft, ultrawhite beachfront with gently lapping
★ waves makes it a family favorite for running-jumping-frolicking fun. The new, heavily shaded grass grilling area, sand volleyball courts, and aquatic rentals make this a must for the active visitor. The beach fronts Hale Koa Hotel as well as Fort DeRussy. **Amenities:** food and drink; lifeguards; showers; toilets; water sports. **Best for:** swimming; walking. ⊠ *2161 Kalia Rd., Waikiki.*

Gray's Beach. A little guesthouse called Gray's-by-the-Sea stood here in the 1920s; now it's a gathering place for eclectic beach types from sailing pioneers like George Parsons to the "bird men" of Waikiki: stop and watch the show as up to six parrots are placed on the heads, shoulders, and arms of squealing tourists waiting impatiently for their photos to be taken. The tides often put sand space at a premium, but if you want a look back into old Waikiki, have a mai tai at the Shorebird and check out a time gone by. The Halekulani Hotel and Outrigger Reef hotel are on this beach. **Amenities:** food and drink; lifeguards; parking (fee); showers; toilets. **Best for:** partiers; walking. ⊠ *2199 Kalia Rd., Waikiki.*

Kahaloa and Ulukou Beaches. The beach widens back out here, creating the "it" spot for the bikini crowd—beautiful bodies abound. This is where you find most of the catamaran charters for a spectacular sail out to Diamond Head, or surfboard and outrigger canoe rentals for a ride on the rolling waves of the Canoe surf break. Great music and outdoor dancing beckon the sand-bound visitor to Duke's Canoe Club, where shirt and shoes not only aren't required, they're discouraged. The Royal Hawaiian Hotel and the Moana Surfrider are both on this beach. **Amenities:** food and drink; lifeguards; parking (fee); showers; toilets; water sports. **Best for:** partiers; surfing. ⊠ *2259 Kalakaua Ave., Waikiki.*

FAMILY **Kuhio Beach Park.** This beach has experienced a renaissance after a recent face-lift. Now bordered by a landscaped boardwalk, it's great for romantic walks any time of day. Check out the Kuhio Beach hula mound Tuesday, Thursday, and Saturday at 6:30 (at 6 November–January) for free hula and Hawaiian-music performances and a torch-lighting ceremony at sunset. Surf lessons for beginners are available from the beach center every half hour. **Amenities:** food and drink; lifeguards; showers; toilets; water sports. **Best for:** surfing; walking. ⊠ *2461 Kalakaua Ave., Waikiki* ♦ *Go past Moana Surfrider Hotel to Kapahulu Ave. pier.*

OUTRIGGER CANOES

Outrigger canoes are a simple, cheap, but often-overlooked way to have fun in Waikiki. Everyone clamors to be on the water near Waikiki, and most people go for pricey sailing trips or surf lessons.

The long, funny-looking boats in front of Duke's Canoe Club allow you to get out on the water for much less money. At $20 for two rides, the price has changed only a little in the past decade, but the thrill hasn't changed in centuries. You can get a paddle, but no one expects you to use it—the beach boys negotiate you in and out of the break as they have been doing all their lives.

If you think taking off on a wave on a 10-foot board is a rush, wait until your whole family takes off on one in a 30-foot boat!

FAMILY **Queen's Surf Beach.** So named as it was once the site of Queen Liliuokalani's beach house, this beach draws a mix of families and gay couples—and it seems as if someone is always playing a steel drum. There are banyan trees for shade and volleyball nets for pros and amateurs alike. The water fronting Queen's Surf is an aquatic preserve, providing the best snorkeling in Waikiki. **Amenities:** lifeguards; showers; toilets. **Best for:** swimming; walking. ⊠ *2598 Kalakaua Ave., Waikiki* ✦ *Across from the entrance to Honolulu Zoo.*

FAMILY **Sans Souci/Kaimana Beach.** Nicknamed Dig-Me Beach because of its outlandish display of skimpy bathing suits, this small rectangle of sand is nonetheless a good sunning spot for all ages. Children enjoy its shallow, safe waters, which are protected (for now) by the walls of the historic natatorium, an Olympic-size saltwater swimming arena that's been closed for decades. Serious swimmers and triathletes also swim in the channel here, beyond the reef. Sans Souci is favored by locals wanting to avoid the crowds while still enjoying the convenience of Waikiki. The New Otani Kaimana Beach Hotel is next door. **Amenities:** lifeguards; parking (fee); showers; toilets. **Best for:** swimming; walking. ⊠ *2776 Kalakaua Ave., Waikiki* ✦ *Across from Kapiolani Park, between New Otani Kaimana Beach Hotel and Waikiki War Memorial Natatorium.*

ALA MOANA

Honolulu proper only has one beach: Ala Moana. Popular with locals, it hosts everything from Dragon Boat competitions to the Aloha State Games.

FAMILY **Ala Moana Beach Park.** A protective reef makes Ala Moana essentially a ½-mile-wide saltwater swimming pool. Very smooth sand and no waves create a haven for families and stand-up paddle surfers. After Waikiki, this is the most popular beach among visitors, and the free parking area can fill up quickly on sunny weekend days. On the Waikiki side is a peninsula called Magic Island, with shady trees and paved sidewalks ideal for jogging. Ala Moana also has playing fields, tennis courts, and a couple of small ponds for sailing toy boats. This beach is for everyone, but only in the daytime; it's a high-crime area, with lots

BEACH SAFETY ON OAHU

Hawaii's world-renowned, beautiful beaches can be dangerous at times due to large waves and strong currents—so much so that the state rates wave hazards using three signs: a yellow square (caution), a red stop sign (high hazard), and a black diamond (extreme hazard). Signs are posted and updated three times daily or as conditions change.

Visiting beaches with lifeguards is strongly recommended, and you should swim only when there's a normal caution rating. Never swim alone or dive into unknown water or shallow breaking waves. When admiring the waves close to the shoreline, don't turn your back to the ocean. Waves can come in suddenly and wash beachgoers out to sea. If you're unable to swim out of a rip current, don't fight the pull but instead tread water and wave your arms in the air to signal for help.

Even in calm conditions, there are other dangerous things in the water to be aware of, including razor-sharp coral, jellyfish, eels, and sharks.

Jellyfish cause the most ocean injuries, and signs are posted along beaches when they're present. If you're stung, pick off the tentacles with tweezers, rinse the affected area with vinegar, and apply heat.

Shark attacks in Hawaii are rare. Of the 40 species of sharks found near Hawaii, tiger sharks are considered the most dangerous because of their size and indiscriminate feeding behavior. They're easily recognized by their blunt snouts and vertical bars on their sides. Here are a few tips to reduce your shark-attack risk:

■ Swim, surf, or dive with others at beaches patrolled by lifeguards.

■ Avoid swimming at dawn, dusk, and night, when some shark species may move inshore to feed.

■ Don't enter the water if you have open wounds or are bleeding.

■ Avoid murky waters, harbor entrances, areas near stream mouths (especially after heavy rains), channels, or steep drop-offs.

■ Don't wear high-contrast swimwear or shiny jewelry.

■ Don't swim near dolphins, which are often prey for large sharks.

■ If you spot a shark, leave the water quickly and calmly; never provoke or harass a shark, no matter how small.

The website ⊕ *oceansafety.soest.hawaii.edu* provides statewide beach-hazard maps as well as weather and surf advisories, listings of closed beaches, and safety tips.

of homeless people, after dark. **Amenities:** food and drink; lifeguards; parking (fee); showers; toilets. **Best for:** swimming; walking. ⊠ *1201 Ala Moana Blvd., Ala Moana* ✢ *From Waikiki take Bus No. 8 to Ala Moana Shopping Center and cross Ala Moana Blvd.*

DIAMOND HEAD

Diamond Head Beach Park. You have to like a little hiking to like Diamond Head Beach. This beautiful, remote spot is at the base of Diamond Head crater. The beach is just a small strip of sand with lots of coral in the water. This said, the views looking out from the point are breathtaking, and it's amazing to watch the windsurfers skimming along, driven by the gusts off the point. From the parking area, look for an opening in the wall where an unpaved trail leads down to the beach. Even for the unadventurous, a stop at the lookout point is well worth the time. **Amenities:** parking (no fee); showers. **Best for:** solitude; sunset; surfing; windsurfing. ⊠ *At base of Diamond Head, 3500 Diamond Head Rd., Diamond Head ✛ Park at the crest of Diamond Head Rd. and walk down.*

3

SOUTHEAST OAHU

Much of Southeast Oahu is surrounded by reef, making most of the coast uninviting to swimmers, but the spots where the reef opens up are true gems. The drive along this side of the island is amazing, with its sheer lava-rock walls on one side and deep-blue ocean on the other. There are plenty of restaurants in the suburb of Hawaii Kai, so you can make a day of it, knowing that food isn't far away.

Halona Cove. Also known as *From Here to Eternity* Beach and "Pounders," this little beauty is never crowded due to the short, treacherous climb down to the sand. But for the intrepid, what a treat this spot can be. It's in a break in the ocean cliffs, with the surrounding crags providing protection from the wind. Open-ocean waves roll up onto the beach (thus the second nickname), but unlike at Sandy Beach, a gently sloping sand bottom takes much of the punch out of them before they hit the shore. Turtles frequent the small cove, seeking respite from the otherwise blustery coast. It's great for packing a lunch and holing up for the day. ⚠ **The current is mellow inside the cove but dangerous once you get outside it. Amenities:** parking (no fee). **Best for:** sunrise. ⊠ *8699 Kalanianaole Hwy., Hawaii Kai ✛ Below the Halona Blow Hole Lookout parking lot.*

FAMILY
Fodor's Choice
★

Hanauma Bay Nature Preserve. Picture this as the world's biggest open-air aquarium. You go here to see fish, and fish you'll see. Due to their exposure to thousands of visitors every week, these fish are more like family pets than the skittish marine life you might expect. An old volcanic crater has created a haven from the waves where the coral has thrived. There's an educational center where you must watch a nine-minute video about the nature preserve before being allowed down to the bay. ■ TIP➜ **The bay is best early in the morning (around 7), before the crowds arrive; it can be difficult to park later in the day.**

Snorkel equipment and lockers are available for rent, and there's an entry fee for nonresidents. Smoking is not allowed, and the beach is closed on Tuesday. Wednesday to Monday, the beach is open 6 am–6 pm (until 7 pm June–August). There's a tram from the parking lot to the beach, or you can walk the short distance on foot. Need transportation? Take TheBus each way from anywhere on the island. Alternatively, Hanauma Bay Snorkeling Excursions runs snorkeling tours to Hanauma Bay, with equipment and transportation from Waikiki hotels. **Amenities:** food and drink; lifeguards; parking (fee); showers;

Not a water baby? Come to Sandy Beach—otherwise known as Break-Neck Beach—to watch the massive ocean swells and awesome pounding surf.

toilets. **Best for:** snorkeling; swimming. ✉ *7455 Kalanianaole Hwy., Hawaii Kai* ☎ *808/396–4229* ⊕ *www.honolulu.gov/cms-dpr-menu/site-dpr-sitearticles/1716-hanauma-bay-home.html* 🎫 *Nonresidents $7.50; parking $1; mask and snorkel $12, with fins $20; tram from parking lot to beach $2.25 round-trip.*

Sandy Beach Park. Probably the most popular beach with locals on this side of Oahu, the broad, sloping beach is covered with sunbathers there to watch the "Show" and soak up rays. The Show is a shore break that's like no other in the Islands. Monster ocean swells rolling into the beach combined with the sudden rise in the ocean floor causes waves to jack up and crash magnificently on the shore. Expert surfers and bodyboarders young and old brave this danger to get some of the biggest barrels you can find for bodysurfing. ⚠ **But keep in mind that the beach is nicknamed Break-Neck Beach for a reason: many neck and back injuries are sustained here each year.** Use extreme caution when swimming here, or just kick back and watch the drama unfold from the comfort of your beach chair. **Amenities:** lifeguards; parking (no fee); showers; toilets. **Best for:** bodyboarding; walking. ✉ *7850 Kalanianaole Hwy., Hawaii Kai* ⚓ *Makai (toward ocean) of Kalanianaole Hwy., 2 miles east of Hanauma Bay.*

WINDWARD OAHU

The windward side lives up to its name, with ideal spots for windsurfing and kiteboarding, or for the more intrepid, hang gliding. For the most part the waves are mellow, and the bottoms are all sand—making for nice spots to visit with younger kids. The only drawback is that this side of Oahu does tend to get more rain. But the vistas are so beautiful that a little sprinkling of "pineapple juice" shouldn't dampen your experience; plus, it benefits the waterfalls that cascade down the Koolaus.

FodorsChoice ★ Bellows Beach Park. Bellows is the same beach as Waimanalo, but it's under the auspices of the military, making it more friendly for visitors—though that also limits public beach access to weekends. The park area is excellent for camping, and ironwood trees provide plenty of shade. ■**TIP→** The beach is best before 2 pm. After 2, trade winds bring clouds that get hung up on steep mountains nearby, causing overcast skies. There are no food concessions, but McDonald's and other take-out fare are right outside the entrance gate. **Amenities:** lifeguards; parking (no fee); showers; toilets. **Best for:** solitude; walking; swimming. ⊠ *520 Tinker Rd., Waimanalo ✛ Enter on Kalanianaole Hwy. near Waimanalo town center.*

FAMILY Kahana Bay Beach Park. Local parents often bring their children here to wade in safety in the very shallow, protected waters. This pretty beach cove, surrounded by mountains, has a long arc of sand that is great for walking and a cool, shady grove of tall ironwood and pandanus trees that is ideal for a picnic. An ancient Hawaiian fishpond, which was in use until the 1920s, is visible nearby. The water here is not generally a clear blue due to the runoff from heavy rains in the valley. **Amenities:** parking (no fee); showers; toilets. **Best for:** swimming; walking. ⊠ *52-201 Kamehameha Hwy., Kaneohe ✛ North of Kualoa Park.*

FAMILY FodorsChoice ★ Kailua Beach Park. A cobalt-blue sea and a wide continuous arc of powdery sand make Kailua Beach Park one of the island's best beaches, illustrated by the crowds of local families who spend their weekend days here. This is like a big Lanikai Beach, but a little windier and a little wider, and a better spot for spending a full day. Kailua Beach has calm water, a line of palms and ironwoods that provide shade on the sand, and a huge park with picnic pavilions where you can escape the heat. This is the "it" spot if you're looking to try your hand at windsurfing or kiteboarding. You can rent kayaks nearby at Kailua Beach Adventures (130 Kailua Rd.) and take them to the Mokulua Islands for the day. **Amenities:** lifeguards; parking (no fee); showers; toilets; water sports. **Best for:** walking; swimming; windsurfing. ⊠ *437 Kawailoa Rd., Kailua ✛ Near Kailua town, turn right on Kailua Rd. After the market, cross bridge, then turn left into beach parking lot.*

Kualoa Park. Grassy expanses border a long, narrow stretch of beach with spectacular views of Kaneohe Bay and the Koolau Mountains, making Kualoa one of the island's most beautiful picnic, camping, and beach areas. Dominating the view is an islet called Mokolii, better known as Chinaman's Hat, which rises 206 feet above the water. You can swim in the shallow areas of this rarely crowded beach year-round. The one drawback is that it's usually windy here, but the wide-open spaces are ideal for kite flying. **Amenities:** lifeguards; showers; toilets. **Best for:** solitude; swimming. ⊠ *49-479 Kamehameha Hwy., Kaaawa ✛ North of Waiahole.*

Kailua Beach Park is long and wide, with ample space to accommodate the families that flock here on the weekends. On some weekdays, you may have to share the sand with just a few others.

Lanikai Beach Park. Think of the beaches you see in commercials: peaceful jade-green waters, powder-soft white sand, families and dogs frolicking mindlessly, and offshore islands in the distance. It's an ideal spot for camping out with a book. Though the beach hides behind multimillion-dollar houses, by state law there is public access every 400 yards. Street parking is available but difficult to find (and prohibited on holiday weekends. ■ **TIP→** Look for walled or fenced pathways every 400 yards, leading to the beach. Be sure not to park in the marked bike/jogging lane. There are no shower or bathroom facilities here—but you'll find both a two-minute drive away at Kailua Beach Park. **Amenities:** none. **Best for:** swimming; walking; sunrise. ⊠ *974 Mokulua Dr., Kailua* ✛ *Past Kailua Beach Park.*

Makapuu Beach Park. A magnificent beach protected by Makapuu Point welcomes you to the windward side. Hang gliders circle above the beach, and the water is filled with body boarders. Just off the coast you can see Bird Island, a sanctuary for aquatic fowl, jutting out of the blue. The currents can be heavy, so check with a lifeguard if you're unsure of safety. Before you leave, take the prettiest (and coldest) outdoor shower available on the island. Being surrounded by tropical flowers and foliage while you rinse off that sand will be a memory you will cherish from this side of the rock. **Amenities:** lifeguards; parking (no fee); showers; toilets. **Best for:** sunrise; walking. ⊠ *41-095 Kalanianaole Hwy., Waimanalo* ✛ *Across from Sea Life Park, 2 miles south of Waimanalo.*

Malaekahana Beach Park. The big attraction here is tiny Goat Island, a bird sanctuary just offshore. At low tide the water is shallow enough—never more than waist-high—so that you can wade out to it. Wear sneakers or aqua socks so you don't cut yourself on the coral. The beach itself is fairly narrow but long enough for a 20-minute stroll, one-way. The waves are never too big, and sometimes they're just right for the beginning bodysurfer. The entrance gates, which close at 7:45 pm in summer and 6:45 pm the rest of the year, are easy to miss, and you can't see the beach from the road. Families love to camp in the groves of ironwood trees at Malaekahana State Park. Cabins are also available here, making a perfect rural getaway. **Amenities:** parking (no fee); showers; toilets. **Best for:** swimming; walking. ⊠ *56-207 Kamehameha Hwy., Laie ✛ Enter at gates ½ mile north of Laie on Kamehameha Hwy.*

3

Punaluu Beach Park. If you're making a circle of the island, this is a great stopping point to jump out of your car and stretch your legs and get your toes wet. It's easy, because the sand literally comes up to your parked car, and nice, because there is a sandy bottom and mostly calm conditions. Plus there are full facilities, shops for picnic supplies, and lots of shade trees. Often overlooked, and often overcast, Punaluu can afford you a moment of fresh air before you get back to your sightseeing. **Amenities:** parking (no fee); showers; toilets. **Best for:** solitude; swimming. ⊠ *53-400 Kamehameha Hwy., Hauula.*

FAMILY **Waimanalo Beach Park.** One of the most beautiful beaches on the island, Waimanalo is a local pick, busy with picnicking families and active sports fields. Expect a wide stretch of sand; turquoise, emerald, and deep blue seas; and gentle shore-breaking waves that are fun for all ages. Theft is an occasional problem, so lock your car. **Amenities:** lifeguards; parking (no fee); showers; toilets. **Best for:** sunrise; swimming; walking. ⊠ *41-849 Kalanianaole Hwy., Waimanalo ✛ South of Waimanalo town center.*

NORTH SHORE

"North Shore, where the waves are mean, just like a washing machine," sing the Kaau Crater Boys about this legendary side of the island. And in winter they are absolutely right. At times the waves overtake the road, stranding tourists and locals alike. When the surf is up, there are signs on the beach telling you how far to stay back so that you aren't swept out to sea. The most prestigious big-wave contest in the world, the Eddie Aikau, is held at Waimea Bay on waves the size of a five- or six-story building. The Triple Crown of Surfing roams across three North Shore beaches in the winter months.

All this changes come summer when this tiger turns into a kitten, with water smooth enough to water-ski on and ideal for snorkeling. The fierce Banzai Pipeline surf break becomes a great dive area, allowing you to explore the coral heads that, in winter, have claimed so many lives on the ultrashallow but big, hollow tubes created here. Even with the monster surf subsided, this is still a time for caution: lifeguards are scarce, and currents don't subside just because the waves do.

That said, it's a place like no other on Earth, and must be explored. From the turtles at Mokuleia to the tunnels at Shark's Cove, you could spend your whole trip on this side and not be disappointed.

Ehukai Beach Park. What sets Ehukai apart is the view of the famous Banzai Pipeline. Here the winter waves curl into magnificent tubes, making it an experienced wave-rider's dream. It's also an inexperienced swimmer's nightmare. Spring and summer waves on the other hand are more accommodating to the average person, and there's good snorkeling. Except when the surf contests are going on, there's no reason to stay on the central strip. Travel in either direction from the center, and the conditions remain the same but the population thins out, leaving you with a magnificent stretch of sand all to yourself. **Amenities:** lifeguards; parking (no fee); showers; toilets. **Best for:** snorkeling; surfing. ⊠ *59-406 Kamehameha Hwy., Haleiwa ✤ 1 mile north of Foodland at Pupukea.*

FAMILY **Haleiwa Alii Beach Park.** The winter waves are impressive here, but in summer the ocean is like a lake, ideal for family swimming. The beach itself is big and often full of locals. Its broad lawn off the highway invites volleyball and Frisbee games and groups of barbecuers. This is also the opening break for the Triple Crown of Surfing, and the grass is often filled with art festivals or carnivals. **Amenities:** lifeguards; parking (no fee); showers; toilets. **Best for:** surfing; swimming. ⊠ *66-162 Haleiwa Rd., Haleiwa ✤ North of Haleiwa town center and past harbor.*

Mokuleia Beach Park. There is a reason why the producers of the TV show *Lost* chose this beach for their set. On the remote northwest point of the island, it is about 10 miles from the closest store or public restroom. Its beauty is in its lack of facilities and isolation—all the joy of being stranded on a deserted island without the trauma of the plane crash. The beach is wide and white, the waters bright blue (but a little choppy) and full of sea turtles and other marine life. Mokuleia is a great secret find; just remember to pack supplies and use caution, as there are no lifeguards. **Amenities:** parking (no fee) **Best for:** walking, sunset. ⊠ *68-67 Farrington Hwy., Haleiwa ✤ West of Haleiwa town center, across from Dillingham Airfield.*

Fodor's Choice **Pupukea Beach Park/Shark's Cove.** Surrounded by shady trees, Pupukea ★ Beach Park is pounded by surf in the winter months but offers great diving and snorkeling in summer (March through October). The cavernous lava tubes and tunnels are great for both novice and experienced snorkelers and divers. It's imperative that you wear reef shoes at all times since there are a lot of sharp rocks. Sharp rocks also mean that this beach isn't the best for little ones. Some dive-tour companies offer round-trip transportation from Waikiki. Equipment rentals and dining options are nearby. **Amenities:** parking (no fee); showers; toilets. **Best for:** diving; snorkeling; swimming. ⊠ *Haleiwa ✤ 3.5 miles north of Haleiwa, across the street from Foodland.*

Sunset Beach Neighborhood Park. The beach is broad, the sand is soft, the summer waves are gentle—making for good snorkeling—and the winter surf is crashing. Many love searching this shore for the puka shells that adorn the necklaces you see everywhere. **Amenities:** lifeguards; parking (no fee); showers; toilets. **Best for:** snorkeling; sunset; surfing. ⊠ *59 Kamehameha Hwy., Haleiwa ✤ 1 mile north of Ehukai Beach Park.*

DID YOU KNOW?

If you're vacationing with kids, Lanikai Beach is a good choice, with calm water and soft sand.

FAMILY **Turtle Bay.** Now known more for its resort (the Turtle Bay Resort) than its magnificent beach, Turtle Bay is mostly passed over on the way to the better-known beaches of Sunset and Waimea. But for the average visitor with average swimming capabilities, this is a good place to be on the North Shore. The crescent-shaped beach is protected by a huge sea wall. You can see and hear the fury of the northern swell while blissfully floating in cool, calm waters. The convenience of this spot is also hard to pass up—there is a concession selling sandwiches and sunblock right on the beach. The resort has free parking for beach guests. **Amenities:** food and drink; parking (no fee); showers; toilets. **Best for:** sunset; swimming. ⊠ *57-20 Kuilima Dr., 4 miles north of Kahuku, Kahuku ✛ Turn into Turtle Bay Resort, and let guard know where you are going.*

Fodor'sChoice **Waimea Bay Beach Park.** Made popular in that old Beach Boys song ★ "Surfin' U.S.A.," Waimea Bay Beach Park is a slice of big-wave heaven, home to king-size 25- to 30-foot winter waves. Summer is the time to swim and snorkel in the calm waters. The shore break is great for novice bodysurfers. Due to its popularity, the postage-stamp parking lot is quickly filled, but it's also possible to park along the side of the road and walk in. **Amenities:** lifeguards; parking (no fee); showers; toilets. **Best for:** snorkeling (in summer); surfing (in winter); swimming (in summer). ⊠ *61-31 Kamehameha Hwy., Haleiwa ✛ Across from Waimea Valley, 3 miles north of Haleiwa.*

WEST (LEEWARD) OAHU

The North Shore may be known as "country," but the west side is truly the rural area on Oahu. There are commuters from this side to Honolulu, but many are born, live, and die on this side with scarcely a trip to town. For the most part, there's little hostility toward outsiders, but occasional problems have flared up, mostly due to drug abuse, which has ravaged the fringes of the island—generally on the order of car break-ins, not violence. So, in short, lock your car, don't bring valuables, and enjoy the amazing beaches.

The beaches on the west side are expansive and empty. Most Oahu residents and tourists don't make it to this side simply because of the drive; in traffic it can take almost 90 minutes to make it to Kaena Point from downtown Honolulu. But you'll be hard-pressed to find a better sunset anywhere.

Electric Beach. Directly across from the electricity plant—hence the name—Electric Beach (also known as Kahe Point) is a haven for tropical fish, making it a great snorkeling spot. The expulsion of hot water from the plant raises the temperature of the ocean, attracting Hawaiian green sea turtles, spotted moray eels, and spinner dolphins. Although the visibility is not always the best, the crowds are often small, but growing, and the fish are guaranteed. It's best to wear reef shoes here because of the sharp rocks. Unfortunately, there can be a strong current here, so it's not very kid-friendly. This is also a great place to stop for a picnic and admire the views. **Amenities:** parking (no fee); showers; toilets. **Best for:** snorkeling; sunset. ⊠ *Farrington Hwy., Kapolei ✛ 1 mile west of Ko Olina Resort.*

DID YOU KNOW?

Beach Boys fans flock to Waimea Bay, the beach with winter waves reaching 30 feet, made popular in "Surfin' U.S.A."

FAMILY **Ko Olina.** This is the best spot on the island if you have small kids. The resort area commissioned a series of four man-made lagoons, but, as it has to provide public beach access, you are the winner. Huge rock walls protect the lagoons, making them into perfect spots for the kids to get their first taste of the ocean without getting bowled over. The large expanses of seashore grass and hala trees that surround the semicircle beaches are made-to-order for nap time. A 1½-mile jogging track connects the lagoons. Due to its appeal for *keiki* (children), Ko Olina is popular, and the parking lot fills up quickly when school is out and on weekends, so try to get here before 10 am. The biggest parking lot is at the farthest lagoon from the entrance. There are actually three resorts here: Aulani (the Disney resort), Four Seasons Resort Oahu, and the Ko Olina Beach Villas Resort (which has a time-share section as well). **Amenities:** food and drink; parking (no fee); showers; toilet. **Best for:** sunset; swimming; walking. ⊠ *92 Aliinui Dr., 23 miles west of Honolulu, Kapolei* ✛ *Take Ko Olina exit off H1 West and proceed to guard shack.*

Makaha Beach Park. This beach provides a slice of local life most visitors don't see. Families string up tarps for the day, fire up hibachis, set up lawn chairs, get out the fishing gear, and strum ukulele while they "talk story" (chat). Legendary waterman Buffalo Keaulana can be found in the shade of the palms playing with his grandkids and spinning yarns of yesteryear. In these waters Buffalo not only invented some of the most outrageous methods of surfing, but also raised his world-champion son Rusty. He also made Makaha the home of the world's first international surf meet in 1954 and still hosts his Big Board Surfing Classic. With its long, slow-building waves, it's a great spot to try out longboarding. The swimming is generally decent in summer, but avoid the big winter waves. The only parking is along the highway, but it's free. **Amenities:** lifeguards; showers; toilets. **Best for:** surfing; swimming. ⊠ *84-450 Farrington Hwy., Waianae* ✛ *Go 32 miles west of Honolulu on the H1, then exit onto Farrington Hwy. The beach will be on your left.*

Papaoneone Beach. You may have to do a little exploring to find Papaoneone Beach, which is tucked behind three condos. Duck through a wide, easy to-spot hole in the fence, and you find an extremely wide, sloping beach that always seems to be empty. You'll have to park on the street. The waters are that eerie blue found only on the west side. Waves can get high here (it faces the same direction as the famed Makaha Beach), but, for the most part, the shore break makes for great easy rides on your bodyboard or belly. The only downside is that, with the exception of a shower, all facilities are for the condos at the adjacent Beach Lovers Hawaii, so it's just you and the big blue. **Amenities:** showers. **Best for:** solitude; swimming. ⊠ *84-946 Farrington Hwy., Waianae* ✛ *In Makaha, across from Jade St.*

Pokai Bay Beach Park. This gorgeous swimming and snorkeling beach is protected by a long breakwater left over from a now-defunct boat harbor. The beach's entire length is sand, and a reef creates smallish waves perfect for novice surfers. **Amenities:** parking (no fee); showers; toilets. **Best for:** snorkeling; swimming. ⊠ *85-027 Waianae Valley Rd., Waianae* ✛ *Off Farrington Hwy.*

FAMILY

Fodor's Choice

★

White Plains Beach Park. Concealed from the public eye for many years as part of the former Barbers Point Naval Air Station, this beach is reminiscent of Waikiki but without the condos and the crowds. It is a long, sloping beach with numerous surf breaks, but it is also mild enough at shore for older children to play freely. It has views of Pearl Harbor and, over that, Diamond Head. Although the sand lives up to its name, the real joy of this beach comes from its history as part of a military property for the better part of a century. Expansive parking, great restroom facilities, and numerous tree-covered barbecue areas make it a great day-trip spot. As a bonus, a Hawaiian monk seal takes up residence here several months out of the year (seals are rare in the Islands). **Amenities:** lifeguards; parking (no fee); showers; toilets. **Best for:** surfing; swimming. ⊠ *Essex Rd. and Tripoli Rd., Kapolei* ✢ *Take Makakilo exit off H1 West, then turn left. Follow it into base gates, make left. Blue signs lead to beach.*

Yokohama Bay. You'll be one of the few outsiders at this Waianae Coast beach at the very end of the road. If it weren't for the little strip of paved road, it would feel like a deserted isle: no stores, no houses, just a huge sloping stretch of beach and some of the darkest-blue water off the island. Locals come here to fish and swim in waters calm enough for children in summer. Early morning brings with it spinner dolphins by the dozens just offshore. Although Makua Beach up the road is the best spot to see these animals, it's not nearly as beautiful or sandy as "Yokes." **Amenities:** lifeguards; parking (no fee); showers; toilets. **Best for:** solitude; sunset; swimming. ⊠ *81-780 Farrington Hwy., Waianae* ✢ *About 7 miles north of Makaha.*

4

WHERE TO EAT

Updated by
Powell Berger

Oahu is undergoing something of a renaissance at both ends of the dining spectrum. You can splurge on world-class contemporary cuisine at destination restaurants and explore local flavors at popular, very affordable holes in the wall. Whatever your taste and budget, you'll find places that pique your interest and palate.

You may wish to budget for a pricey dining experience at the very top of the restaurant food chain, where chefs Alan Wong, Roy Yamaguchi, George Mavrothalassitis, Chris Kajioka, and others you've seen on the Food Network and Travel Channel put a sophisticated spin on local foods and flavors. Savor dishes that take cues from Japan, China, Korea, the Philippines, the United States, and Europe, then are filtered through an Island sensibility. Take advantage of the location and order the superb local fish—mahimahi, opakaka, ono, and opah.

Spend the rest of your food dollars where budget-conscious locals do: in plate-lunch places and small ethnic eateries, at roadside stands and lunch wagons, or at window-in-the-wall delis. Snack on a *musubi* (a handheld rice ball wrapped with seaweed and often topped with Spam), slurp shave ice with red-bean paste, or order Filipino pork adobo with two scoops of rice and macaroni salad.

In Waikiki, where most visitors stay, you can find choices from upscale dining rooms with a view to Japanese noodle shops. When you're ready to explore, hop in the car, or on the trolley or bus—by going just a few miles in any direction, you can save money and eat like a local.

Kaimuki's Waialae Avenue, for example, is a critical mass of good eats and drinks. There you'll find an espresso bar, a Chinese bakery, a patisserie, an Italian bistro, a dim-sum restaurant, Mexican food, and a Hawaiian regional-cuisine standout (3660 on the Rise)—all in three blocks, and 10 minutes from Waikiki. Chinatown, 15 minutes in the other direction and easily reached by the Waikiki Trolley, is another dining (and shopping) treasure, not only for Chinese but also Vietnamese, Filipino, Malaysian, and Indian food, and even a chic little tea shop. Kakaako, the developing urban area between Waikiki and Chinatown, also offers a mix of local eateries, upscale restaurants, and ethnic takeout.

Outside Honolulu and Waikiki there are fewer dining options, but restaurants tend to be filled with locals and are cheaper and more casual. Windward Oahu's dining scene has improved greatly in recent years due to the visitors to Kailua and Lanikai beaches, so everything from plate lunches to Latin foods to creative regional offerings can be found there. Across the rest of the island, the cuisine is mainly American—great if you're traveling with kids—but there are a handful of Italian and Asian places worth trying as well.

OAHU DINING PLANNER

WITH KIDS
Hawaii is a kid-friendly destination in many regards, and many restaurants welcome the little ones (*keiki* in Hawaiian). That said, there are probably a few places in Waikiki where you're better off dining sans kids and taking advantage of your hotel's child care.

SMOKING
Smoking is prohibited except in places where liquor revenues exceed food sales.

PARKING
In Waikiki, walk or take a cab or call Uber; it's cheaper than parking or valet rates. Elsewhere on Oahu—including the new, hip Kakaako area—free, validated, and reasonably priced parking is widely available. Exceptions: parking downtown during the day is expensive—take the trolley or TheBus; Chinatown parking is also expensive and tough to find, especially at night. Consider the bus, a cab, or Uber.

RESERVATIONS
If you expect to dine at Alan Wong's, Chef Mavro, Roy's, or Vintage Cave Honolulu, book your table from home weeks in advance, particularly if you are looking to celebrate a special event and want a specific date or time. As in any other city, new restaurants tend to be jammed during their first few months. Otherwise, reserve when you get into town. Even some of the most coveted reservations can often be had if you can be flexible.

WHAT TO WEAR
Although people on Oahu dress up for dinner more than on any other Hawaiian island, casual still reigns supreme; most top restaurants abide by the dressy casual (i.e., "aloha wear") standard, where dark jeans are acceptable as long as they're not worn with sneakers. T-shirts and shorts are generally not welcome for dinner in nicer restaurants, and a few of Honolulu's nicest spots ask gentlemen to wear a jacket.

HOURS AND PRICES
People dine early here—the most sought-after dinner reservations are between 6 and 7, but you can usually have your pick of tables by 8. Exceptions: sushi bars and Japanese taverns, a few 24-hour diners, and some younger-spinning restaurants. Takeout places still open at dawn and close shortly after midday. Standard tipping for good service is 20%.

WHAT IT COSTS AT DINNER			
$	$$	$$$	$$$$
Under $17	$17–$26	$27–$35	Over $35

HONOLULU

There's no lack of choices when it comes to dining in Honolulu, where everything from the haute cuisine of heavy-hitting top-notch chefs to a wide variety of Asian specialties to reliable and inexpensive American favorites can be found.

WAIKIKI

As Honolulu's tourist hub, Waikiki is dense with restaurants. There are notable steak houses and grills in Waikiki as well, serving upscale American cuisine. But thanks to the many Japanese nationals who stay here, Waikiki is blessed with lots of cheap, filling, authentic Japanese food, particularly noodle houses. Plastic representations of food in the window outside are an indicator of authenticity and a help in ordering. It's not uncommon for a server to accompany a guest outside so that the selection can be pointed to.

$$ ITALIAN 🍴 **Arancino di Mare.** Three locations in town offer fresh seafood, hand-trimmed beef, pastas cooked to order, handmade pizza dough and bread, house-made desserts, and meats and cheeses imported from Italy. Locals as well as tourists come here to enjoy dishes that use only fresh, authentic ingredients. **Known for:** excellent spaghetti pescatore with shrimp, calamari, mussels, and clams; local favorite; small and casual in Waikiki, elegant date-night setting in Kahala. [$] *Average main: $26* ✉ *Waikiki Beach Marriott Resort, 2552 Kalakaua Ave., Waikiki* ☎ *808/931–6273* 🌐 *www.arancino.com.*

$$$$ STEAKHOUSE 🍴 **Bali Steak & Seafood.** This many-windowed, multilevel room takes delightful advantage of the restaurant's perch above the beach, facing Diamond Head. The chef creates uncomplicated contemporary cuisine—grilled fish, steaks, and chops accented with East–West fusion flavors. **Known for:** partnerships with local farmers for farm-to-table offerings; attentive staff; splurge prices. [$] *Average main: $40* ✉ *Hilton Hawaiian Village, 2005 Kalia Rd., Waikiki* ☎ *808/941–2254* 🌐 *www.hiltonhawaiianvillage.com/dining/bali-steak-and-seafood* 🕒 *Closed Sun. and Mon. No lunch.*

$$$$ STEAKHOUSE 🍴 **BLT Steak.** BLT Steak remains one of the swankiest rooms in town, where chef Fred DeAngelo blends global fare with local ingredients. From the tables of resined Makassar ebony, striped like a zebra, to the black-leather booths, this is a place for an intimate tête-à tête over a jalapeño-cilantro margarita, while you decide to go surf or turf. **Known for:** bar menu with excellent burgers, swanky cocktails, and raw oysters; creative sides like jalapeño mashed potatoes and spicy barbecue Kahuku corn; lofty prices deserving of a soothing cocktail. [$] *Average main: $48* ✉ *Trump International Hotel Waikiki Beach Walk, 223 Saratoga*

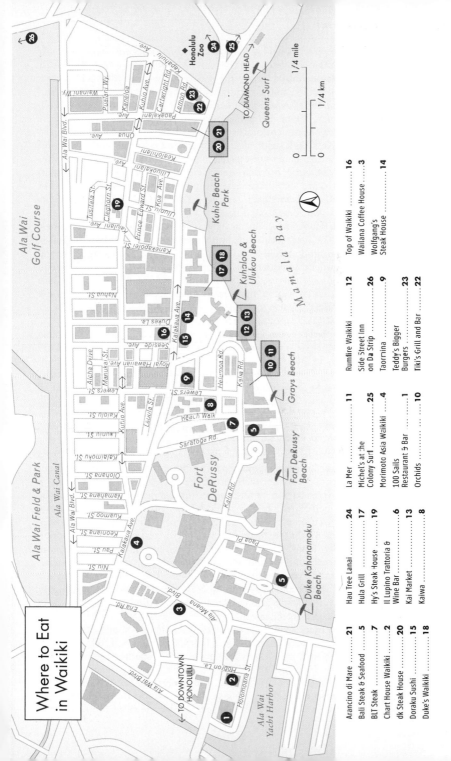

Where to Eat in Waikiki

Arancino di Mare **21**
Bali Steak & Seafood **5**
BLT Steak **7**
Chart House Waikiki **2**
dk Steak House **20**
Doraku Sushi **15**
Duke's Waikiki **18**

Hau Tree Lanai **24**
Hula Grill **17**
Hy's Steak House **19**
Il Lupino Trattoria &
  Wine Bar **6**
Kai Market **13**
Kaiwa **8**

La Mer **11**
Michel's at the
  Colony Surf **25**
Morimoto Asia Waikiki **4**
100 Sails
  Restaurant & Bar **1**
Orchids **10**

Rumfire Waikiki **12**
Side Street Inn
  on Da Strip **26**
Taormina **9**
Teddy's Bigger
  Burgers **23**
Tiki's Grill and Bar **22**

Top of Waikiki **16**
Wailana Coffee House **3**
Wolfgang's
  Steak House **14**

Ala Wai
Golf Course

Ala Wai Field & Park

Ala Wai Canal

Honolulu
Zoo

TO DIAMOND HEAD →

Queens Surf

Kuhio Beach
Park

Kuhaloa &
Ulukou Beach

M a m a l a   B a y

Grays Beach

Fort DeRussy
Beach

Fort
DeRussy

Duke Kahanamoku
Beach

Ala Wai
Yacht Harbor

TO DOWNTOWN
HONOLULU →

1/4 mile

1/4 km

Rd., Waikiki ☎ *808/683–7440* 🌐 *www.bltrestaurants.com/blt-steak/waikiki/* 🕒 *No lunch.*

$$$$ AMERICAN 🍴 **Chart House Waikiki.** Enjoy the sunset views over the yacht harbor as you take in live music nightly while sipping a signature "Guy-Tai" cocktail at this Waikiki landmark. The restaurant opened in 1969, and the menu retains the midcentury notion of "fine dining"—oysters Rockefeller, shrimp cocktail, and steaks (from a garlicky tenderloin to a wagyu New York strip), along with island nods such as ahi wontons, poke, and macadamia-nut-crusted mahimahi. **Known for:** sought-after tables on the lanai; old-time steak house atmosphere with dim lighting and strong cocktails; generations of regulars. [$] *Average main: $48* ✉ *1765 Ala Moana Blvd., Waikiki* ☎ *808/941–6669* 🌐 *www.charthousehonolulu.com* 🕒 *No lunch.*

$$$$ STEAKHOUSE 🍴 **dk Steak House.** Honolulu has its share of national-chain steak houses, but D.K. Kodama's local steak house serves steaks free from hormones, antibiotics, and steroids straight from Oahu's first dry-aging room. **Known for:** addictive potatoes au gratin topped with Maui onions and Parmesan; local flavors, local ownership, and locally sourced produce and select meats; sunset views from outdoor tables. [$] *Average main: $55* ✉ *Waikiki Beach Marriott Resort & Spa, 2552 Kalakaua Ave., Waikiki* ☎ *808/931–6280* 🌐 *www.dksteakhouse.com* 🕒 *No lunch.*

$$ JAPANESE 🍴 **Doraku Sushi.** From entrepreneur Kevin Aoki, son of Benihana founder Rocky Aoki, comes this low-lit bells-and-whistles sushi-roll chain (Miami and Atlanta have other branches) aimed at a nightclubbing crowd. There's better sushi in town, but the nightlife, bar scene, and late-night hours keep the place packed. **Known for:** a happening bar scene, with both early and late happy hours; tempura everything, including brownies; creative rolls like the Emperor seafood roll. [$] *Average main: $25* ✉ *Royal Hawaiian Center, 2233 Kalakaua Ave., Waikiki* ☎ *808/922–3323* 🌐 *www.dorakusushi.com.*

$$$ AMERICAN FAMILY 🍴 **Duke's Waikiki.** Locals often take visiting friends and family from the mainland to this popular open-air hotel restaurant for the beachfront setting—it's right in front of the famed Canoes surf break in Waikiki—and bar scene and *pupu* (hors d'oeuvres) more than the food. Named for the father of modern surfing and filled with Duke Kahanamoku memorabilia, it's got a great salad bar and a crowd-pleasing menu that includes fish, prime rib, and *huli huli* (rotisserie). **Known for:** iconic local spot with great views, great bar scene, and perfect location in Waikiki; Duke's on Sunday is so popular musician Henry Kapono wrote a song about it (Duke's on Sunday); bar seating for better service and better prices. [$] *Average main: $28* ✉ *Outrigger Waikiki on the Beach, 2335 Kalakaua Ave., Waikiki* ☎ *808/922–2268* 🌐 *www.dukeswaikiki.com.*

$$$$ AMERICAN 🍴 **Hau Tree Lanai.** Countless anniversaries, birthdays, and family milestones have been celebrated under this spectacular *hau* tree, where it's said that even Robert Louis Stevenson found shade as he mused and wrote about Hawaii. Still today, diners are captivated by the shade, the beach views, the romantic setting, and a menu that delivers everything from eggs Benedict to a sizzling steak. **Known for:** the romantic beach dining spot folks dream about; spectacular views of the beach and

water by day and by night; a solid menu, big portions, and attentive service. [$] *Average main: $48* ✉ *New Otani Kaimana Beach Hotel, 2863 Kalakaua Ave., Waikiki* ☎ *808/921–7066* 🌐 *www.kaimana.com/hautreelanai.htm.*

$$$ HAWAIIAN 🍴 **Hula Grill.** The placid younger sister of boisterous Duke's, downstairs, this restaurant and bar resemble an open-air plantation-period summer home with kitschy decor, stone-flagged floors, warm wood, and floral prints. The food is carefully prepared and familiar—standard breakfast items, steaks and grilled seafood at dinner—but with local and Asian touches that add modest interest. **Known for:** spectacular views from the window tables; reliable local dining experience with the kitsch to know you're in Waikiki; nice bar scene for drinks and snacks. [$] *Average main: $28* ✉ *Outrigger Waikiki on the Beach, 2335 Kalakaua Ave., Waikiki* ☎ *808/923–4852* 🌐 *www.hulagrillwaikiki.com.*

4

$$$$ STEAKHOUSE 🍴 **Hy's Steak House.** If the Rat Pack reconvened for big steaks and a bigger red, they'd feel right at home at Hy's, which hasn't changed much since it opened in 1976. The formula: prime-grade beef cooked over an open kiawe-wood fire (aka mesquite), old-style service, a men's-club atmosphere (but ladies very welcome), and a wine list recognized for excellence by *Wine Spectator.* Aside from the signature steaks, specialties include beef Wellington, Caesar salad, and those flambéed desserts rarely seen these days—the last two are prepared tableside, of course. **Known for:** dark woods, club chairs, banquettes, and that fabulous 1970's feel; a wine list fit for the most persnickety palate; desserts flambéed tableside. [$] *Average main: $54* ✉ *Waikiki Park Heights Hotel, 2440 Kuhio Ave., Waikiki* ☎ *808/922–5555* 🌐 *www.hyshawaii.com* ⏲ *No lunch.*

$$$ ITALIAN 🍴 **Il Lupino Trattoria & Wine Bar.** Il Lupino doesn't reinvent Italian cuisine—you get pretty good renditions of tried-and-true favorites such as fried calamari, caprese salad, four-cheese pizza, bucatini all'amatriciana, and a grilled veal chop. But when you put all the elements together—the yellow awning, the brigade of white-shirted servers, the well-appointed wine locker, the patio seating, and long wood bar that doglegs out to the open air, not to mention the decent food—you get a well-rounded, enjoyable dining experience. **Known for:** happy hour all afternoon, with small plates and good pricing; suprisingly nice spot for breakfast; crowds, so get a reservation or prepare to wait. [$] *Average main: $33* ✉ *Royal Hawaiian Center, 2233 Kalakaua Ave., Waikiki* ☎ *808/922–3400* 🌐 *www.illupino.com.*

$$$$ ECLECTIC 🍴 **Kai Market.** A buffet in a giant resort hotel might send some discerning diners running, but the mass-market Sheraton Waikiki has pulled off this farm-to-table smorgasbord of Island and international flavors with considerable success. Yes, there is the obligatory prime rib carving station (locals are loco for prime rib), but there's also cilantro-laden Chinese-style steamed fish, clams in a ginger-black-bean sauce, osso bucco, and Korean-style braised short ribs. **Known for:** enough buffet options to make everyone happy; popular seafood and barbecue nights; hotel entertainment and people-watching. [$] *Average main: $55* ✉ *Sheraton Waikiki Hotel, 2255 Kalakaua Ave., Waikiki* ☎ *808/922–4422* 🌐 *www.sheraton-waikiki.com/dining/kai* ⏲ *No lunch.*

$$$$ JAPANESE 🍴 **Kaiwa.** At this sleek, contemporary Japanese restaurant, choose from the teppan bar, the sushi bar, the main dining room, or the sexy *zashiki* room, curtained off by strands of lights. You can try *okonomiyaki,* the famous savory pancakes that are a specialty of Osaka, with mix-and-match ingredients scrambled on a griddle, then drizzled with piquant sauces, or jewel-like appetizers such as dashi gelée topped with tender abalone and sea urchin served in martini glasses. **Known for:** visually captivating, from the decor to the plating perfection; happy hour includes a nice menu with varied options; authentic experience that brings loyal diners back. [$] *Average main: $43* ✉ *Waikiki Beach Walk, 226 Lewers St., Waikiki* ☎ *808/924–1555* 🌐 *kai-wa.com.*

$$$$ FRENCH 🍴 **La Mer.** Looking out on its namesake, La Mer is the most romantic dining room on Oahu, with carved wooden screens setting an elegant art deco–ish tone. The window tables—and most of the restaurant's tables are windowside or very close—open to the fresh air, and sounds of the beach just below are sufficiently captivating that guests often forgive the tired classic haute-cuisine French food. **Known for:** it doesn't get more romantic than this; an impressive wine list and a sommelier to match; a classy bar scene that includes the romance at a less staggering price. [$] *Average main: $142* ✉ *Halekulani, 2199 Kalia Rd., Waikiki* ☎ *808/923–2311* 🌐 *www.halekulani.com/living/dining/la_mer* 🕒 *No lunch* 👔 *Jacket required.*

$$$$ FRENCH 🍴 **Michel's at the Colony Surf.** Often called Waikiki's most romantic spot, Michel's is an old-school French favorite on Waikiki's tranquil Gold Coast, where you pay for a spectacular beachside sunset view and classic French fare. Opened in 1962, the place retains a *Mad Men* feel, with lots of wood and stone and bow-tied servers preparing things like steak tartare tableside. **Known for:** the sound of the surf and the intoxicating smell of the islands; classic French cuisine with some local twists; a vibe that steps back in time, in all the right ways. [$] *Average main: $55* ✉ *Colony Surf, 2895 Kalakaua Ave., Waikiki* ☎ *808/923–6552* 🌐 *michelshawaii.com* 🕒 *No lunch.*

$$$$ JAPANESE 🍴 **Morimoto Asia Waikiki.** Locals were surprised when chef Masahara Morimoto vacated the Modern for new digs at the renovated and rebranded Alohilani Resort (formerly the Pacific Beach hotel), but loyalists have not been disappointed. The sleek space includes an open-air lanai and gorgeous bar, as well as a dining room designed for entertaining clients or celebrating with friends. **Known for:** attentive service and great food; casual elegance in a lovely spot in Waikiki; new menu with enough to draw loyalists. [$] *Average main: $41* ✉ *Alohilani Resort, 2490 Kalakaua Ave., Waikiki* ☎ *808/922–0022* 🌐 *www.morimotoasiawaikiki.com.*

$$$$ ECLECTIC 🍴 **100 Sails Restaurant & Bar.** With the top-to-bottom renovations of the Prince Hotel, the former Prince Court (known for its buffet and views) has become the 100 Sails, a new take with the same commitment to great food and great views. Slightly more casual than its predecessor, 100 Sails continues the everything-you-can-imagine buffet tradition (with crab legs and prime rib of course) along with à la carte "small bites." But the chef never loses focus on locally sourced ingredients and knock-out presentation. **Known for:** international buffet for every meal;

CLOSE UP

Honolulu's Food Trucks

Lunch wagons, or food trucks, as they are now known around the country, have been an island staple for plate lunches for decades. With the taco-truck craze and the emergence of social media, Oahu's fleet is growing like crazy. Some make it, some don't, but the variety and array of flavors make them hard to turn down.

You can check the trucks' locations and daily menus on Twitter or Instagram, or try a sampling from more than two-dozen vendors at the monthly Eat the Street food-truck rally. Visit ⊕ *www.eatthestreethawaii.com* for details. Also check out the assortment of trucks that gather for the monthly Honolulu Night Market in Kakaako, the free monthly outdoor film screenings at the iconic IBM building in Kakaako, and the assortment of food trucks that gather at the Wednesday-evening farmers' market at Blaisdell Center or the Saturday-morning market at Ward Village.

Here are some of our favorite lunch wagons:

Elena's (⊕ *www.elenasrestaurant.com*) is an extension of the popular, family-run Filipino restaurant in Waipahu. There are three trucks, in Campbell, Mililani, and the airport area. Try the AFRO, an adobo–fried rice omelet, or the famous *lechón* (roast pork with onions and tomatoes) special.

The Girls Who Bake Next Door (⊕ *www.thegirlswhobakenextdoor.com*) are just that—two friends who love to bake. Their cupcakes, cookies, and other sweet treats show up at events all over Honolulu.

Chubbie's Burgers Burgers and fries, every which way. Sometimes the staff even set up tables and chairs and play some music. ⊕ *www.chubbies-burgers.com*).

Sweet Revenge (⊕ *www.sweetrevengehonolulu.com*) serves up pies of all types, all in the individual size, and all for around $8. Everything from quiche to chicken potpie to s'mores pies and chocolate Twix pies.

4

---

views and sunsets to rival any other Waikiki location; free valet parking at the hotel. $ *Average main: $58* ⊠ *Hawaii Prince Hotel Waikiki, 100 Holomoana St., Waikiki* ☎ *808/944–4494* ⊕ *www.princewaikiki.com/dining/honolulu-american-restaurant/.*

$$$$ ✕ **Orchids.** Perched along the seawall at historic Gray's Beach, Orchids
SEAFOOD in the luxe Halekulani resort is open all day—it's a locus of power breakfasters, ladies who lunch, celebrating families at the over-the-top Sunday brunch, and the gamut at dinner. The louvered walls are open to the breezes, sprays of orchids add color, the seafood is perfectly prepared, and the wine list is intriguing. **Known for:** island breezes, ocean sounds, and five-star service and food; great service and even better food; a menu with something for just about everyone. $ *Average main: $42* ⊠ *Halekulani, 2199 Kalia Rd., Waikiki* ☎ *808/923–2311* ⊕ *www.halekulani.com/dining/orchids-restaurant.*

$$ ✕ **Rumfire Waikiki.** If the perfect sunset happy hour means cocktails,
ASIAN FUSION bite-size shareable plates, tropical breezes, ocean sounds, and flaming oversized torches, then "Meet me at Rumfire" should be your calling card. Eat inside perched on ottomans in front of floor-to-ceiling

windows or outside, steps from the beach, grazing on sliced coffee-rubbed rib steak, fish tacos, or spicy Szechuan baby back ribs. **Known for:** beachside nightlife scene with great food and cocktails; fabulous location right on the beach; gathering spot for young professionals. [$] *Average main: $25* ✉ *Sheraton Waikiki, 2255 Kalakaua Ave., Waikiki* ☎ *808/922–4422* 🌐 *www.rumfirewaikiki.com.*

$$ ECLECTIC FAMILY 🍴 **Side Street Inn on Da Strip.** The original Hopaka Street pub is famous as the place where celebrity chefs gather after hours; this second location is on bustling Kapahulu Avenue, closer to Waikiki. Local-style bar food—salty panfried pork chops with a plastic tub of ketchup; lup cheong fried rice; and passion fruit–glazed ribs—comes in huge, shareable portions. **Known for:** portions that can seemingly feed you for a week; regulars have reserved seats at the bar; diner feel with really good food. [$] *Average main: $20* ✉ *614 Kapahulu Ave., Waikiki* ☎ *808/739–3939* 🌐 *www.sidestreetinn.com* 🕓 *No lunch.*

PUPU

Entertaining Hawaii-style means having a lot of *pupu*—the local term for appetizers or hors d'oeuvres. Locals eat these small portions of food mostly as they wind down from their workday, relax, and enjoy a couple of drinks. Popular pupu include sushi, tempura, teriyaki chicken or beef skewers, barbecued meat, and our favorite: *poke* (pronounced "po-keh"), or raw fish, seasoned with seaweed, shoyu, and other flavorings.

$$$$ ITALIAN 🍴 **Taormina.** Honolulu has its share of Italian restaurants, and Taormina, taking its culinary cues from Sicily, is considered one of the best by foodies, locals, and visitors alike. In a sleek, elegant room (there is outdoor seating, but this is one place we recommend staying indoors), the menu includes clean, well-executed classics, from porcini risotto with sautéed foie gras to a giant veal Parmesan. **Known for:** intimate quiet respite in bustling Waikiki; authentic Sicilian cuisine; extensive wine list. [$] *Average main: $36* ✉ *Waikiki Beach Walk, 227 Lewers St., Waikiki* ☎ *808/926–5050* 🌐 *www.taorminarestaurant.com.*

$ BURGER 🍴 **Teddy's Bigger Burgers.** Modeled after 1950s diners, this local franchise serves classic moist and messy burgers, along with turkey and veggie burgers, as well as chicken breast and fish sandwiches. The fries are crisply perfect, the shakes rich and sweet. **Known for:** messy burgers, great fries, and rich milk shakes; diner-style service, with food to go; dependable quick lunch across the island. [$] *Average main: $11* ✉ *Waikiki Grand Hotel, 134 Kapahulu Ave., Waikiki* ☎ *808/926–3444* 🌐 *www.teddysbb.com.*

$$$ MODERN HAWAIIAN 🍴 **Tiki's Grill and Bar.** Tiki's is the kind of place people come to Waikiki for: a retro–South Pacific spot with a back-of-the-bar faux volcano, open-air lounge with live local music, indoor-outdoor dining, and a view of the beach across the street. Chef Ronnie Nasuti, who for years helmed the Roy's flagship, stronghold of Hawaiian regional cuisine, turns out beautifully composed plates and manages to put fresh twists on the super familiar—like lilikoi wasabi-grilled wings, watermelon and Naked Cow feta salad, and Thai-style shrimp puttanesca. **Known for:** surpisingly good food in a made-for-TV setting; Pacific Rim menu

inspired by a noted island chef; can get pricey, but a fun experience worthy of a hana hou (encore). [$] *Average main: $27* ✉ *Aston Waikiki Beach Hotel, 2570 Kalakaua Ave., Waikiki* ☎ *808/923–8454* 🌐 *www.tikisgrill.com.*

$$$$ MODERN AMERICAN 🍴 **Top of Waikiki.** Top of Waikiki, which opened in 1965, remains one of the best spots in town to take in Honolulu's stunning panorama. Lance Kosaka, who was executive chef at Alan Wong's Pineapple Room, turns out contemporary American dishes with island flavor, and his menu includes staples like garlic shrimp, beet, avocado, and goat cheese salad, and steaks and fish that bring guests back again and again. **Known for:** rotating restaurant views; creative cuisine for varied tastes; nice remodel, but still feels like a midcentury rotating restaurant. [$] *Average main: $40* ✉ *Waikiki Business Plaza, 2270 Kalakaua Ave., Waikiki* ☎ *808/923–3877* 🌐 *www.topofwaikiki.com.*

$ AMERICAN 🍴 **Wailana Coffee House.** Plenty of local gossip, drama, family feuds, and stories fill the history of Wailana Coffee House, a staple in Honolulu since 1969. Budget-conscious snowbirds, night owls with a yen for karaoke, all-day drinkers of both coffee and the stronger stuff, hearty eaters, and post-clubbing club kids all crowd this venerable, family-run diner and cocktail lounge—which recently underwent a renovation of the dining room and kitchen—at the edge of Waikiki. **Known for:** never changing; always open 24/7/365; karaoke bar and stiff cocktails. [$] *Average main: $12* ✉ *1860 Ala Moana Blvd., at Ena Rd., Waikiki* ☎ *808/955–1764.*

$$$$ STEAKHOUSE 🍴 **Wolfgang's Steak House.** Sequestered in the Royal Hawaiian Shopping Center, this open-air New York-style steak house brings loyalists back for beautifully aged steaks, attentive service, and its unique gruff New Yorker attitude. This Honolulu outpost of the NY-based original serves good steaks that have been dry-aged on-site, with classics like shrimp cocktail, slabs of Canadian bacon, crab cakes, creamed spinach, and the token grilled fish selection. **Known for:** classic NY steak house vibe, food, and service; great location in the heart of Waikiki; suprisingly varied brunch menu (with a killer Bloody Mary, of course). [$] *Average main: $55* ✉ *Royal Hawaiian Center, 2201 Kalakaua Ave., Waikiki* ☎ *808/922–3600* 🌐 *www.wolfgangssteakhouse.net/waikiki/.*

MALASADAS

Malasadas are a contribution of the Portuguese, who came to the Islands to work on the plantations. Roughly translated, the name means "half-cooked," which refers to the origin of these deep-fried, heavily sugared treats said to have been created as a way to use up scraps of rich, buttery egg dough. A handful of bakeries specialize in them (Leonard's on Kapahulu, Agnes in Kailua, Champion on Beretania); restaurants sometimes serve an upscale version stuffed with fruit puree; and they're inevitable at food trucks, fairs, and carnivals. Eat them hot or not at all.

DOWNTOWN

$$ AMERICAN 🍴 **Honolulu Museum of Art Café.** The Honolulu Museum of Art's cool courtyards and galleries filled with works by masters from Monet to Hokusai are well worth a visit and, afterward, so is this popular lunch restaurant. The open-air café is flanked by a burbling water feature and 8-foot-tall ceramic "dumplings" by artist Jun Kaneko—a tranquil setting in the shade of a 75-year-old monkeypod tree in which to eat your salade niçoise (featuring seared coriander-crusted ahi) or fork-tender filet mignon sandwich with dijon-caper relish. **Known for:** wonderfully chic setting; limited but beautifully prepared menu of soups, salads, sandwiches, and mains; nice spot for Sunday brunch. [$] *Average main: $17* ✉ *Honolulu Museum of Art, 900 S. Beretania St., Downtown* ☎ *808/532–8734* 🌐 *www.honolulumuseum.org/394-museum_cafe* ⏲ *Closed Mon. No dinner.*

$ AMERICAN FAMILY 🍴 **Murphy's Bar & Grill.** Located on the edge between the financial district and Chinatown, Honolulu's go-to Irish bar serves Guinness on tap and an Irish-American menu of pubby favorites such as spicy chicken wings, jalapeño poppers, fish 'n' chips, corned beef and cabbage, and grilled New York steak—without that Waikiki price tag. But probably the most popular menu item is the Blarney Burger, gooey with Guinness-infused cheddar cheese. **Known for:** stick-to-your-ribs Irish fare; creative salads that add diversity (and heart relief) to an otherwise heavy menu; fun setting that has you smiling on the way out the door. [$] *Average main: $16* ✉ *2 Merchant St., Downtown* ☎ *808/531–0422* 🌐 *www.murphyshawaii.com.*

$$ WINE BAR 🍴 **Vino Italian Tapas & Wine Bar.** Vino has a lock on local oenophiles, who make a beeline for this wine bar and restaurant, and neighborhood regulars who gather for pau hana with friends and co-workers. Chef Keith Endo creates his take on contemporary Mediterranean-inspired cuisine, including house-made pastas, jumbo shrimp in a resonant cioppino sauce, and Big Island smoked pork, all paired with wines selected by the nationally recognized sommelier Chuck Furuya. **Known for:** excellent wines, with wine tastings regularly; casual atmosphere with excellent food; house-made pastas, breads, and sausages. [$] *Average main: $25* ✉ *Waterfront Plaza, 500 Ala Moana Blvd., Suite 6F, Kakaako* ☎ *808/524–8466* 🌐 *www.vinohawaii.com* ⏲ *Closed Mon. No lunch.*

$$$ JAPANESE 🍴 **Yanagi Sushi.** One of relatively few restaurants to serve the complete menu until 2 am (until 10 pm on Sunday), Yanagi is a full-service Japanese restaurant offering not only sushi and sashimi around a small bar, but also *teishoku* (combination menus), tempura, stews, and grill-it-yourself shabu-shabu. The fish can be depended on for freshness and variety. **Known for:** late hours, making it a favorite among night owls; well-priced combo dinners; a local favorite for sushi. [$] *Average main: $28* ✉ *762 Kapiolani Blvd., Downtown* ☎ *808/597–1525* 🌐 *www.yanagisushi-hawaii.com.*

CHINATOWN

$$ HAWAIIAN

🍴 **Fete Hawaii.** Fete slipped into its cozy brick-walled space amidst the Chinatown culinary boom in 2016, and it's been packing in regulars ever since. Folks come for the burgers and specials at lunch; for dinner, try one of the pastas, seafood, or to-die-for twice-fried chicken with grits and collard greens. **Known for:** tiny, chic space with a hipster vibe; twice-fried chicken that regulars swear by; craft cocktails and beer. [$] *Average main: $23* ✉ *2 N. Hotel St., Chinatown* ☎ *808/369–1390* 🌐 *fetehawaii.com.*

$$ BISTRO

🍴 **HASR Bistro.** This country-style European bistro in the middle of bustling Chinatown brings a fun, playful attitude to fine dining ("HASR" stands for Highly Allocated Spoiled Rotten). Owner Terry Kakazu brings her wine expertise to the restaurant, while executive chef Rodney Uyehara adds his culinary flair to this quaint eatery with lunch sandwiches like the Crabby Melt (a tuna melt but with crab) and dinner specialities like cioppino and Kurobuta pork chop. **Known for:** bistro-style comfort food; live entertainment on weekends; small with lots of charm. [$] *Average main: $25* ✉ *31 N. Pauahi St., Chinatown* ☎ *808/533–4277* 🌐 *www.hasrbistro.com* 🕑 *Closed Sun. No lunch Mon.*

$ CHINESE

🍴 **Legend Seafood Restaurant.** Use your best cab-hailing technique and sign language to make the cart ladies stop at your table and show you their fare at this large, loud Hong-Kong-style dim sum spot. The pork-filled steamed buns, spinach dumplings, taro-and-pork *gok* (bite-size fried balls), and still-warm custard tarts are excellent pre-shopping fortification. **Known for:** loud and chaotic atmosphere (and that's the fun); dim sum that draws in both locals and visitors; breakfast before a busy day. [$] *Average main: $13* ✉ *Chinese Cultural Plaza, 100 N. Beretania St., Suite 108, Chinatown* ☎ *808/532–1868* 🌐 *www.legendseafoodhonolulu.com.*

$$ CHINESE

🍴 **Little Village Noodle House.** Unassuming and budget-friendly, Little Village is so popular with locals that it expanded to the space next door. The extensive Pan-Asian menu is filled with crowd-pleasers like spicy panfried beef, eggplant with garlic sauce, Singapore rice noodles, honey-walnut shrimp, crispy orange chicken, and dried string beans with pork. **Known for:** the best Chinese food in Chinatown; budget-friendly prices and extensive menu; BYOB. [$] *Average main: $18* ✉ *1113 Smith St., Chinatown* ☎ *808/545–3008* 🌐 *www.littlevillagehawaii.com.*

$$ AMERICAN
Fodor's Choice ★

🍴 **Livestock Tavern.** Livestock scores big with its seasonal menu of comfort foods, craft cocktails, and cowboy-minimalist decor. Although meat commands the menu, offerings like burrata, creative salads, and crispy snapper round out the possibilities. **Known for:** nice bar scene with good craft cocktails; a hamburger that draws locals again and again; creative dishes ranging from comfort food to trendy salads. [$] *Average main: $20* ✉ *49 N. Hotel St., Chinatown* ☎ *808/537–2577* 🌐 *www.livestocktavern.com* 🕑 *Closed Sun.*

$$ ASIAN

🍴 **Lucky Belly.** A hip local crowd sips cocktails and slurps familiar noodle dishes with a modern twist at this popular fusion ramen bar. Try the Belly Bowl with smoked bacon, sausage, and pork belly in a savory broth loaded with noodles, as well as the trendy small plates such as pork belly buns, oxtail dumplings, and steak tartare spiced with

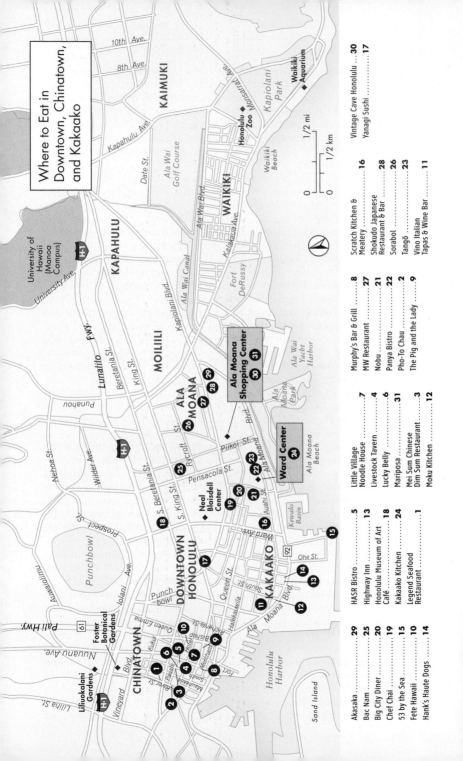

Where to Eat in Downtown, Chinatown, and Kakaako

Akasaka 29
Bac Nam 25
Big City Diner 20
Chef Chai 19
53 by the Sea 15
Fete Hawaii 10
Hank's Haute Dogs ... 14

HASR Bistro 5
Highway Inn 13
Honolulu Museum of Art
Café 18
Kakaako Kitchen 24
Legend Seafood
Restaurant 1

Little Village
Noodle House 7
Livestock Tavern 4
Lucky Belly 6
Mariposa 31
Mei Sum Chinese
Dim Sum Restaurant 3
Moku Kitchen 12

Murphy's Bar & Grill 8
MW Restaurant 27
Nobu 21
Panya Bistro 22
Pho-To Chau 2
The Pig and the Lady 9

Scratch Kitchen &
Meatery 16
Shokudo Japanese
Restaurant & Bar 28
Sorabol 26
Tangō 23
Vino Italian
Tapas & Wine Bar 11

Vintage Cave Honolulu ... 30
Yanagi Sushi 17

Japanese chili powder. **Known for:** huge portions of unique, tasty fusion cuisine; attentive and casual service; hang out for local hipsters and downtown professionals. [$] *Average main: $20* ✉ *50 N. Hotel St., Chinatown* ☎ *808/531–1888* 🌐 *www.luckybelly.com* 🕒 *Closed Sun.*

$ CHINESE

🍴 **Mei Sum Chinese Dim Sum Restaurant.** In contrast to the sprawling, noisy halls in which dim sum is generally served, Mei Sum is compact and shiny bright, not to mention a favorite of locals who work in the area. Be ready to guess and point at the color photos of dim sum favorites; not much English is spoken, but the charades pay off when you get your delicate buns and tasty bites. **Known for:** all-day dim sum until 9 pm; not much English spoken, but it will be a social experience; dim sum, but with a more wide-ranging menu. [$] *Average main: $11* ✉ *1170 Nuuanu Ave., Suite 102, Chinatown* ☎ *808/531–3268.*

$ VIETNAMESE

🍴 **Pho-To Chau.** Those people lined up on River Street know where to get bowls of steaming *pho* (Vietnamese beef noodle soup) with all the best trimmings. This divey storefront was the go-to pho spot long before hipsters and foodies found Chinatown. **Known for:** a local institution with long lines; when they run out, they close, regardless of the time; large pho can be easily shared. [$] *Average main: $8* ✉ *1007 River St., Chinatown* ☎ *808/533–4549* 💳 *No credit cards* 🕒 *No dinner.*

$$ MODERN ASIAN
Fodor's Choice ★

🍴 **The Pig and the Lady.** Chef Andrew Le's casual noodle house attracts downtown office workers by day, but by night it becomes a creative contemporary restaurant, pulling in serious chowhounds. Drawing on both his Vietnamese heritage and multicultural island flavors, the talented, playful Le is a wizard with spice and acid, turning out dishes of layered flavor such as "coffee can bread" (which is baked in Café du Monde coffee cans) with chicken-liver paté, Kyoho grapes, and pink peppercorns. **Known for:** masterful fusion mash-up of Vietnamese tastes, spices, and local foods; house-made soft-serve and sorbets, including unexpected flavors; sister location, Piggy Smalls, in Kakaako. [$] *Average main: $20* ✉ *83 N. King St., Chinatown* ☎ *808/585–8255* 🌐 *www.thepigandthelady.com* 🕒 *Closed Sun.*

KAKAAKO

$$$$ CONTEMPORARY

🍴 **53 by the Sea.** Housed in a McVilla aimed at attracting a Japanese wedding clientele, this restaurant serves contemporary Continental food that focuses primarily on well-prepared standards you'd find at a reception (crab cakes in lemon puree, mahimahi with a mango beurre blanc, lamb chops in a red wine reduction)—albeit with a million-dollar view of Honolulu, from Kakaako to Diamond Head. Perched at water's edge, with famed surf break Point Panic offshore, 53 by the Sea uses its setting to great advantage—the crescent-shaped dining room faces the sea, so even if you're not at a table nestled against the floor-to-ceiling windows, you have a fine view. **Known for:** views, especially at sunset; odd villa decor that somehow works; wedding chapel on-site in case the mood strikes. [$] *Average main: $50* ✉ *53 Ahui St., Kakaako* ☎ *808/536–5353* 🌐 *www.53bythesea.com.*

$ HOT DOG FAMILY

🍴 **Hank's Haute Dogs.** Owner Hank Adaniya's idea of a hot dog involves things like wild boar sausage with cran-apple relish. Originally a true hole-in-the-wall, the gentrified Hank's is still a tiny spot where you can go classic with the Chicago Dog, made with the traditional fixings (including neon-green relish), or gourmet with the butter-seared lobster sausage topped with garlic-relish aioli. **Known for:** 11 varieties of dogs daily, plus another 6 as daily specials; fries, truffle fries, and onion rings to die for; part of Kakaako's SALT area. $ Average main: $9 ⊠ 324 Coral St., Kakaako ☎ 808/532–4265 ⊕ www.hankshautedogs. com ⟲ Remember to get parking validated.

$ ✕ **Highway Inn.** Highway Inn serves up what it does best: local favorites
MODERN like Kalbi ribs, *kalua* (roasted in an underground oven) pork sliders,
HAWAIIAN beef stew, and old-fashioned hamburger steaks. It's a local favorite for
FAMILY breakfast, a great lunch spot, and happening at dinner. **Known for:** local Hawaiian food done right; near the cruise terminal; the place for poi, lau lau, and other Hawaiian staples you can't get back home. $ Average main: $15 ⊠ 680 Ala Moana Blvd., Kakaako ☎ 808/954–4955 ⊕ www. myhighwayinn.com.

$ ✕ **Kakaako Kitchen.** Kakaako has grown up around Russell Siu's master-
MODERN piece kitchen, where he serves high-quality plate lunches utilizing local,
HAWAIIAN farm-to-table ingredients. Here, you can get a crab-and-avocado salad
FAMILY on toasted ciabatta or deep-fried pork chops topped with caramelized onion gravy and served with two scoops of either brown or white rice, and green salad instead of the usual mayo-laden macaroni salad. **Known for:** fresh, local food with a twist; lunchtime favorite for area workers; brown gravy, a staple on the menu, made from scratch. $ Average main: $14 ⊠ Ward Village Shops, 1200 Ala Moana Blvd., Kakaako ☎ 808/596–7488 ⊕ www.kakaakokitchen.com.

$$ ✕ **Moku Kitchen.** In the hip SALT complex, Moku's draws locals, includ-
HAWAIIAN ing both foodies and families, as well as visitors looking for authentic
FAMILY farm-to-table cuisine in a laid-back, urban setting. It's one of legend-ary chef Peter Merriman's restaurants. **Known for:** local, farm-to-table menu with something for everyone; impressive list of craft cocktails and beers; live music that can get loud. $ Average main: $19 ⊠ SALT at Our Kakaako, 660 Ala Moana Blvd., Kakaako ☎ 808/591–6658 ⊕ www.mokukitchen.com.

$$$$ ✕ **Nobu.** Always a local favorite, Nobu's move from Waikiki to the
JAPANESE chic Kakaako high-rise Waiea has only made it better. It remains a
FUSION magnet for visiting celebrities and local bigwigs—and its new location now draws a local after-work crowd to sip cocktails in the open-air bar. **Known for:** casual elegance at serious prices; consistently good and creative cuisine; a bar scene that rarely disappoints. $ Average main: $38 ⊠ Waiea at Ward Village, 1118 Ala Moana Blvd., Kakaako ☎ 808/237–6999 ⊕ www.noburestaurants.com/honolulu ⊘ No lunch.

$$ ✕ **Panya Bistro.** This easy-breezy café run by Hong Kong–born sisters
ECLECTIC Alice and Annie Yeung offers a crowd-pleasing menu of contemporary American (salads, sandwiches, pastas) and Asian (Thai-style steak salad, Japanese-style fried chicken, Singaporean *laksa*), served in a disco-tinged space (there's also a full bar). A gourmet pizza chef turns out custom pizzas on the lanai every Thursday night. **Known for:** French-style pastries and cakes; gourmet pizzas cooked on the lanai every Thursday; great spot for breakfast. $ Average main: $18 ⊠ Hokua, 1288 Ala Moana Blvd., Kakaako ☎ 808/946–6388 ⊕ www.panyagroup.com.

$$ ✕**Scratch Kitchen & Meatery.** Tucked into the chic South Shore Market
HAWAIIAN in Kakaako's Ward Village, this former Chinatown spot has moved
uptown with its hipster decor, open kitchen, and creative menu. For
breakfast, you'll be drawn to milk-and-cereal pancakes; for dinner
it's small plates that might include foi gras loco moco or chicken and
waffles. **Known for:** locally popular breakfast and brunch; perhaps a
bit too much hipster vibe; spicy (and good) chicken and waffles. $ *Average main: $18 ⊠ South Shore Market at Ward Village, 1170 Auahi
St., Kakaako ✛ Entrance on the side of the building, along Queen St.*
☎ *808/589–1669 ⊕ www.scratch-hawaii.com ⊗ No dinner weekends.*

$$ ✕**Tangö.** On the ground floor of a glass-sheathed condominium, Tangö's
ECLECTIC spare contemporary setting stays humming at breakfast, lunch, and
dinner. Finnish chef Göran Streng has a couple of nods to his heritage
in unfussy dishes such as gravlax with crispy skin and mustard-dill
sauce, but the menu is by and large "general bistro," running from
bouillabaisse to herb-crusted rack of lamb with some Asian nods.
Known for: celebrity-filled power breakfasts; loco moco (unlike any
you'll have elsewhere); attentive staff. $ *Average main: $25 ⊠ Hokua
Building, 1288 Ala Moana Blvd., Kakaako ☎ 808/593–7288 ⊕ www.
tangocafehawaii.com.*

ALA MOANA

$$ ✕**Akasaka.** Step inside this tiny sushi bar tucked between the strip clubs
JAPANESE behind the Ala Moana Hotel, and you'll swear you're in an out-of-the-
way Edo neighborhood in some indeterminate time. Don't be deterred
by its dodgy neighbors or its reputation for inconsistent service. **Known
for:** great spot for before or after concerts at nearby Republik; local
favorite; no pretense, nothing fancy. $ *Average main: $21 ⊠ 1646 B
Kona St., Suite B, Ala Moana ☎ 808/942–4466.*

$ ✕**Bac Nam.** Tam and Kimmy Huynh's menu is much more extensive
VIETNAMESE than most, ranging far beyond the usual pho and *bun* (cold noodle
dishes) found at many Vietnamese restaurants. Lamb curry, tapioca
dumplings, tamarind head-on shrimp, an extraordinary crab noodle
soup, and other dishes hail from North and South Vietnam. **Known for:**
favorite of neighborhood workers; free parking behind the restaurant;
no frills hole-in-the-wall. $ *Average main: $12 ⊠ 1117 S. King St., Ala
Moana ☎ 808/597–8201.*

$ ✕**Big City Diner.** Part of a local chain of retro diners, Big City offers
AMERICAN Hawaii-style comfort favorites for breakfast, lunch, and dinner. In the
FAMILY morning you get rice instead of potatoes, the option of fish or Portu-
guese sausage instead of bacon, and roasted macadamia nut pancakes
smothered in *haupia* (coconut) sauce—with generous portions and low
prices. **Known for:** perfect for families; huge portions, and all of it good;
a few outdoor tables nice on a sunny morning for breakfast and the
paper. $ *Average main: $16 ⊠ Ward Entertainment Center, 1060 Auahi
St., Ala Moana ☎ 808/591–8891 ⊕ www.bigcitydinerhawaii.com.*

$$$ ✕**Chef Chai.** This sleek, contemporary dining room on the edge of
FUSION Kakaako offers an eclectic, fusion mix of seafood, meats, and creative
starters and salads. Committed to healthier options, Chef Chai cut
back his dependence on butter and cream, creating menu items like a

4

delicious lobster bisque thickened with squash puree, and ahi tartare cones that look like tiny ice-cream cones but taste like sashimi with avo and wasabi. **Known for:** pre- and post-theater crowds from the Blaisdell; creative fusion cuisine melding local flavors with global influences; excellent desserts. $ *Average main: $30 ⊠ Pacifica Honolulu, 1009 Kapiolani Blvd., Ala Moana ☎ 808/585–0011 ⊕ www.chefchai.com.*

$$$
ASIAN
✕ **Mariposa.** Yes, the popovers and the wee cups of bouillon are there at lunch, but in every other regard, this Neiman Marcus restaurant menu departs from the classic model, incorporating a clear sense of Pacific place. The breezy open-air veranda, with a view of Ala Moana Beach Park, twirling ceiling fans, and life-size hula-girl murals say Hawaii. **Known for:** the go-to spot for the local "ladies who lunch" crowd; warm lilikoi pudding cake; lovely interiors reminiscent of Hawaii plantation days. $ *Average main: $35 ⊠ Neiman Marcus, Ala Moana Center, 1450 Ala Moana Blvd., Ala Moana ☎ 808/951–3420 ⊕ www. neimanmarcushawaii.com.*

$$$
HAWAIIAN
Fodor's Choice
★
✕ **MW Restaurant.** The "M" and "W" team of husband-and-wife chefs Michelle Karr-Ueko and Wade Ueko bring together their collective experience (20 years alongside chef Alan Wong, a side step to the famed French Laundry, and some serious kitchen time at comfort food icon Zippy's) to create a uniquely local menu with a decidedly upscale twist. Don't miss the mochi-crusted opakapaka and the garlic steamed onaga. **Known for:** scrumptious desserts (save room); small bar that turns out nice craft cocktails; valet parking only. $ *Average main: $35 ⊠ 1538 Kapiolani Blvd., Suite 107, Ala Moana ✛ Behind the strip shopping center; walk down the side towards the lights in the back ☎ 808/955–6505 ⊕ www.mwrestaurant.com.*

$$
JAPANESE
✕ **Shokudo Japanese Restaurant & Bar.** With a soaring ceiling, crazy red mobile sculpture, contemporary Japanese grazing plates, fruity vodka "sodas," and hungry young people, Shokudo is a culinary house of fun. Whether you go for new-wave fusion dishes such as sushi pizza (a flat, baked square of rice topped with salmon, scallop, crab, and pickled jalapeño), or more traditional noodle bowls and sushi, the food is all good. **Known for:** honey toast for dessert; vibe and decor to keep you entertained; popular, but losing charm for old-timers. $ *Average main: $21 ⊠ Ala Moana Pacific Center, 1585 Kapiolani Blvd., Ala Moana ☎ 808/941–3701 ⊕ www.shokudojapanese.com ☾ Closed Mon.*

$$
KOREAN
✕ **Sorabol.** Open 24 hours a day on weekends and until 1 am on weeknights, with a tiny parking lot and a maze of booths and private rooms, Sorabol offers a vast menu encompassing the entirety of day-to-day Korean cuisine, plus sushi. English menu translations are cryptic at best, and the decor is a bit tired and off-putting. **Known for:** late-night dining; simple but good Korean food; inconsistent service. $ *Average main: $24 ⊠ 805 Keeaumoku St., Ala Moana ☎ 808/947–3113 ⊕ www. sorabolhawaii.com.*

$$$$
CONTEMPORARY
Fodor's Choice
★
✕ **Vintage Cave Honolulu.** One of Oahu's priciest and most exclusive creative dining options is Vintage Cave, a luxurious, art-filled reinvention of what was once the brick-lined basement of Shirokyua department store. The restaurant now offers two options: the more casual Vintage Cave Café (for mere mortals) and the ultra luxe Vintage Cave

Club for those looking for an over-the-top experience. **Known for:** an elaborate dining experience; spectacular art; pampering, decadence, and romance. [$] *Average main: $300* ✉ *Ala Moana Shopping Center, 1450 Ala Moana Blvd., Suite 2250, Level B, Row D, Ala Moana* ☎ *808/441–1744* 🌐 *www.vintagecave.com* 👔 *Jacket required.*

IWILEI

$$ AMERICAN FAMILY 🍴 **La Mariana Restaurant & Sailing Club.** The last of Honolulu's old-school tiki bars is tucked away in the industrial area of Sand Island. A mix of salty-dog sailors (the place looks out on sailboats bobbing in the Keehi Lagoon marina) and hipsters drink stiff mai tais (cocktails are all made with bottled mixers—no handcrafted anything here) sitting at the bar lit by hanging puffer-fish lamps or in peacock chairs in the dining room. **Known for:** throwback to a simpler era; live sing-along piano music; pufferfish lamps that cast a particular glow. [$] *Average main: $20* ✉ *50 Sand Island Access Rd., Iwilei* ☎ *808/848–2800* 🌐 *www.lamarianasailingclub.com.*

$$ SEAFOOD FAMILY 🍴 **Nico's at Pier 38.** Lyonnaise chef Nico Chaiz's harborside restaurant is steps from the Honolulu Fish Auction, which explains his "line to plate" concept—superfresh fish at a reasonable price. The signature dish is an ahi steak crusted in *furikake* (a Japanese mix of toasted nori and sesame seeds) and pan-seared, but he lets his French flag fly with steak frites and bouillabaisse, too. **Known for:** fresh-off-the-line fish, perfectly cooked; excellent double cheeseburger; lunch at the bar with a cold beer. [$] *Average main: $21* ✉ *1133 N. Nimitz Hwy., Pier 38, Iwilei* ☎ *808/540–1377* 🌐 *www.nicospier38.com.*

$ DINER 🍴 **Sugoi Bento & Catering.** This breakfast-and-lunch spot was among the first of a new wave of plate-lunch places to take particular care with quality and nutrition, offering brown rice and green salad instead of the usual white rice and mayo-loaded mac salad. Sweet-and-spicy garlic chicken and *mochiko* (rice-batter-dipped and fried) chicken, adapted from traditional Japanese dishes, are specialties that bring locals back again and again. **Known for:** local favorites like mochiko fried chicken, garlic chicken, and loco moco; grab and go for the beach; ample parking. [$] *Average main: $11* ✉ *City Square Shopping Center, 1286 Kalani St., Iwilei* ☎ *808/841–7984* 🌐 *www.sugoihawaii.com* 💳 *No credit cards* 🕒 *No dinner.*

MAKIKI HEIGHTS

$ BURGER FAMILY Fodor's Choice ★ 🍴 **Honolulu Burger Co.** Owner Ken Takahashi retired as a nightclub impresario on the Big Island to become a real-life burger king. This modest storefront is the home of the locavore burger, made with range-fed beef, Manoa lettuce, tomatoes, and a wide range of toppings, all island-grown—and you can taste the difference. **Known for:** burgers made with the best local ingredients; popular food truck; excellent truffle fries. [$] *Average main: $11* ✉ *1295 S. Beretania St., Makiki Heights* ☎ *808/626–5202* 🌐 *www.honoluluburgerco.com.*

$ AMERICAN 🍴 **Spalding House Cafe.** In the exclusive Makiki Heights neighborhood above the city, the Honolulu Museum of Art Spalding House's casual café spills out of the ground floor of the museum onto the lush,

OAHU'S BEST SHAVE ICE

Islands-style shave ice (never *shaved* ice—it's a pidgin thing) is said to have been born when neighborhood kids hung around the icehouse, waiting to pounce on the shavings from large blocks of ice, carved with ultrasharp Japanese planes that created an exceptionally fine-textured granita.

In the 1920s, according to the historian for syrup manufacturer Malolo Beverages & Supplies, Ltd., Chinese vendors developed sweet fruit concentrates to pour over the ice.

The evolution continued with mom-and-pop shops adding their own touches, such as hiding a nugget of Japanese sweet bean paste in the center; placing a small scoop of ice cream at the bottom; and adding *li hing* powder (a Chinese seasoning used on preserved fruits).

There's nothing better on a sticky hot day. Here are two great places to try:

Waiola. Waiola Shave Ice, off Kapahulu Avenue, is known for its finely shaved ice and wide variety of flavors, and more recently has become famous through its regular appearances in the reboot of *Hawaii Five-0.* In real life, the service is a bit surly and the prices are slightly higher than for most other shave ice, but it's close to Waikiki. ✉ *525 Kapahulu Ave., Kapahulu.*

Uncle Clay's House of Pure Aloha. Located in a strip mall in the residential neighborhood of Aina Haina, Uncle Clay's is a happy place. They specialize in house-made all-natural syrups made from cane sugar and locally sourced fruits. They've even got a flavor called "kalespin"—a combination of kale and spinach. ✉ *Aina Haina Shopping Center, 820 W. Hind Dr., Aina Haina (right off Kalanianaole Hwy.)*

expansive lawn with a million-dollar view of the city and Diamond Head. Sit inside when it's hot, grab an outdoor table when the trade winds are blowing. **Known for:** picnic for two on the museum grounds; deviled eggs; BYOB (and no corkage). [$] *Average main: $14* ✉ *Honolulu Museum of Art Spalding House, 2411 Makiki Heights Dr., Makiki Heights* ☎ *808/237–5225* 🌐 *www.honolulumuseum.org/12001-spalding_house* 🕒 *Closed Mon. No dinner.*

MOILIILI

$$$$ MODERN HAWAIIAN Fodor's Choice ★

🍴 **Alan Wong's Restaurant Honolulu.** James Beard Award–winning Alan Wong is the undisputed king of Hawaiian regional cuisine, earning love and respect for his humble demeanor and practice as much as for his food. The "Wong Way," as it's not-so-jokingly called by his staff, includes an ingrained understanding of the aloha spirit, evident in the skilled but unstarched service and creative and playful interpretations of Islands cuisine. **Known for:** well-deserved awards and accolades, which line the walls; island-inspired dishes, especially seafood; bland location (but it's all about the food). [$] *Average main: $43* ✉ *McCully Court, 1857 S. King St., 3rd fl., Moiliili* ☎ *808/949–2526* 🌐 *www.alanwongs.com* 🕒 *No lunch.*

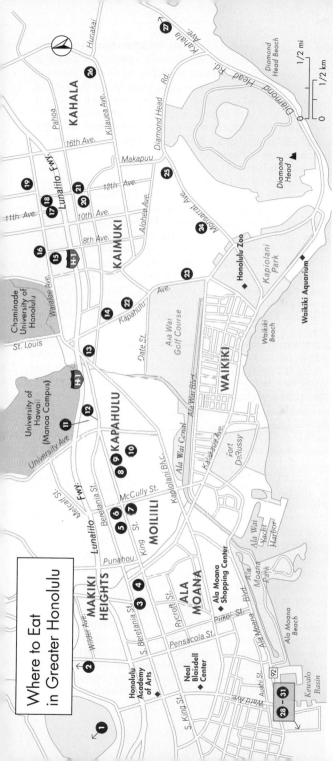

Where to Eat in Greater Honolulu

$$$$ MODERN EUROPEAN Fodor's Choice ★ 🍴 **Chef Mavro.** George Mavrothalassitis, who took two hotel restaurants to the top of the ranks before opening this well-regarded restaurant in 1998, admits he's crazy. Crazy because of the care he takes to draw out the truest and most concentrated flavors, to track down the freshest fish, to create one-of-a-kind wine pairings, and marry French technique with global flavors and local ingredients. **Known for:** exquisite prix-fixe cuisine; understated location; wine pairings unmatched on Oahu. [$] *Average main: $130* ✉ *1969 S. King St., Moiliili* ☎ *808/944–4714* 🌐 *www.chefmavro.com* ⏲ *No lunch.*

$$ THAI 🍴 **Chiang Mai.** Long beloved for its Thai classics based on family recipes, such as spicy curries and stir-fries and sticky rice in woven-grass baskets, Chiang Mai is a short cab ride from Waikiki. Some dishes, like the signature Cornish game hen in lemongrass and spices, show how acculturation can create interesting pairings. **Known for:** excellent Thai food in a home-style environment; limited parking in a small lot in back; local business-lunch favorite. [$] *Average main: $25* ✉ *2239 S. King St., Moiliili* ☎ *808/941–1151* ⏲ *No lunch weekends.*

$ JAPANESE 🍴 **Fukuya Delicatessen.** Get a taste of local Japanese culture at this family operation on the main thoroughfare in local-style Moiliili, a mile or so *mauka* out of Waikiki. Open since 1939, the delicatessen offers take-out breakfasts and lunches, Japanese snacks, noodle dishes, and confections—and it's a local favorite for catering, from parties to funeral gatherings. **Known for:** family-run business for generations; mochi tray, offering samples of everything; kid-friendly menu. [$] *Average main: $8* ✉ *2710 S. King St., Moiliili* ☎ *808/946–2073* 🌐 *www.fukuyadeli.com* ⏲ *Closed Mon. and Tues. No dinner.*

$$$ JAPANESE 🍴 **Imanas Tei.** Nihonjin (Japanese nationals) and locals flock to this tucked-away, bamboo-ceilinged restaurant for its tasteful, simple decor and equally tasteful—and perfect—sushi, sashimi, *nabe* (hot pots prepared at the table), and grilled dishes. You assemble your meal dish by dish, and the cost can add up if you aren't careful. **Known for:** simple food that some feel is better than in Japan; long waits; traditional izakaya experience. [$] *Average main: $30* ✉ *2626 S. King St., Moiliili* ☎ *808/941–2626, 808/934–2727* ⏲ *Closed Sun. No lunch.*

$ VEGETARIAN 🍴 **Peace Café.** This tranquil little storefront with a rustic country communal table is a nurturing sanctuary on a fast-food-loving island. Place your order at the counter, serve yourself lemon-infused water from a large glass beverage jar, and wait for your Yogini plate (a mountain of brown rice, beans, greens, and seaweed), soy soba salad, Moroccan chickpea stew, barbecue tempeh sandwich, and other vegan bites. **Known for:** tiny refuge with a devoted clientele; innovative menu; mellow and calming setting. [$] *Average main: $10* ✉ *2239 S. King St., Moiliili* ☎ *808/951–7555* 🌐 *www.peacecafehawaii.com* ⏲ *No dinner Sun.*

$ ECLECTIC 🍴 **Pint + Jigger.** Dining trends like the gastro pub are typically late to arrive in Honolulu, but Pint + Jigger was worth the wait. Sit at one of the "beer garden" communal benches or perch at a hightop in this welcoming wood-and-brick room for farm-to-glass cocktails, craft beers, and creative small bites. **Known for:** great craft beer and good cocktails; Sunday morning NFL games (7 am kickoff); convivial vibe, but hit-or-miss service. $ *Average main: $13* ✉ *1936 S. King St., Moiliili* ☎ *808/744–9593* ⊕ *www.pintandjigger.com* ☽ *No lunch weekdays.*

$$$$ ✕ **Sushi Sasabune.** Try to get a coveted seat at the counter, and prepare
JAPANESE for an unforgettable sushi experience—if you behave. This is the home of Seiji Kumagawa—Honolulu's Sushi Nazi, who prefers that diners eat omakase-style, letting the chef send out his choices of his favorites for the night, each priced individually (prices add up quickly). **Known for:** one of Honolulu's top sushi spots; a strict chef who expects you to follow directions; all sushi priced by the course until you stop. $ *Average main: $115* ✉ *1417 S. King St., Moiliili* ☎ *808/947–3800* ☽ *Closed Sun. and Mon. No lunch Sat.*

$$$$ ✕ **The Willows.** Old-time locals come to this buffet-only spot to celebrate
HAWAIIAN things like graduations, showers, and centennials, and it hosts its share of wedding receptions (there's a chapel on-site), not to mention a full acre of pavilions overlooking a network of ponds (once natural streams flowing from mountain to sea). The Island-style comfort food includes signature chicken-and-shrimp curry (*Joy of Cooking*–style, not Indian), crab legs and lobster claws, along with local favorites such as *laulau* (a steamed bundle of ti leaves containing pork, butterfish, and taro tops), oxtail soup, and kalua pig. **Known for:** particularly lovely grounds; a buffet that seems to never end; dated decor that is somehow still charming in its own way. $ *Average main: $40* ✉ *901 Hausten St., Moiliili* ☎ *808/952–9200* ⊕ *www.willowshawaii.com.*

KAPAHULU

$$$ ✕ **Izakaya Nonbei.** Teruaki Mori designed this pub, one of the most
JAPANESE traditional of Honolulu's izakayas, to make you feel that you're in a northern inn during winter in his native Japan. Dishes not to miss—*aji tataki* (seared, vinegar-marinated jack mackerel topped with ginger); *karei kara-age* (delicate deep-fried flounder); *dobinmushi* (mushroom consommé presented in a teapot); fried *gobo* (burdock) chips; and crab, avocado, and bacon salad. **Known for:** local favorite for happy hour and quick bites; tiny spot but a huge menu; being busy (reservations strongly recommended). $ *Average main: $30* ✉ *3108 Olu St., Kapahulu* ☎ *808/734–5573.*

$$$$ ✕ **Tokkuri Tei.** A local favorite for the playful atmosphere that belies the
JAPANESE quality of the food created by chef Hideaki "Santa" Miyoshi, best to just say *Omakase, kudasai* ("Chef's choice, please"), and he'll order for you. Famous for his quirky menu names (Spider Poke, for example, where the menu reports, "There's a spider in da poke"), the chef delivers creative options that can intimidate at first glance. Just be aware that some of the more rare seafood dishes can cost up to $45 (each). **Known for:** Japanese food that delivers time and again; expensive rare seafood dishes; ahi tartare poke, which is is everything locals dream about. $ *Average main: $40* ✉ *449 Kapahulu Ave., Kapahulu* ☎ *808/732–6480* ⊕ *www.tokkuritei-hawaii.com.*

$ ✕ **Waiola.** Off Kapahulu Avenue, longtime local favorite Waiola Shave
CAFÉ Ice, known for its powdery shave ice (or snow cone) and wide variety
FAMILY of flavors, has become nationally known through its regular appearance on the reboot of *Hawaii Five-0*. In real life, the service at this

4

little house with a takeout window is a bit surly, and the prices are slightly higher than those at most other shave ice places, but it's close to Waikiki. **Known for:** regular appearances on "Hawaii 5-0"; an excellent example of a Hawaii classic; surly service (but that's part of the charm). [$] *Average main: $4* ✉ *3113 Mokihana St., Kapahulu* ☎ *808/735–8886* 🌐 *www.waiolashaveice.com.*

KAIMUKI

Ten minutes beyond Kapahulu is this commercial thoroughfare that runs through an old neighborhood filled with cool old Craftsman bungalows (that are slowly being knocked down to make room for ticky-tacky boxes). It may have the highest and most diverse concentration of eateries on the island, from a Jamaican restaurant and a shabu-shabu house to a chic contemporary bistro and a nougat manufacturer.

$$ WINE BAR 🍴 **Formaggio Wine Bar.** All but invisible on the back side of a strip mall, this neighborhood wine bar goes for an Italian-catacomb feel, with dim lighting and soft, warm design tones. You'll find an extensive selection of wines by the glass or bottle that can be paired with the varied small plates and pizzas. **Known for:** open kitchen; delicious short ribs in red wine; hit or miss service. [$] *Average main: $17* ✉ *Market City Shopping Center, 2919 Kapiolani Blvd., lower level in the rear, Kaimuki* ☎ *808/739–7719* 🌐 *www.formaggiohonolulu.com.*

$$ VIETNAMESE 🍴 **Hale Vietnam.** One of Oahu's first Vietnamese restaurants, this neighborhood spot, initially popular with budget-minded college kids, expresses its friendly character with its name: *hale* (hah-lay) is the Hawaiian word for house or home. As Kaimuki has gentrifed, Hale Vietnam has remained an anchor spot, albeit with prices that reflect the changing times. **Known for:** neighborhood staple; friendly, helpful staff who will help first-timers; local family favorite that welcomes kids. [$] *Average main: $17* ✉ *1140 12th Ave., Kaimuki* ☎ *808/735–7581.*

$$ ASIAN 🍴 **Himalayan Kitchen.** Owned by a Nepalese chef, Himalayan Kitchen aims to serve all the cuisines of that high-altitude region, and the menu tries to stretch a bit beyond Indian standards—curries, biriyanis, tandoori grills. Hawaii is not an epicenter of Indian cuisine, so this joint does what it can to introduce new flavors while staying true to the standbys. **Known for:** a welcome departure from standard local restaurants; cozy neighborhood atmosphere; challenging parking. [$] *Average main: $17* ✉ *1137 11th Ave., Kaimuki* ☎ *808/735–1122* 🌐 *www.kaimukihawaii.com/d/c/himalayan-kitchen-kaimuki.html.*

$ MODERN HAWAIIAN Fodor's Choice ★ 🍴 **Koko Head Cafe.** When Lee Anne Wong, best known as a competitor on the first season of Bravo's "Top Chef," moved to the Islands, foodies waited with bated breath for her first brick-and-mortar restaurant. And this is it: a lively and laid-back café in Kaimuki, where she took the concept of breakfast and flipped it, creating innovative dishes like the miso-smoked pork-and-onion omelet, cornflake French toast with billionaire's bacon and frosted flake gelato, and kimchi bacon cheddar scones. **Known for:** cornflake French Toast; creative cocktail menu; crazy busy weekends. [$] *Average main: $13* ✉ *1145c 12th Ave., Kaimuki* ☎ *808/732–8920* 🌐 *www.kokoheadcafe.com* ⏲ *No dinner.*

$$ 🍴 **Mud Hen Water.** The name of this restaurant perched on busy Waialae Avenue is the English translation of *Waialae* (meaning a gathering spot around a watering hole). Chef Ed Kenney (of 12th Avenue Grill fame) explores modern interpretations of the Hawaiian foods he remembers from his childhood: line-caught, local seafood, roasted-beet poke with gorilla *ogo* (seaweed), and opah buried in coals and steamed in banana leaves with local vegetables and coconut cream. **Known for:** constantly changing menu of what's fresh, local, and available; spot where locals and visitors actually mingle; small plates and snacks. [$] *Average main: $17* ✉ *3452 Waialae Ave., Kaimuki* ☎ *808/737–6000* 🌐 *www.mudhenwater.com* 🕒 *Closed Mon. No lunch Tues.–Fri.*
HAWAIIAN

$$$$ 🍴 **3660 on the Rise.** Named for its address on Honolulu's premier Waialae Avenue, this restaurant brought fresh dining to Kaimuki when it opened in 1992, inspiring a neighborhood dining renaissance. Loyalists swear by the New York Steak Alaea (grilled with Hawaiian clay salt), potato-crusted crab cakes, and the signature ahi katsu wrapped in *nori* (seaweed) and deep-fried with a wasabi-ginger butter sauce. **Known for:** local favorite for special occasions; ahi katsu that sets the local bar for this favorite dish; good desserts. [$] *Average main: $38* ✉ *3660 Waialae Ave., Kaimuki* ☎ *808/737–1177* 🌐 *www.3660.com* 🕒 *Closed Mon. No lunch.*
MODERN HAWAIIAN

$$ 🍴 **Town.** Town remains a hot spot for Honolulu's creative class and farm-to-table diners, where chef-owner Ed Kenney and his partner Dave Caldiero offer a Mediterranean-eclectic menu ranging from hand-cut pastas and refreshing, composed salads (pastas and salads) to clean preparations of fish and meat (polenta with egg and asparagus or buttermilk panna cotta). The menu is constantly changing, reflecting what's fresh and available. **Known for:** eclectic menu that suits both meat eaters and vegetarians; indoor-outdoor seating; great burger and fries. [$] *Average main: $25* ✉ *3435 Waialae Ave., Kaimuki* ☎ *808/735–5900* 🌐 *www.townkaimuki.com* 🕒 *Closed Sun.*
INTERNATIONAL
Fodor's Choice ★

$$$ 🍴 **12th Avenue Grill.** A local favorite since the doors opened over a decade ago, this award-winning American brasserie from chef-owner Kevin Hanney keeps surprising loyalists with an expanding menu and lively bar scene.The longtime favorite grilled pork chop is joined on the menu by shwarma-spiced Niihau lamb shanks with house-made yogurt, pan-roasted U-10 Hokkaido scallops with Kaffir-Kahuku corn puree, and beautifully prepared soups, salads, and small plates. The specials are always excellent, and the passion-fruit mochi cake with vanilla-ginger syrup is one of the best desserts in town. **Known for:** Kevin Hanney, who is a local icon; commitment to locally sourced ingredients; innovative craft cocktails. [$] *Average main: $28* ✉ *1120 12th Ave., Kaimuki* ☎ *808/732–9469* 🌐 *www.12thavegrill.com* 🕒 *No lunch.*
MODERN HAWAIIAN
Fodor's Choice ★

DIAMOND HEAD

$ 🍴 **Diamond Head Market & Grill.** Just five minutes from Waikiki hotels is Kelvin Ro's one-stop food shop—indispensable if you have accommodations with a kitchen or if you want a quick grab-and-go meal. Join surfers, beach goers, and Diamond Head hikers at the take-out window to order gourmet sandwiches and plates such as hand-shaped burgers, portobello steaks, Korean kalbi ribs, and grilled ahi with wasabi-ginger
AMERICAN

sauce, rice, and salad. Grab-and-go selections include sandwiches, bentos, and salads. **Known for:** excellent desserts and scones; picnic fare for the beach; well-priced grab-and-go dinners. [$] *Average main: $11* ✉ *3158 Monsarrat Ave., Diamond Head* ☎ *808/732–0077* 🌐 *www.diamondheadmarket.com.*

$ AMERICAN 🍴 **South Shore Grill.** Just a couple of minutes out of Waikiki on trendy Monsarrat Avenue near the base of Diamond Head, South Shore Grill is an affordable counter-service spot coveted by locals for the fish tacos, cajun shrimp tacos, and plate lunches. Sandwiches (on ciabatta rolls), entrée salads, stuffed burritos, six different burger options, and a plate of ono (wahoo) coated with macadamia-nut pesto and served with a tangy slaw are worth the repeat visits. **Known for:** casual surfer vibe; takeout for the beach; peanut butter temptation for dessert. [$] *Average main: $12* ✉ *3114 Monsarrat Ave., Diamond Head* ☎ *808/734–0229* 🌐 *www.southshoregrillhawaii.com.*

KAHALA

$$$$ ASIAN FUSION 🍴 **Hoku's.** Everything about this room speaks of quality and sophistication: the wall of windows with their beach views, the avant-garde cutlery and dinnerware, the solicitous staff, and the carefully constructed Euro-Pacific cuisine. The menu constantly changes, but you can count on chef Wayne Hirabayashi to use fresh, local ingredients (including herbs from the hotel's on-site herb garden) in his innovative dishes that include braised short-rib tempura, salt-crusted rack of lamb with basil pesto, and butter-poached lobster with passion-fruit jus. **Known for:** relaxed elegance in the grande dame of Hawaii's social scene; panoramic views from every table; setting and service that can outshine the food. [$] *Average main: $55* ✉ *The Kahala Hotel & Resort, 5000 Kahala Ave., Kahala* ☎ *808/739–8760* 🌐 *www.kahalaresort.com/honolulu_restaurants/hokus* ⏲ *Closed Tues. No lunch.*

$ GREEK 🍴 **Olive Tree Cafe.** An Iranian Hellenophile owns this bustling, self-serve café that dishes up the best taramasalata, falafel, and souvlaki in town. Stand in line at the counter to order while your companion tries to finagle one of the outdoor tables. **Known for:** seriously good Greek food; unpretentious and somehow still charming; BYOB (borrow their corkscrew). [$] *Average main: $14* ✉ *4614 Kilauea Ave., Suite 107, Kahala* ☎ *808/737–0303* 💳 *No credit cards* ⏲ *No lunch.*

MAPUNAPUNA

$$$$ SUSHI 🍴 **Mitch's Sushi Restaurant.** This microscopic sushi bar (15 seats) is an adjunct of a wholesale seafood market operated by gregarious South African expatriate Douglas Mitchell, who oversees the sushi chefs and keeps customers chatting. The fish, air-freighted from around the world, is ultrafresh, well cut (into huge pieces—to the regret of those who follow the one-bite rule), and prepared for the serious sushi lover. **Known for:** hole-in-the-wall atmosphere; BYOB; being busy and closing by 8:30 (reservations recommended). [$] *Average main: $60* ✉ *524 Ohohia St., near Honolulu International Airport, Mapunapuna* ☎ *808/837–7774* 🌐 *www.mitchsushi.com.*

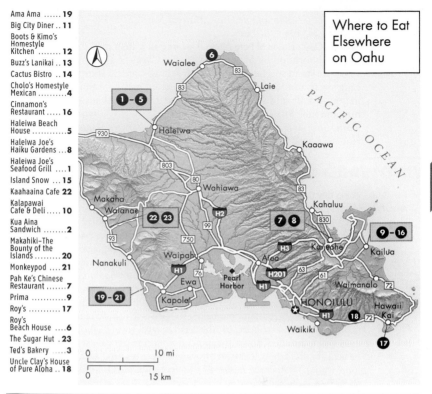

Where to Eat Elsewhere on Oahu

4

KAPALAMA

$ ✗ **Mitsu-Ken.** Mitsu-Ken's garlic chicken may haunt your dreams, which
HAWAIIAN makes it worth the trek to a downscale neighborhood to find the joint. Line up and order the plate lunch with rice and salad, or chicken only, and sink your teeth into this crispy, profoundly garlicky masterpiece drizzled with a sweet glaze. **Known for:** showstopper garlic chicken and delicious breakfast bentos; cash only; good stop before the Swap Meet (it opens at 5 am and closes by 1 pm). $ *Average main: $7* ✉ *2300 N. King St., Kalihi* ☎ *808/848–5573* ═ *No credit cards* ✆ *Closed Sun. and Mon. No dinner.*

SOUTHEAST OAHU

$$$ ✗ **Roy's.** Roy Yamaguchi is one of the 12 founding chefs of Hawaiian
MODERN regional cuisine, a culinary movement that put Hawaii on the food
HAWAIIAN map back in 1991. Opened in 1988, his flagship restaurant across the highway from Maunalua Bay is still packed every night with food-savvy visitors mixing with well-heeled residents. **Known for:** spectacular sunset views and a tiki torch–lit lanai and bar area; small and large portions available for many dishes; signature menu items like blackened ahi with a cultlike following. $ *Average main: $34* ✉ *Hawaii Kai Corporate*

Plaza, 6600 Kalanianaole Hwy., Hawaii Kai ☎ *808/396–7697* ⊕ *www. royshawaii.com* ☺ *No lunch.*

$ ✕ **Uncle Clay's House of Pure Aloha.** Located in a strip mall in the residen-
HAWAIIAN tial neighborhood of Aina Haina, Uncle Clay's is a happy place. This
FAMILY shave-ice stand specializes in house-made all-natural syrups made from
cane sugar and locally sourced fruits, including "kalespin"—a combi-
nation of kale and spinach. **Known for:** shave ice that's gone trendy;
fun, and kids love it; uninspiring location. $ *Average main: $4* ⊠ *Aina
Haina Shopping Center, 820 W. Hind Dr., right off Kalanianaole Hwy.,
Hawaii Kai* ☎ *808/373–5111* ⊕ *www.houseofpurealoha.com.*

WINDWARD OAHU

$ ✕ **Big City Diner.** This outlet of the popular retro diner chain has outdoor
AMERICAN lanai seating, a bar, and is across the street from a small bird sanctuary.
FAMILY It's a hot spot for breakfast and Sunday football; popular dinner items
include grilled steak with onions and mushrooms, baby back ribs, meat
loaf, and salads. **Known for:** happy families returning again and again;
nice indoor and outdoor bar; big portions. $ *Average main: $16* ⊠ *108
Hekili St., Kailua* ☎ *808/263–8880* ⊕ *bigcitydinerhawaii.com.*

$ ✕ **Boots & Kimo's Homestyle Kitchen.** Sometimes you wait an hour for
AMERICAN a table here since the restaurant's fervent followers come back again
and again for the banana pancakes topped with thick macadamia-nut
sauce. And it's no wonder: brothers Ricky and Jesse Kiakona treat their
guests like family. **Known for:** macadamia nut pancakes; long lines of
patient regulars; new location offering a nicer waiting area (but still the
long waits). $ *Average main: $11* ⊠ *151 Hekili St., Suite 102, Kailua*
☎ *808/263–7929* ☺ *No dinner.*

$$$ ✕ **Buzz's Lanikai.** Virtually unchanged since owners Bobby Lou and Buzz
STEAKHOUSE opened it in 1967, this neighborhood institution opposite Kailua Beach
Park is filled with the aroma of grilling steaks and plumeria blooms.
Sadly, Buzz has passed on, but you can now enjoy a predinner drink
on Stan's Deck, a salute to Bobby Lou's second husband. **Known for:**
local institution; the views from the lanai at lunch; excellent fruity
beach cocktails. $ *Average main: $35* ⊠ *413 Kawailoa Rd., Kailua*
☎ *808/261–4661* ⊕ *www.buzzsoriginalsteakhouse.com.*

$$ ✕ **Cactus Bistro.** This casual Pan-Latin spot brings much-needed and cre-
LATIN AMERICAN ative flavors to Kailua's beach soul. Check out maple leaf Muscovy duck
carnitas, smoked jidori chicken coyotas, and an assortment of *pinchos*
(small plates) to accompany the nice happy hour menu. **Known for:**
Latin flavors; great stop to or from the beach; nice array of margaritas
and sangrias. $ *Average main: $21* ⊠ *Davis Building, 767 Kailua Rd.,
Kailua* ☎ *808/261–1000* ⊕ *www.cactusbistro.com.*

$ ✕ **Cinnamon's Restaurant.** Known for uncommon variations on common
AMERICAN breakfast themes (pancakes, eggs Benedict, French toast, home fries, and
eggs), this neighborhood favorite is tucked into a hard-to-find Kailua
office park (call for directions). Lunch features local-style plate lunches,
which are good, but the main attraction is breakfast. **Known for:** endless variations on pancakes, eggs Benedict, and waffles; cinnamon rolls

(of course); long waits. $ *Average main: $14* ⊠ *315 Uluniu St., Kailua* ☎ *808/261–8724* ⊕ *www.cinnamons808.com.*

$$ ✕ **Haleiwa Joe's Haiku Gardens.** The Haleiwa location may be the name-
AMERICAN sake and claim the surf, but this Windward-side spot offers all the same friendly vibe and grilled seafood with knock-'em-dead views and a tiki torch–lit atmosphere after dark. The chef promotes a daily special preparation for the day's catch delivered straight from the Honolulu Fish Auction, along with the signature turf favorites. **Known for:** stunning views of Haiku Gardens; reliable for both seafood and meat; excellent daily specials. $ *Average main: $26* ⊠ *44-336 Haiku Rd., Kaneohe* ☎ *808/247–6671* ⊕ *www.haleiwajoes.com.*

$ ✕ **Island Snow.** This hole in the wall has been creating shave ice perfec-
HAWAIIAN tion in its tiny original spot since 1979, but when two young girls named Obama discovered the luscious flavors in 2008, it was really put on the map. A favorite spot for both locals and storied visitors (and these days lots of regular tourists), they make a mean shave ice, whether you stick with standard flavors like cherry or go for lilikoi guava with a snowcap on top. **Known for:** the best shave ice on the Windward side; the Obama girls, who grew up on this stuff (look for their photos on the wall); long lines of local kiteboarders and surfers. $ *Average main: $5* ⊠ *130 Kailua Rd., Kailua* ☎ *808/263–6339* ⊕ *islandsnow.com.*

$$ ✕ **Kalapawai Cafe & Deli.** This one-stop Mediterranean-leaning café, wine
ECLECTIC bar, bakery, and gourmet deli is the creation of the Dymond family, two generations of restaurateurs who have shaken up the Windward food scene with their signature green-and-white market and café. Come in on your way to the beach for a cup of coffee and bagel, and stop back for a gourmet pizza or bruschetta (how does eggplant confit, sweet peppers, honey, and goat cheese sound?) for lunch or a candlelit dinner at night. **Known for:** candlelight dinners and signature dishes by night; good coffee and sandwiches by day; impressive wine list for such a small spot. $ *Average main: $19* ⊠ *750 Kailua Rd., Kailua* ☎ *808/262–3354* ⊕ *www.kalapawaimarket.com.*

$$ ✕ **Pah Ke's Chinese Restaurant.** If you happen to be on the Windward side
CHINESE at dinner time, this out-of-the-ordinary Chinese restaurant—named for the local pidgin term for Chinese (literally translated, this is "Chinese's Chinese Restaurant")—is a good option. Ebullient owner and chef Raymond Siu, a former hotel pastry chef, focuses on healthier cooking techniques and local ingredients. **Known for:** dependable spot for the family; house specials that are usually better than standard menu fare; a big dining room with bright lights and not much atmosphere. $ *Average main: $22* ⊠ *46-018 Kamehameha Hwy., Kaneohe* ☎ *808/235–4505* ⊕ *www.pahke.com.*

$$ ✕ **Prima.** The beautifully blistered pies are cooked in a white-tiled Ferrara
PIZZA kiawe wood-burning oven that you can see in the open kitchen of this bright, light pizzeria with robin's egg–blue Eames shell chairs. This is as Neapolitan as it gets on Oahu, and these are the best pizzas on the island, topped with such ingredients as soppressata, prosciutto, and spicy meatballs, paired with fresh, local produce. **Known for:** a once-hidden gem now discovered; hit-or-miss service; the pizza … don't worry about the rest. $ *Average main: $18* ⊠ *Kailua Foodland Marketplace, 108 Hekili St., Kailua* ☎ *808/888–8933* ⊕ *www.primahawaii.com.*

4

CLOSE UP

Shrimp Snacks

No drive to the North Shore is complete without a shrimp stop. Shrimp stands dot Kamehameha Highway from Kahaluu to Kahuku. For about $12, you can get a shrimp plate lunch or a snack of chilled shrimp with cocktail sauce, served from a rough hut or converted van (many permanently parked) with picnic-table seating.

The shrimp-shack phenomenon began with a lost lease and a determined restaurateur. In 1994, when Giovanni and Connie Aragona couldn't renew the lease on their Haleiwa deli, they began hawking their best-selling dish—an Italian-style scampi preparation involving lemon, butter, and lots of garlic—from a truck alongside the road. About the same time, aquaculture was gaining a foothold in nearby Kahuku, with farmers raising sweet, white shrimp and huge, orange-whiskered prawns in shallow freshwater ponds. The ready supply and the success of the first shrimp truck led to many imitators.

Although it's changed hands, that first business lives on as Giovanni's Original Shrimp Truck, parked in Kahuku town. Signature dishes include the garlic shrimp and a spicy shrimp sauté, both worth a stop.

But there's plenty of competition: at least a dozen stands, trucks, or stalls are operating at any given time, with varying menus (and quality).

Not all of that shrimp comes fresh from the ponds; much of it is imported. The only way you can be sure you're buying local, farm-raised shrimp is if the shrimp is still kicking. Romy's Kahuku Prawns and Shrimp Hut (Kamehameha Highway, near Kahuku) is an arm of one of the longest-running aquaculture farms in the area; it sells live shrimp and prawns and farm-raised fish along with excellent plate lunches. The award-winning Macky's serves some of the juiciest, tastiest plates on the North Shore; if you're lucky, you'll be greeted by the gregarious Macky Chan himself.

THE NORTH SHORE

$
MEXICAN

✕ **Cholo's Homestyle Mexican.** There are a few institutions on the North Shore that are the area's great gathering places. Foodland (the great grocery store) is one, and the other is Cholo's. **Known for:** excellent sashimi-grade ahi tacos; a good breakfast burrito when you need it; fresh mango margaritas. $ *Average main: $15* ⊠ *North Shore Marketplace, 66-250 Kamehameha Hwy., Haleiwa* ☎ *808/637-3059* ⊕ *www.cholos.mx.*

$$
AMERICAN

✕ **Haleiwa Beach House.** The newest restaurant on the North Shore, Haleiwa Beach House takes full advantage of its epic views of the water and the glorious building it calls home. Once the local icon Jamesons, this beautifully restored spot puts diners on the lanai, up the spiral wood staircase at the bar, and always within view of the surf and the sounds of the ocean. **Known for:** view and setting that can't be beat; solid, reliable beef, seafood, salads, and kids options; craft beers on draft and a nice wine list. $ *Average main: $25* ⊠ *62-540 Kamehameha Hwy, Haleiwa* ☎ *808/637-3435* ⊕ *www.haleiwabeachhouse.com.*

$$$ AMERICAN 🍴 **Haleiwa Joe's Seafood Grill.** After the long drive to the North Shore, Haleiwa Joe's open-air lanai and a mai tai may be just what you need as you watch boats and surfers come and go from the harbor. This casual little joint rarely changes (and to some, that might feel dated), but regulars show up for the crunchy coconut shrimp, a fish sandwich, or the fresh fish special. **Known for:** reliable food with a nice harbor setting; never changing; good daily fish specials. [$] *Average main: $27* ✉ *66-011 Kamehameha Hwy., Haleiwa* ☎ *808/637-8005* 🌐 *www.haleiwajoes.com.*

$ BURGER 🍴 **Kua Aina Sandwich.** This North Shore spot has gone from funky burger shack (it first opened in 1975) to institution, with crowds of tourists and locals standing in line to order the large, hand-formed burgers heaped with bacon, cheese, salsa, and pineapples. Frankly, there are better burgers to be had around the island, but this place commands a loyal following who return again and again. **Known for:** a pilgrimage stop on the North Shore surf circuit; tourists by the busload; decent burgers and fries. [$] *Average main: $10* ✉ *66-160 Kamehameha Hwy., Haleiwa* ☎ *808/637-6067.*

4

$$$$ MODERN HAWAIIAN 🍴 **Roy's Beach House.** Loyalists of Roy Yamaguchi's iconic spots in Hawaii Kai and Waikiki are thrilled that he's also represented on the North Shore, in this rustic-beam-and-concrete-floor pavilion literally on the sand at Turtle Bay. All the favorites are served at this more beach-casual spot, from the miso butterfish to the beef short ribs, along with a more casual lunch menu. **Known for:** casual, romantic setting right on the beach; Roy's signature dishes; special-occasion celebrations. [$] *Average main: $42* ✉ *Turtle Bay Resort, 57-091 Kamehameha Hwy., Kahuku* ☎ *808/293-0801* 🌐 *www.roysbeachhouse.com.*

$ AMERICAN 🍴 **Ted's Bakery.** No North Shore trek is complete without a stop at a shrimp truck and a slice of Ted's pie. Sunburned tourists and salty surfers rub shoulders in their quest for Ted's famous chocolate *haupia* pie (layered coconut and dark chocolate puddings topped with whipped cream) and hearty plate lunches—like gravy-drenched hamburger steak and mahimahi. **Known for:** Ted's pies, which seem to show up at every Oahu pot luck; reliable all-day dining; plate lunches. [$] *Average main: $9* ✉ *59-024 Kamehameha Hwy., Haleiwa* ☎ *808/638-8207* 🌐 *www.tedsbakery.com.*

WEST (LEEWARD) OAHU

$$$$ MODERN HAWAIIAN 🍴 **Ama Ama.** There's nothing "Mickey Mouse" about the food at the fine-dining restaurant of this Disney resort. Add to that the views of the Ko Olina lagoons and Pacific Ocean—and live music by top local performers Friday–Sunday nights—and you have an evening worth the pretty penny. **Known for:** outstanding views and setting; consistently good food; hit-or-miss service. [$] *Average main: $40* ✉ *Aulani, a Disney Resort & Spa, 92-1185 Aliinui Dr., Ko Olina* ☎ *808/674-6200* 🌐 *www.disneyaulani.com/dining.*

$ HAWAIIAN 🍴 **Kaahaaina Cafe.** Hidden behind the Waianae Coast Comprehensive Health Center, this café offers what most every other hospital café in the world doesn't: good food, breathtaking views, and a space of calm amidst walking trails and coastline views. Open for breakfast and lunch, this local favorite offers plate lunches (huli huli chicken with rice and a salad, for example), standard breakfast fare, burgers, and daily specials (always worth asking about). **Known for:** local food-truck chef who put down roots; otherworldly views; locally sourced, healthy food. [$] *Average main: $8* ✉ *Waianae Coast Comprehensive Health Center, 86-260 Farrington Hwy., Waianae* ☎ *808/697–3488* ⏲ *Closed weekends. No dinner.*

$$$$ HAWAIIAN FAMILY 🍴 **Makahiki—The Bounty of the Islands.** The buffet restaurant at Disney's Aulani resort offers a wide variety of locally produced items, as well as familiar dishes from stateside and the rest of the world. You'll find sustainable Hawaiian seafood, Asian selections, familiar grilled meats and vegetables, and a kids' menu. **Known for:** true reflection of Hawaii; wide array of food to please every member of the family; popular character breakfasts (which book up months in advance). [$] *Average main: $52* ✉ *Aulani, a Disney Resort & Spa, 92-1185 Aliinui Dr., Ko Olina* ☎ *808/674–6200* 🌐 *www.disneyaulani.com/dining* ⏲ *No lunch.*

$$ HAWAIIAN 🍴 **Monkeypod Kitchen.** Local farm-to-table guru Peter Merriman is known throughout Hawaii for his inventive and popular restaurants. Monkeypod at Ko Olina captures his creativity and locally inspired food mantra perfectly. **Known for:** lobster deviled eggs and fresh fish tacos; indoor/outdoor setting; life-changing strawberry cream pie. [$] *Average main: $17* ✉ *Ko Olina Resort, 92-1048 Olani St., Kapolei* ☎ *808/380–4086* 🌐 *www.monkeypodkitchen.com.*

$ BAKERY 🍴 **The Sugar Hut.** The only bakery and dessert shop in Waianae, this tiny little storefront whips up a couple dozen flavors of French macarons, truffles, cupcakes, pies, parfaits, and cream puffs daily. You can also find standard desserts like cookies, brownies, and Rice Krispies treats. **Known for:** macarons and other excellent baked goods and desserts; lots of sweet tooth in a tiny package; bargain-priced "ugly ducklings". [$] *Average main: 4* ✉ *87-070 Farrington Hwy., Waianae* ✥ *Look for the Crab Shack restaurant and park in the tiny lot out front* ☎ *808/722–7539* 🌐 *www.sugarhuthawaii.com.*

WHERE TO STAY

Updated by
Powell Berger

As in real estate, location matters. And although Oahu is just 44 miles long and 30 miles wide—meaning you can circle the entire island before lunch—it boasts neighborhoods and lodgings with very different vibes and personalities. If you like the action and choices of big cities, consider Waikiki, a 24-hour playground with everything from surf to karaoke bars. Those who want an escape from urban life look to the island's leeward or windward sides, or to the North Shore, where the surf culture creates a laid-back atmosphere.

Most of the island's major hotels and resorts are in Waikiki, which has a lot to offer within a small area—namely shopping, restaurants, nightlife—and nearly 3 miles of sandy beach. You don't need a car in Waikiki; everything is nearby, including the Honolulu Zoo and Waikiki Aquarium, the 300-acre Kapiolani Park, running and biking paths, grocery stores, and access to public transportation that can take you to museums, shopping centers, and historic landmarks around the island.

You'll find places to stay along the entire stretch of both Kalakaua and Kuhio avenues, with smaller and quieter hotels and condos at the eastern end, and more business-centric accommodations on the western edge of Waikiki, near the Hawaii Convention Center, Ala Moana Center, and downtown Honolulu.

The majority of tourists who come to Oahu stay in Waikiki, but choosing accommodations in downtown Honolulu affords you the opportunity to be close to shopping and restaurants at Ala Moana Center, the largest shopping mall in the state. It also provides easy access to the airport.

If you want to get away from the bustle of the city, consider a stay on Oahu's Leeward Coast. Consider the Ko Olina resort area, about 20 minutes from the Honolulu International Airport and 40 minutes from Waikiki. Here, there are great golf courses and quiet beaches and coves that make for a relaxing getaway. But you'll need a car to get off the property if you want to explore the rest of the island.

Other, more low-key options are on Windward Oahu or the North Shore. Both regions are rustic and charming, with quaint eateries and coffee shops, local boutiques, and some of the island's best beaches. One of Oahu's premier resorts, Turtle Bay, is located here, too.

OAHU LODGING PLANNER

LODGING PROPERTY TYPES

HOTELS AND RESORTS

Oahu offers more accommodation choices than any other Hawaiian island, and for many visitors, staying at a top-notch resort or hotel here—such as the luxe Turtle Bay Resort on the North Shore or the posh Halekulani in Waikiki—is the ultimate Islands-style pampering experience.

Keep in mind that most Waikiki and Ko Olina hotels charge $10 or more per day for parking. Consider renting a car only on the days that you wish to go exploring or factor the parking costs into your budget.

B&BS AND INNS

There are dozens of B&Bs on Oahu, primarily located in Kailua, on the windward side of the island. Several are located within walking distance of world-famous Kailua Beach, and a handful have pools. A few serve simple continental breakfasts with pastries, coffee, and fresh island fruit and juices, while others provide breakfast items in the units for guests to enjoy at their leisure during their stay. *In addition to the listings below, check the Oahu Visitors Bureau website (⊕ www.gohawaii.com/oahu) for additional B&B options.*

CONDOS AND VACATION RENTALS

Vacation rentals give you the convenience of staying at a home away from home and getting to know Oahu the way the locals do. You can often save money as well, since you have a kitchen, can cook your meals, and don't pay for hotel parking. Prices, amenities, and locations of vacation homes vary considerably, meaning you should be able to find the perfect getaway on Oahu. Properties managed by individual owners can be found at online vacation-rental directories, as well as on the Oahu Visitors Bureau website. There also are several Oahu-based management companies with vacation rentals. Don't be surprised to find the same homes advertised on different sites, and with different names. The major online sites such as ⊕ VRBO.com and ⊕ AirBnB. com offer a plethora of options, but by working with a local agency, you may be able to better compare homes to get the one that works best for you. Compare companies, as some offer Internet specials and free nights when booking, and make sure that there will be an on-island point of contact for you should there be any issues during your stay. Also remember to ask your booking agent about the home's licensing as a vacation rental, since not all properties advertised carry the necessary license. Technically, rentals of less than 30 days are illegal on Oahu unless the property has a license for short-term vacation rentals or is a

5

hotel with apartment units, yet another reason to go with a knowledgable, experienced broker instead of doing the rental on your own. The state does take a stand from time to time to enforce vacation rental laws, and you'll have more protection and assurance that you aren't out there on your own if something goes wrong.

Private Homes Hawaii. This boutique agency represents only properties that hold a vacation rental license as issued by the City and County of Honolulu. Although the selection of homes isn't as vast as some of the other sites, they do represent some of the island's most storied properties and offer signature service to their guests. One of their properties, Walker's Lanikai Beach House, has a history of welcoming visitors and returning *kamaaiana* for decades. ☎ *808/896–9580* ⊕ *www.privatehomeshawaii.com.*

Hawaiian Villa Rentals. With offices on Oahu and Maui, this local company specializes in vacation homes around Oahu but with an emphasis on the Windward Coast and the Kahala area. Their offerings include everything from luxurious estates to more modest cottages and homes. They provide on-island points of contact and can work with you to provide additional conciergelike services. ☎ *808/247–7521* ⊕ *www.hawaiianvillarentals.com.*

PRICES

After your online research but before you book a room, try calling hotels directly. Sometimes on-property reservationists can get you the best deals, and they usually have the most accurate information about rooms, availability, and hotel amenities. If you use a toll-free number, ask for the location of the calling center you've reached. If it's not in Oahu, double-check information and rates by calling the hotel's local number.

The lodgings we list are the cream of the crop in each price category. Assume that hotels have private bath, phone, and TV unless we state otherwise. We always list facilities but not whether you'll be charged an extra fee to use them, so when pricing accommodations, find out what's included.

WHAT IT COSTS			
$	$$	$$$	$$$$
For two people	Under $180	$180–$260	$261–$340	Over $340

Hotel prices are for two people in a standard double room in high season, excluding taxes. Condo price categories reflect studio and one-bedroom rates.

HONOLULU

The vast majority of hotels in Honolulu are in Waikiki, but there are also a few in downtown Honolulu and in the Ala Moana area between downtown and Waikiki. Away from the hopping scene of Waikiki or busy downtown, accommodations on the rest of Oahu range from quiet and romantic bed-and-breakfasts and cottages to less expensive hotels

WHERE TO STAY ON OAHU

Neighborhood	Local Vibe	Pros	Cons
Honolulu	Lodging options are limited in downtown Honolulu, but if you want an urban feel or to be near Chinatown, look no farther.	Access to a wide selection of art galleries, boutiques, and new restaurants as well as Chinatown.	No beaches within walking distance. If you're looking to get away from it all, this is not the place.
Waikiki	Lodgings abound in Waikiki, from youth hostels to five-star accommodations. The area is always abuzz with activity and anything you desire is within walking distance.	You can surf in front of the hotels, wander miles of beach, and explore hundreds of restaurants and bars.	This is tourist central. Prices are high, and you are not going to get the true Hawaii experience.
Windward Oahu	More in tune with the local experience, here is where you'll find most of the island's B&Bs and enjoy the lush side of Oahu.	From beautiful vistas and green jungles, this side really captures the tropical paradise most people envision when dreaming of a Hawaiian vacation.	The lushness comes at a price—it rains a lot on this side. Also, luxury is not the specialty here; if you are looking to get pampered, stay elsewhere.
The North Shore	This is true country living, with one luxurious resort exception. It's bustling in the winter (when the surf is up) but pretty slow-paced in the summer.	Amazing surf and long stretches of sand truly epitomize the beach culture in Hawaii. Historic Haleiwa has enough stores to keep shopaholics busy.	There is no middle ground for accommodations; you're either in backpacker cabanas or $300-a-night suites. There is also zero nightlife, and traffic can get heavy during winter months.
West (Leeward) Oahu	This is the resort side of the rock; there is little outside of these resorts, but plenty on the grounds to keep you occupied for a week.	Ko Olina's lagoons offer the most kid-friendly swimming on the island, and the golf courses on this side are magnificent. Rare is the rainy day out here.	You are isolated from the rest of Oahu, with little in the way of shopping or jungle hikes.

that are a great value. There are a few luxury resorts as well, where you'll truly feel like you're getting away from it all.

For expanded hotel reviews, visit Fodors.com.

WAIKIKI

Hotels in Waikiki range from superluxe resorts to the kind of small, beachy places where shirtless surfers hang out in the lobby. It's where the heart of the visitor action is on Oahu. Those traveling with families might want to take into consideration easy access to the beach, restaurants, and other activities, as parking in the area can sometimes be difficult and pricey. For those looking to be slightly removed from the scene, choose accommodations on the *ewa* (western) end of Waikiki.

$ HOTEL **Aqua Aloha Surf Waikiki.** This affordable property just two blocks from Waikiki Beach offers surfer-chic accommodations at a great value. **Pros:** refrigerators in all rooms; pool with sundeck and cabanas; on-site coin-operated laundry. **Cons:** no view; traffic noise; 10-minute walk to beach. [$] *Rooms from: $110 ✉ 444 Kanekapolei St., Waikiki ☎ 866/970–4160, 808/954–7410 🌐 www.alohasurfhotelwaikiki.com 🛏 202 rooms 🍴 Free Breakfast.*

$ HOTEL **Aqua Oasis.** A trellised open-air lobby of Italian marble, a koi pond, hanging egg chairs, and a guava smoothie greet you on arrival at this Lewers Street hideaway, about a five-minute stroll from Kalakaua Avenue and through one of the many public-access ways to the beach. **Pros:** all rooms have lanai; on-site coin-operated laundry; karaoke lounge in the lobby. **Cons:** rooms are slightly dated; valet parking only; $25 per night resort fee. [$] *Rooms from: $125 ✉ 320 Lewers St., Waikiki ☎ 808/923–2300, 866/767–4528, 808/441–7781 🌐 www.aquaoasishotel.com 🛏 94 rooms 🍴 Free Breakfast.*

$$ RENTAL **Aqua Pacific Monarch.** One block from the western end of Waikiki Beach, this 34-story high-rise condominium resort has a rooftop deck—with a freshwater pool, hot tub, and sauna—with sweeping views of Waikiki and the Pacific Ocean. **Pros:** fantastic view from rooftop pool; hospitality lounge; all rooms have lanai and views. **Cons:** stairs to the pool deck are fairly steep and may be difficult for some; street noise; older property with the wear to show for it. [$] *Rooms from: $183 ✉ 2427 Kuhio Ave., Waikiki ☎ 808/923–9805, 866/940–2782 🌐 www.aquaresorts.com 🛏 216 rooms 🍴 No meals.*

$ RENTAL **Aqua Palms Waikiki.** Across from the Hilton Hawaiian Village on Ala Moana Boulevard, just as it curves toward Waikiki's Kalakaua Avenue, the 12-story Aqua Palms offers studio and luxury one-bedroom-suite accommodations. **Pros:** full kitchens in suites; location easily walkable to park, beach, and activities; hotel shuttle to shopping and throughout Waikiki. **Cons:** closest beach access is through the Hilton Hawaiian Village, across the street; older property with the dings to show for it; not all rooms have lanai. [$] *Rooms from: $129 ✉ 1850 Ala Moana Blvd., Waikiki ☎ 808/954–7424, 866/970–4165, 808/947–7256 🌐 www.aquapalms.com 🛏 267 rooms 🍴 No meals.*

$$ RENTAL FAMILY **Aston at the Waikiki Banyan.** Families and active travelers love the convenience and action of this hotel, just a block from Waikiki Beach, the aquarium, the zoo, and bustling Kalakaua Avenue. **Pros:** many rooms have great views with kitchens; walking distance to shops, beach, restaurants, and activities; fabulous recreation deck for the entire family. **Cons:** room conditions can vary greatly; no on-site restaurant; sharing hotel with residents. [$] *Rooms from: $200 ✉ 201 Ohua Ave., Waikiki ☎ 808/922–0555, 877/997–6667 🌐 www.astonwaikikibanyan.com 🛏 876 suites 🍴 No meals.*

$$ HOTEL FAMILY **Aston Waikiki Beach Hotel.** A good choice for families, this large hotel is directly across the street from a protected stretch of Kuhio Beach and near Kapiolani Park. **Pros:** fun for families; great beach access; cooler bags for packing picnic breakfast. **Cons:** active lobby area and crowded elevators;

Where to Stay in Waikiki

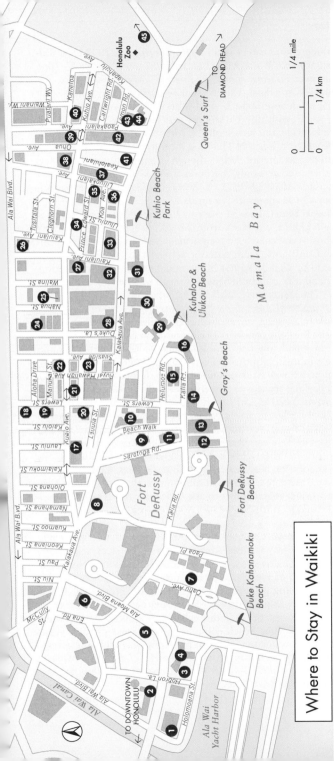

no self-parking; rooms can be small. $ *Rooms from: $229* ✉ *2570 Kalakaua Ave., Waikiki* ☎ *808/922–2511, 877/997–6667, 800/877–7666* ⊕ *www.astonwaikikibeach.com* ⇨ *685 rooms* ⦿ *Free Breakfast.*

$ ⬚ **Aston Waikiki Circle Hotel.** This unusual 14-story circular hotel—built
HOTEL   to resemble a Chinese lantern—is a Waikiki landmark, though the rooms are small, with tiny bathrooms that have only showers. **Pros:** unbeatable location and views; on-site surfboard lockers and complimentary beach gear; Eggs 'N Things, a local icon, is right downstairs. **Cons:** small rooms; interior design, though charming to some, may feel dated to others; showers only. $ *Rooms from: $165* ✉ *2464 Kalakaua Ave., Waikiki* ☎ *808/923–1571, 877/997–6667* ⊕ *www.astonwaikikicircle.com* ⇨ *104 rooms* ⦿ *No meals.*

$$ ⬚ **Aston Waikiki Sunset.** This 38-story high-rise condominium resort is
RENTAL near Diamond Head, one block from Waikiki Beach, and on the city's
FAMILY bus line. **Pros:** spectacular views; apartment-style living; heated swimming pool. **Cons:** noise from outdoor activities can be a distraction; at the far end of Waikiki so not in the middle of the action; interiors show wear and tear and could benefit from an update. $ *Rooms from: $189* ✉ *229 Paoakalani Ave., Waikiki* ☎ *808/922–0511, 877/997–6667* ⊕ *www.astonwaikikisunset.com* ⇨ *435 suites* ⦿ *No meals.*

$ ⬚ **The Breakers.** Despite an explosion of high-rise construction all
RENTAL around it, the Breakers continues to transport guests back to 1960s-era Hawaii in this small, low-rise complex a mere half-block from Waikiki Beach. **Pros:** intimate atmosphere with fabulous poolside courtyard; great location; a throw back to a different era. **Cons:** a bit worn down and dated; parking space is extremely limited (but free); showers only. $ *Rooms from: $170* ✉ *250 Beach Walk, Waikiki* ☎ *808/923–3181, 800/923–7174* ⊕ *www.breakers-hawaii.com* ⇨ *63 rooms* ⦿ *No meals.*

$$$ ⬚ **Castle Waikiki Shore.** Nestled between Fort DeRussy Beach Park and
RENTAL the Outrigger Reef on the Beach, this is the only condo hotel directly
FAMILY on Waikiki Beach. **Pros:** right on the beach; great views from spacious private lanai; location near beach and lush park areas. **Cons:** units can vary and some are dated; two-night minimum stay; not all suites have all amenities listed, so remember to ask. $ *Rooms from: $270* ✉ *2161 Kalia Rd., Waikiki* ☎ *808/952–4500, 800/367–5004* ⊕ *www.castleresorts.com* ⇨ *168 suites* ⦿ *No meals.*

$ ⬚ **Coconut Waikiki Hotel.** Overlooking the Ala Wai Canal, this reasonably
HOTEL   priced boutique hotel has a more residential feel than a typical resort, with a cobblestone driveway, a lobby with rattan living room–style furnishings, a wall of French doors that open up to a gazebo garden, and a tiny swimming pool tucked in a backyard. **Pros:** a small and economical hotel in Waikiki; free Wi-Fi throughout hotel; on-site coin-operated laundry. **Cons:** the walk through busy Waikiki gets tiring when you're carrying all your beach equipment; only valet parking available; area is more residential and can be a long way from the action, particularly at night. $ *Rooms from: $149* ✉ *450 Lewers St., Waikiki* ☎ *866/974–2626, 808/923–8828* ⊕ *www.coconutwaikikihotel.com* ⇨ *81 rooms* ⦿ *Free Breakfast.*

$ B&B/INN **Diamond Head Bed and Breakfast.** Many travelers and residents would love to own a home like this art-filled B&B at the base of Waikiki's famous Diamond Head crater, one of the city's most exclusive neighborhoods; however, there are only three rooms available, so you may have to work a bit to stay here. **Pros:** secluded and peaceful; very homey; history and charm. **Cons:** small and therefore difficult to book; doesn't accept credit cards; no air-conditioning. [$] *Rooms from: $160* ✉ *3240 Noela Dr., Waikiki* ☎ *808/923–3360, 800/262–9912 for reservations* 🌐 *www.diamondheadbnb.com* 💳 *No credit cards* 🛏 *3 rooms* 🍴 *Free Breakfast.*

$$ HOTEL **Doubletree by Hilton Alana Waikiki Beach.** A convenient location—10 minutes' walk from the Hawaii Convention Center—a professional staff, pleasant public spaces, and a 24-hour business center and gym draw a global business clientele to this reliable chain hotel. **Pros:** walkable to the beach and Ala Moana mall; walk-in glass showers with oversize rain showerheads; heated outdoor pool and 24-hour fitness center. **Cons:** a 10-minute walk to the beach; little local flavor; valet parking only. [$] *Rooms from: $209* ✉ *1956 Ala Moana Blvd., Waikiki* ☎ *808/941–7275* 🌐 *doubletree3.hilton.com* 🛏 *317 rooms* 🍴 *No meals.*

$$$ RESORT FAMILY **Embassy Suites Waikiki Beach Walk.** In a place where space is at a premium, this all-suites resort offers families and groups traveling together a bit more room to move about, with two 21-story towers housing one- and two-bedroom suites. **Pros:** great location next to Waikiki Beach Walk and all its shops and restaurants; spacious and modern rooms; complimentary hot breakfast and evening reception daily. **Cons:** no direct beach access; not steeped in Waikiki charm; property can seem busy and noisy. [$] *Rooms from: $319* ✉ *201 Beachwalk St., Waikiki* ☎ *800/362–2779, 808/921–2345* 🌐 *www.embassysuiteswaikiki.com* 🛏 *369 suites* 🍴 *Free Breakfast.*

$$ HOTEL **The Equus Hotel.** This small, boutique hotel has been completely renovated with a Hawaiian country theme that pays tribute to Hawaii's polo-playing history. **Pros:** casual and fun atmosphere; attentive staff; nicely furnished rooms. **Cons:** busy, hectic area; must cross a major road to get to the beach; limited on-site dining (coffee shop and bar only). [$] *Rooms from: $190* ✉ *1696 Ala Moana Blvd., Waikiki* ☎ *808/949–0061* 🌐 *www.equushotel.com* 🛏 *67 rooms* 🍴 *No meals.*

$$$$ RESORT Fodor's Choice ★ **Halekulani.** The luxurious Halekulani exemplifies the translation of its name—the "house befitting heaven"—and from the moment you step into the lobby, the attention to detail and impeccable service wrap you in privilege at this beachfront location away from Waikiki's bustle. **Pros:** heavenly interior and exterior spaces; wonderful dining opportunities in-house; world-class service. **Cons:** might feel a bit formal for Waikiki; pricey; can seem busy with events and formal gatherings. [$] *Rooms from: $500* ✉ *2199 Kalia Rd., Waikiki* ☎ *808/923–2311, 800/367–2343, 844/288–8022* 🌐 *www.halekulani.com* 🛏 *453 rooms* 🍴 *No meals.*

$$$$ HOTEL **Hawaii Prince Hotel & Golf Club Waikiki.** This slim, renovated high-rise with 538 oceanfront rooms including 57 luxury suites fronts Ala Wai Yacht Harbor at the *ewa* (western) edge of Waikiki. **Pros:** fantastic views from all rooms; elegant and sophisticated; location

avoids complicated-to-maneuver Waikiki. **Cons:** no free Internet; no beach access; between weddings and functions, property can seem very busy. ⓢ *Rooms from: $500* ✉ *100 Holomoana St., Waikiki* ☎ *888/977–4623, 808/956–1111* ⊕ *www.hawaiiprincehotel.com* ⟴ *538 rooms* ❘❍❘ *No meals.*

$$
HOTEL
FAMILY

Hilton Garden Inn Waikiki Beach. In 2016, four hotels opened on Oahu, three in the heart of Waikiki, and the largest of them—and most moderately priced—is the Hilton Garden Waikiki Beach. **Pros:** new hotel; central location near International Market Place, shopping, and dining; moderately priced and no resort fee. **Cons:** the large resort can feel impersonal; valet-only parking; two-block walk to the beach. ⓢ *Rooms from: $189* ✉ *2330 Kuhio Ave., Waikiki* ☎ *808/892–1820* ⊕ *www.hiltongardeninn.com* ⟴ *623 rooms* ❘❍❘ *No meals.*

$$
RESORT
FAMILY

Hilton Hawaiian Village Beach Resort & Spa. Location, location, location: this megaresort and convention destination sprawls over 22 acres on Waikiki's widest stretch of beach, with the green lawns of neighboring Fort DeRussy creating a buffer zone to the high-rise lineup of central Waikiki. **Pros:** activities and amenities can keep you and the kids busy for weeks; stellar spa; Friday-night fireworks. **Cons:** size of property can be overwhelming; resort fee $30 (plus tax) per room per night; parking is expensive ($43 per day for self parking). ⓢ *Rooms from: $239* ✉ *2005 Kalia Rd., Waikiki* ☎ *808/949–4321, 800/774–1500* ⊕ *www.hiltonhawaiianvillage.com* ⟴ *4499 rooms* ❘❍❘ *No meals.*

$$
HOTEL

Hilton Waikiki Beach Hotel. Two blocks from Kuhio Beach, this 37-story high-rise, located on the Diamond Head end of Waikiki, is great for travelers who want to be near the action, but not right in it. **Pros:** central location; helpful staff; pleasant, comfortable public spaces. **Cons:** long walk to the beach; very few rooms have views; older property that shows some wear. ⓢ *Rooms from: $219* ✉ *2500 Kuhio Ave., Waikiki* ☎ *808/922–0811, 888/370–0980* ⊕ *www.hiltonwaikikibeach.com* ⟴ *609 rooms* ❘❍❘ *No meals.*

$$
HOTEL

Hotel Renew. Located a block from world-famous Waikiki Beach, this 72-room boutique hotel managed by Aston Hotels & Resorts is a casual but chic change from the big resorts that dominate the oceanfront here. **Pros:** free Wi-Fi; personalized service; close to zoo, aquarium, and beach. **Cons:** no pool; new hotel but older refurbished facility requires constant upkeep; rooms on the small side. ⓢ *Rooms from: $180* ✉ *129 Paoakalani Ave., Waikiki* ☎ *808/687–7700, 877/997–6667* ⊕ *www.hotelrenew.com* ⟴ *72 rooms* ❘❍❘ *Free Breakfast.*

$$$
RESORT
FAMILY

Hyatt Regency Waikiki Resort & Spa. This large high-rise hotel, where the lively atrium-style lobby is the focal point, is across the street from Kuhio Beach, but there's no resort between it and the Pacific Ocean. **Pros:** public spaces are open; elegant and very professional spa; kid-friendly and close to the beach. **Cons:** in a very busy and crowded part of Waikiki; on-site pool is quite small; can feel a bit like you're staying in a shopping mall. ⓢ *Rooms from: $300* ✉ *2424 Kalakaua Ave., Waikiki* ☎ *808/923–1234, 800/633–7313* ⊕ *www.hyattregencywaikiki.com* ⟴ *1,248 rooms* ❘❍❘ *No meals.*

$$$
RESORT

Ilikai Hotel & Suites. At the *ewa* (western) edge of Waikiki overlooking the Ala Wai Small Boat Harbor, this iconic high-rise resort stands at the entrance to Waikiki and is a Honolulu landmark, having celebrated its 50th birthday in 2014. **Pros:** views of sunset from most rooms on the ewa side; western edge of Waikiki keeps you out of the chaos while still close to everything; Wi-Fi throughout the property. **Cons:** very slow elevators; five-minute walk to the beach; despite renovations, it still shows its age. [$] *Rooms from: $300* ✉ *1777 Ala Moana Blvd., Waikiki* ☎ *808/949–3811, 866/406–2782* 🌐 *www.ilikaihotel.com* 🛏 *779 rooms* 🍴 *No meals.*

ASK FOR A LANAI

Islanders love their porches, balconies, and verandas—all wrapped up in a single Hawaiian word: *lanai.* You may not want to look at a parking lot, so when booking, ask about the lanai and be sure to specify the view (understanding that top views command top dollars). Also, check that the lanai is not merely a step-out or Juliet balcony, with just enough room to lean against a railing—you want a lanai that is big enough for patio seating.

$ RENTAL 🏨 **Ilima Hotel.** Tucked away on a residential side street near Waikiki's Ala Wai Canal, this locally owned 17-story condominium-style hotel is a throwback to old Waikiki, offering large units that are ideal for families. **Pros:** free parking in Waikiki is a rarity; great value; free Wi-Fi. **Cons:** furnishings are dated; 10-minute walk to the beach; no ocean views. [$] *Rooms from: $160* ✉ *445 Nohonani St., Waikiki* ☎ *808/923–1877, 800/801–9366* 🌐 *www.ilima.com* 🛏 *98 units* 🍴 *No meals.*

$ HOTEL FAMILY 🏨 **Luana Waikiki.** At the entrance to Waikiki near Fort DeRussy is this welcoming hotel offering both rooms and condominium units. **Pros:** coin-operated laundry facilities on-site; sundeck with barbecue grills; free Wi-Fi. **Cons:** no direct beach access; area can be busy and noisy; pool is small. [$] *Rooms from: $175* ✉ *2045 Kalakaua Ave., Waikiki* ☎ *808/955–6000, 866/940–2782, 808/441–7774* 🌐 *www.aqualuanawaikiki.com* 🛏 *225 units* 🍴 *No meals.*

$$$$ RESORT 🏨 **Moana Surfrider, A Westin Resort & Spa.** Outrageous rates of $1.50 per night were the talk of the town when the "First Lady of Waikiki" opened her doors in 1901; today, this historic beauty—the oldest hotel in Waikiki—is still a wedding and honeymoon favorite with a sweeping main staircase and period furnishings in its historic Moana Wing (and considerably more expensive). **Pros:** elegant, historic property; best place on Waikiki Beach to watch hula and have a drink; can't beat the location. **Cons:** you'll likely dodge bridal parties in the lobby; the hotel now charges a mind-boggling resort fee of $37.70 per room per day; expensive parking ($35/day for self parking across the street). [$] *Rooms from: $400* ✉ *2365 Kalakaua Ave., Waikiki* ☎ *808/922–3111, 866/716–8112* 🌐 *www.moana-surfrider.com* 🛏 *796 rooms* 🍴 *No meals.*

$$$$ HOTEL 🏨 **The Modern Honolulu.** The lobby of this edgy, slickly designed hotel has the feel of an upscale jazz club, with recessed lighting and bookcases, making this the best hotel pick in Waikiki for urbanites who like the hip, big-city vibe. **Pros:** excellent design; unpretentious but hip feel; great bars and restaurants. **Cons:** not kid-friendly; on the outer edge of Waikiki; direct beach access a five-minute walk away. [$] *Rooms from: $450* ✉ *1775 Ala Moana Blvd., Waikiki* ☎ *808/943–5800, 888/970–4161*

🌐 *www.themodernhonolulu.com* 🛏 *383 rooms* 🍴 *No meals.*

$$ HOTEL 🏨 **Ohana Waikiki East.** If you want to be in central Waikiki and don't want to pay beachfront lodging prices, consider the Ohana Waikiki East. **Pros:** close to the beach and reasonable rates; decent on-site eateries, including a piano bar; in the middle of the Waikiki action. **Cons:** some rooms with no lanai and very basic public spaces; an older property with signs of wear and tear; limited self-parking at $30/day. [$] *Rooms from: $229* ✉ *150 Kaiulani Ave., Waikiki* ☎ *808/922–5353, 866/956–4262, 800/688–7444* 🌐 *www.ohanahotelsoahu.com/ohana_east* 🛏 *441 rooms* 🍴 *No meals.*

$$ HOTEL 🏨 **Ohana Waikiki Malia.** Close to the *ewa* (western) end of Waikiki, this older hotel comprises a pair of buildings, one with standard rooms, the other with one-bedroom suites that have kitchenettes. **Pros:** central to shopping and dining in Waikiki; on-site coin-operated laundry facilities; good value. **Cons:** views not much to speak of; dated property that shows; small pool. [$] *Rooms from: $200* ✉ *2211 Kuhio Ave., Waikiki* ☎ *808/923–7621, 866/956–4262* 🌐 *www.ohanahotelsoahu.com/ohana_waikiki_malia* 🛏 *332 rooms* 🍴 *No meals.*

$$$ HOTEL FAMILY 🏨 **Outrigger Reef on the Beach.** What had been a plain but pleasant oceanfront bargain now offers an updated experience in keeping with its prime location, and although the decor and feel may not be to everyone's taste, the staff's aloha and attention to guests' needs bring people back again and again. **Pros:** on the beach; direct access to Waikiki Beach Walk; attentive staff. **Cons:** room decor is dated; views from non-oceanfront rooms are uninspiring; can get pricey compared to the value. [$] *Rooms from: $340* ✉ *2169 Kalia Rd., Waikiki* ☎ *808/923–3111, 866/956–4262, 800/688–7444* 🌐 *www.outriggerreef-onthebeach.com* 🛏 *669 rooms* 🍴 *No meals.*

$$$$ RESORT 🏨 **Outrigger Waikiki Beach Resort.** Outrigger's star property sits on one of the finest sections of Waikiki Beach and is a visitor favorite for its array of cultural activites, live music, dining options, and bar scene. **Pros:** the best beach bar in Waikiki; shopping, activities, and services abound on the property; on-site coin-operated laundry. **Cons:** the lobby feels a bit like an airport with so many people using it as a throughway to the beach; valet parking is $38 per day; the property has aged, which can sometimes be felt in guest-room decor. [$] *Rooms from: $450* ✉ *2335 Kalakaua Ave., Waikiki* ☎ *808/923–0711, 808/956–4262, 800/442–7304* 🌐 *www.outriggerwaikikihotel.com* 🛏 *527 rooms* 🍴 *No meals.*

HOTEL CULTURAL PROGRAMS

Hotels, especially in Waikiki, are fueling a resurgence in Hawaiian culture, thanks to repeat visitors who want a more authentic island experience. In addition to lei-making and hula-dancing lessons, you can learn how to strum a ukulele, listen to Grammy Award–winning Hawaiian musicians, watch a revered master *kumu* (teacher) share the art of ancient hula and chant, chat with a marine biologist about Hawaii's endangered species, or get a lesson in the art of canoe making. Check with the concierge for daily Hawaiian activities at the hotel or nearby.

$$$$
RENTAL

The Residences at Waikiki Beach Tower. You'll find the elegance of a luxury all-suites condominium combined with the intimacy and service of a boutique hotel right on bustling Kalakaua Avenue. **Pros:** roomy suites with quality amenities; great private lanai and views; a recreation deck with something for everyone. **Cons:** no on-site restaurants; you must cross a busy street to the beach; space, amenities, and location don't come cheap. $ *Rooms from: $499* ✉ *2470 Kalakaua Ave., Waikiki* ☎ *877/997–6667, 855/776–1766, 808/670–3999* ⊕ *www.theresidencesatwaikikibeach.com* ⤵ *140 suites* ⦿ *No meals.*

LOOKING FOR A PRIVATE BEACH?

The Royal Hawaiian Hotel and Moana Surfrider—the two oldest hotels on Oahu—are the only hotels in Waikiki with property lines that extend into the sand. They have created private roped-off beach areas that can be accessed only by hotel guests. The areas are adjacent to the hotel properties at the top of the beach.

5

$$$$
HOTEL

Ritz-Carlton Residences Waikiki Beach. Ritz-Carlton Residences, Waikiki Beach (the only Ritz-Carlton on Oahu) welcomes well-heeled guests from across the globe with its signature elegance and impeccable service. **Pros:** very private; luxuriously appointed apartments; pampering service. **Cons:** not close to the beach; pricey, particularly given distance from beach; families can sometimes overrun the facilities. $ *Rooms from: $669* ✉ *383 Kalaimoku St., Waikiki* ☎ *808/922–8111* ⊕ *www.ritzcarlton.com* ⤵ *307 units* ⦿ *No meals.*

$
HOTEL

Royal Grove Hotel. Two generations of the Fong family have put their heart and soul into the operation of this tiny (by Waikiki standards), pink six-story hotel that feels like a throwback to the days of boarding houses—an era where rooms were outfitted for function, not style, and served up with a wealth of simple hospitality at a price that didn't break the bank. **Pros:** very economical Waikiki option; lots of character; a throwback to another era. **Cons:** no air-conditioning in some rooms; room decor is dated; no on-site parking. $ *Rooms from: $100* ✉ *151 Uluniu Ave., Waikiki* ☎ *808/923–7691* ⊕ *www.royalgrovehotel.com* ⤵ *87 rooms* ⦿ *No meals.*

$$$$
RESORT
Fodor'sChoice
★

The Royal Hawaiian, a Luxury Collection Resort. There's nothing like the iconic "Pink Palace of the Pacific," on 14 acres of prime Waikiki Beach, which has held fast to the luxury and grandeur that defined the hotel since it began hosting the rich and famous in the 1930s. **Pros:** can't beat it for history; mai tais and sunsets are amazing; luxury, history, and a prime location. **Cons:** history is not cheap; you'd better like pink; be prepared to share the luxury with brides and galas. $ *Rooms from: $650* ✉ *2259 Kalakaua Ave., Waikiki* ☎ *808/923–7311, 866/716–8110* ⊕ *www.royal-hawaiian.com* ⤵ *561 rooms* ⦿ *No meals.*

$$$
HOTEL
FAMILY

Sheraton Princess Kaiulani. Starwood's Princess Kaiulani sits across the street from the regal Moana Surfrider, without some of the more elaborate amenities (such as a spa or a kid's club), but with rates that are considerably kinder to the wallet. **Pros:** in the heart of everything in Waikiki, with beach right across the street; Beach Service with chairs, towels, fruit, and water available on the beach; great value for the location. Cons: lobby area can feel like Grand Central Station; pool closes at 7 pm; resort fee a whopping $34.55/day, with parking an additional $35/day. Ⓢ *Rooms from: $310* ✉ *120 Kaiulani Ave., Waikiki* ☎ *808/922–5811, 866/716–8109* ⊕ *www.princess-kaiulani. com* ⌨ *1,010 rooms* ⎮○⎮ *No meals.*

$$$$ ⬚ **Sheraton Waikiki.** If you don't mind crowds, this could be the place
HOTEL for you: towering over its neighbors on the prow of Waikiki's famous
FAMILY sands, the enormous Sheraton sits right at center stage on the beach.
Pros: location in the heart of everything; variety of on-site activities and dining options; swimming pools often ranked among the Islands' best. Cons: busy atmosphere clashes with laid-back Hawaiian style; pricey resort fee and parking fees; local events routinely fill the ballrooms. Ⓢ *Rooms from: $515* ✉ *2255 Kalakaua Ave., Waikiki* ☎ *808/922–4422, 866/716–8109* ⊕ *www.sheraton-waikiki.com* ⌨ *1,634 rooms* ⎮○⎮ *No meals.*

$$ ⬚ **Shoreline Waikiki.** Situated right on the bustling Seaside Avenue in
HOTEL Waikiki, this 14-story, 1970s-era modernist boutique hotel is another old dame that's been brought back to life as an urban-chic property. Pros: great location in the middle of bustling Waikiki; no resort fee; hipster decor a refreshing break from old-style Hawaiiana. Cons: if the 1970s aren't your thing, skip it; rooms are small and inconsistent, so ask about the details; pool very small. Ⓢ *Rooms from: $250* ✉ *342 Seaside Ave., Waikiki* ☎ *808/931–2444, 855/931–2444* ⊕ *www.shorelinehotelwaikiki.com* ⌨ *135 rooms* ⎮○⎮ *No meals.*

$$$ ⬚ **Surfjack Hotel & Swim Club.** Numerous Waikiki properties have trans-
HOTEL formed their midcentury digs into hip, 21st-century style, but none has done it as well as this 1960s-inspired boutique hotel with a surfing vibe. Pros: hipster, urban-chic vibe that works; retro, locally designed decor; Ed Kenney restaurant on-site. Cons: not much immediately surrounding the hotel; far from the beach; rooms can be inconsistent. Ⓢ *Rooms from: $290* ✉ *412 Lewers St., Waikiki* ☎ *808/923–8882* ⊕ *www.surfjack.com* ⌨ *112 rooms* ⎮○⎮ *No meals.*

$$$$ ⬚ **Trump International Hotel Waikiki Beach Walk.** One of the chicest hotels
HOTEL on the Waikiki scene, the Trump has been drawing visitors since it opened in late 2009. Pros: beautifully appointed rooms; on the edge of Waikiki so a bit quieter; great views of Friday fireworks and nightly sunsets. Cons: must cross street to reach the beach; pricey; small pool often filled with kids. Ⓢ *Rooms from: $550* ✉ *223 Saratoga Rd., Waikiki* ☎ *808/683–7777, 877/683–7401* ⊕ *www.trumphotelcollection.com/ waikiki* ⌨ *462 rooms* ⎮○⎮ *No meals.*

$$$$ ⬚ **Waikiki Beach Marriott Resort & Spa.** On the eastern edge of Waikiki,
RESORT this flagship Marriott sits on about 5 acres across from Kuhio Beach and close to Kapiolani Park, the Honolulu Zoo, and the Waikiki Aquarium. Pros: stunning views of Waikiki; airy, tropical public spaces; unbeatable location. Cons: large impersonal hotel, sometimes confusing to navigate; Kalakaua Avenue can be noisy; pricey parking and resort fee. Ⓢ *Rooms from: $350* ✉ *2552 Kalakaua Ave., Waikiki* ☎ *808/922–6611, 800/367–5370* ⊕ *www.marriottwaikiki. com* ⌨ *1,310 rooms* ⎮○⎮ *No meals.*

$$ HOTEL FAMILY **Waikiki Beachcomber by Outrigger.** Located almost directly across from the Royal Hawaiian Center and next door to the new and revamped International Market Place, the Beachcomber is a well-situated hotel for families as well as those looking for a boutique feel in the heart of the action. **Pros:** Magic of Polynesia live entertainment; airport transportation; no resort fees, free Wi-Fi, and unlimited trolley rides. **Cons:** very busy area in the thick of Waikiki action; a busy property that sometimes shows the wear; valet parking only ($38 per day). [$] *Rooms from: $250* ✉ *2300 Kalakaua Ave., Waikiki* ☎ *808/922–4646, 877/317–5756* 🌐 *www.waikikibeachcomberresort.com* 🛏 *496 rooms* 🍴 *No meals.*

CONDO COMFORTS

The local **Foodland** grocery-store chain has two locations near Waikiki (✉ *Market City, 2939 Harding Ave., near intersection with Kapahulu Ave. and highway overpass, Kaimuki* ☎ *808/734–6303* ✉ *1460 Beretania St., Honolulu* ☎ *808/946–4654*). A smaller version of larger Foodland, **Food Pantry** (✉ *2370 Kuhio Ave., across from Miramar hotel, Waikiki* ☎ *808/923–9831*) also has apparel, beach stuff, and tourist-oriented items.

5

$$ HOTEL **Waikiki Parc.** In contrast to the stately vintage-Hawaiian elegance of her sister hotel, the Halekulani, the Waikiki Parc makes a contemporary statement, offering the same attention to detail in service and architectural design but lacking the beachfront location and higher prices. **Pros:** modern, consistent, and well-appointed; great access to Waikiki Beach and Beach Walk shopping and dining; lots of activities for the active traveler, including at the Halekulani across the street. **Cons:** no direct beach access; rooms can be small; renovations anticipated in 2018, so check before booking. [$] *Rooms from: $240* ✉ *2233 Helumoa Rd., Waikiki* ☎ *808/921–7272, 844/640–0842, 800/422–0450* 🌐 *www.waikikiparc.com* 🛏 *297 rooms* 🍴 *No meals.*

$ HOTEL **Waikiki Sand Villa.** Families and those looking for an economical rate without sacrificing proximity to Waikiki's beaches, dining, and shopping return to the Waikiki Sand Villa year after year. **Pros:** fun bar; pool and foot spa great for lounging; economical choice. **Cons:** the noise from the bar might annoy some; 10-minute walk to the beach; street noise from Ala Wai can get loud. [$] *Rooms from: $165* ✉ *2375 Ala Wai Blvd., Waikiki* ☎ *808/922–4744, 800/247–1903* 🌐 *www.sandvillahotel.com* 🛏 *214 rooms* 🍴 *No meals.*

DOWNTOWN HONOLULU

$$ HOTEL **Aston at the Executive Centre Hotel.** Downtown Honolulu's only hotel is an all-suites high-rise in the center of the business district, within walking distance of the historic Capitol District, museums, and Honolulu's Chinatown, and a 10-minute drive from Honolulu International Airport. **Pros:** central to downtown businesses, transportation, and sights; great restaurant (Hukilau) in the lobby; good spot for overnighting before or after a cruise. **Cons:** no beach within walking distance; area businesses shut down early on weekdays and usually close on weekends; parking is very expensive. [$] *Rooms from: $260* ✉ *1088 Bishop St., Downtown*

☎ *808/539–3000, 877/997–6667* ⊕ *www.astonhotels.com/resort/over-view/aston-at-the-executive-centre-hotel* ➷ *116 suites* ⑪ *No meals.*

ALA MOANA

$$$ ⊡ **Ala Moana Hotel.** A decent value in a pricey hotel market, this well-
HOTEL located and nicely appointed hotel is connected to Oahu's largest mall, the Ala Moana Center, by a pedestrian ramp, and is a 10-minute walk to Waikiki. **Pros:** great value (and no resort fee); rooms are comfortably appointed; quick walk to the beach, convention center, and shopping. **Cons:** outside the heartbeat of Waikiki; some areas and rooms feel dated; large, impersonal hotel. Ⓢ *Rooms from: $269* ⊠ *410 Atkinson Dr., Ala Moana* ☎ *808/955–4811, 866/488–1396* ⊕ *www.alamoana-hotelhonolulu.com* ➷ *1,134 rooms* ⑪ *No meals.*

KAHALA

$$$$ ⊡ **The Kahala Hotel & Resort.** Hidden away in the upscale residential
RESORT neighborhood of Kahala (on the other side of Diamond Head from
FAMILY Waikiki), this elegant oceanfront hotel has played host to celebrities,
Fodor's Choice princesses, the Dalai Lama, and nearly every president since Lyndon
★ Johnson as one of Hawaii's very first luxury resorts. **Pros:** away from hectic Waikiki; beautiful rooms and public spaces; heavenly spa. **Cons:** Waikiki is a drive away; in a residential neighborhood, so not much to do within walking distance of hotel; might be too quiet for some. Ⓢ *Rooms from: $495* ⊠ *5000 Kahala Ave., Kahala* ☎ *808/739–8888, 800/367–2525* ⊕ *www.kahalaresort.com* ➷ *338 rooms* ⑪ *No meals.*

WINDWARD OAHU

$$$ ⊡ **Paradise Bay Resort.** Located right on picturesque Kaneohe Bay amidst
RESORT the junglelike fauna of the windward side, this resort offers apartment-style units ranging from cozy studios to spacious two-bedroom suites with breathtaking views of the majestic Koolau Mountains, and even one stand-alone cottage in a remote area not generally frequented by tourists. **Pros:** local, authentic experience; beautiful views over the bay; pet-friendly (but $25 per night charge). **Cons:** remote location not near most other attractions; neighborhood is a bit run-down; rental car a necessity (but parking included in $35 nightly resort fee). Ⓢ *Rooms from: $295* ⊠ *47-039 Lihikai Dr., Kaneohe* ☎ *800/735–5071, 808/239–5711* ⊕ *www.paradisebayresort.com* ➷ *46 rooms* ⑪ *Free Breakfast.*

$$ ⊡ **Sheffield House Bed & Breakfast.** Literally 10 houses from Kailua Beach
B&B/INN on Oahu's windward side, this cozy bed-and-breakfast has been around since the early 1990s. **Pros:** Windward Oahu offers a uniquely local experience; best beaches on the island; boutiques and dining abound in Kailua. **Cons:** B&Bs aren't for everybody; don't expect luxury; rental car a must. Ⓢ *Rooms from: $180* ⊠ *131 Kuulei Rd., Kailua* ☎ *808/262–0721* ⊕ *www.hawaiisheffieldhouse.com* ➷ *2 rooms* ⑪ *Free Breakfast.*

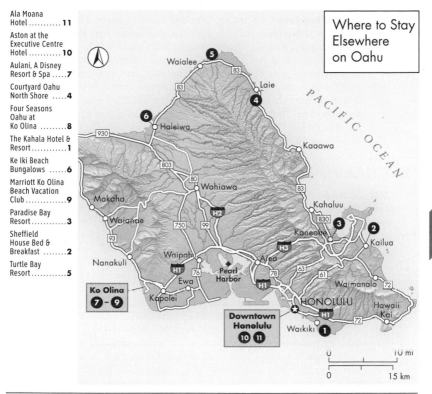

Where to Stay
Elsewhere
on Oahu

5

THE NORTH SHORE

$$ **Courtyard Oahu North Shore.** This property offers reliable and afford-
HOTEL able hotel accommodations close to the Polynesian Cultural Center
and a short drive to some of the North Shore's most iconic beaches
and surfing spots. **Pros:** best bet for North Shore exploring; reliable,
modern, and clean; near the beach. **Cons:** a long drive to the rest of
Oahu's attractions; no alcohol served in the hotel or nearby estab-
lishments; a car is needed, and parking is not free. $ *Rooms from:
$259* ⊠ *55-400 Kamehameha Hwy., Laie* ☎ *808/293–4900* ⊕ *www.
marriott.com/hotels/travel/hnloa-courtyard-oahu-north-shore* ⇨ *144
rooms* ❍| *No meals.*

$ **Ke Iki Beach Bungalows.** At this 1½-acre sloped beachfront lot with
RENTAL six duplex bungalows, you can choose from studios and one- or two-
bedroom units outfitted with breezy beach-house furnishings, individual
grills, hammocks, and picnic tables, and enjoy access to a 200-foot strand
of sugary white-sand beach running between the North Shore's famous
Waimea Bay and Ehukai Beach (Banzai Pipeline). **Pros:** helpful and
friendly staff; great prices; steps to the beach. **Cons:** a bit far from restau-
rants and shopping; can feel dated and rustic; B&Bs aren't for everyone.
$ *Rooms from: $155* ⊠ *59-579 Ke Iki Rd., Haleiwa* ☎ *808/638–8829,
866/638–8229* ⊕ *www.keikibeach.com* ⇨ *11 units* ❍| *No meals.*

$$$$ RESORT **Turtle Bay Resort.** Sprawling over 840 acres of natural landscape on the edge of Kuilima Point in Kahuku, the Turtle Bay Resort boasts spacious guest rooms averaging nearly 500 square feet, with lanai that showcase stunning peninsula views. **Pros:** fabulous open public spaces in a secluded area of Oahu; beautiful two-level spa; excellent location for exploring the North Shore. **Cons:** very remote—even Haleiwa is a 20-minute drive; $48-per-night resort fee; 24/7 resort living isn't for everyone. [$] *Rooms from: $360* ✉ *57-091 Kamehameha Hwy., Kahuku* ☎ *808/293–6000, 800/203–3650, 866/827–5321 for reservations* 🌐 *www.turtlebayresort.com* 🛏 *535 rooms* 🍴 *No meals.*

WEST (LEEWARD) OAHU

$$$$ RESORT FAMILY Fodor's Choice ★ **Aulani, A Disney Resort & Spa.** Disney's first property in Hawaii melds the Disney magic with breathtaking vistas, white sandy beaches, and sunsets that even Mickey stops to watch. **Pros:** tons to do on-site; family-friendly done right; Painted Sky teen spa. **Cons:** a long way from Waikiki; character breakfasts are often sold out (book far in advance); areas and events can get really busy. [$] *Rooms from: $550* ✉ *92-1185 Aliinui Dr., Ko Olina* ☎ *714/520–7001, 808/674–6200, 866/443–4763* 🌐 *www.disneyaulani.com* 🛏 *856 rooms* 🍴 *No meals.*

$$$$ RESORT **Four Seasons Oahu at Ko Olina.** Oahu welcomed this luxurious new property to Ko Olina with great excitement—the first Four Seasons on the island, with nearly every room and suite in the 17-story hotel offering floor-to-ceiling windows and a private lanai, all with an ocean view. **Pros:** luxurious and exclusive; secluded, even in the Ko Olina complex; amenities and options abound. **Cons:** an hour from Waikiki; luxury doesn't come cheap; it doesn't always measure up to other Four Seasons. [$] *Rooms from: $675* ✉ *92-1001 Olani St., in the Ko Olina complex, Kapolei* ☎ *808/679–0079, 844/387–0308* 🌐 *www.fourseasons.com/oahu* 🛏 *371 rooms* 🍴 *No meals.*

$$$$ RENTAL FAMILY **Marriott Ko Olina Beach Vacation Club.** Though primarily a time-share property, Marriott Ko Olina also offers nightly rentals, which range from hotel-style standard guest rooms to expansive and elegantly appointed one- or two-bedroom guest villa apartments, all located within a 642-acre gated community. **Pros:** suites are beautifully decorated and have ample space for families; nice views; resort area offers entertainment, shopping, and dining options beyond the property. **Cons:** an hour to Honolulu and Waikiki; rooms and suites vary, so ask when booking; the coast beyond Ko Olina is rural without a lot for visitors to do. [$] *Rooms from: $450* ✉ *92-161 Waipahe Pl., Ko Olina* ☎ *808/679–4700, 800/307–7312* 🌐 *www.marriott.com* 🛏 *544 units* 🍴 *No meals.*

NIGHTLIFE AND PERFORMING ARTS

Updated by
Tiffany Hill

Gone are the days when there was nothing to do in Honolulu at night. Any guidebook that tells you Honolulu isn't for the night owl is outdated. Most nights it's hard to pick which DJ to see at which nightclub, or which art show opening to attend. In fact, many people who arrive in Oahu expecting to find white-sand beaches and nothing else are surprised at such a vibrant nightlife. Bask in the shade of the swaying palm trees, watch the sunset over Waikiki, and dress up, because more and more clubs in Honolulu enforce a dress code.

Posh bars can be found in many of the larger hotels, but venture outside the strip and into places like Chinatown (which virtually explodes with events on the first Friday of each month) and surrounding neighborhoods, and you'll discover comfortable local watering holes. Every night of the week you can find musicians in venues from Kailua to Ko Olina—and everywhere in between.

And if all-night dancing isn't for you, Oahu also has a thriving arts and culture scene, with community-theater productions, stand-up comedy, outdoor concerts, film festivals, and chamber-music performances. Major Broadway shows, dance companies, rock stars, and comedians come through the Islands, too. Check local newspapers—the *Honolulu Star-Advertiser* or *Midweek*—for the latest events. Websites like ⊕ *www.frolichawaii.com* and ⊕ *www.honolulumagazine.com* also have great information.

Whether you stay out all night or get up early to catch the morning surf, there's something for everyone on Oahu.

NIGHTLIFE

Oahu is the best of all the Islands for nightlife. The locals call it *pau hana*, but you might call it happy hour (the literal translation of the Hawaiian phrase is "done with work"). On weeknights, it's likely that you'll find the working crowd, still in their business-casual attire, downing chilled beers even before the sun goes down. Those who don't have to wake up in the early morning should change into a fresh outfit and start the evening closer to 10 pm.

On the weekends, it's typical to have dinner at a restaurant before hitting the clubs around 9:30. Some bar-hoppers start as early as 7, but partygoers typically don't patronize more than two establishments a night. That's because getting from one Oahu nightspot to the next usually requires transportation. Happily, cab services are plentiful, and rideshares like Uber and Lyft give Honolulu a San Francisco feel.

You can find a bar in just about any area on Oahu. Most of the clubs, however, are in Waikiki, near Ala Moana, and in Chinatown, near downtown Honolulu. The drinking age is 21 on Oahu and throughout Hawaii. Many bars will admit younger people but will not serve them alcohol. By law, all establishments that serve alcoholic beverages must close by 2 am, although you might get lucky and stumble into a secret all-night party. The only exceptions are those with a cabaret license, which can stay open until 4 am. ■TIP➔ Some places have a cover charge of $5–$10, but with many establishments, getting there early means you don't have to pay.

HONOLULU

WAIKIKI

BARS

Duke's Waikiki. Making the most of its spot on Waikiki Beach, Duke's presents live music everyday. Contemporary Hawaiian musicians like Henry Kapono and Maunalua have performed here, as have nationally known musicians like Jimmy Buffett. It's not unusual for surfers to leave their boards outside to step in for a casual drink after a long day on the waves. The bar-and-grill's surf theme pays homage to Duke Kahanamoku, who popularized the sport in the early 1900s. ⊠ *Outrigger Waikiki, 2335 Kalakaua Ave., Suite 116, Waikiki* ☎ *808/922–2268* ⊕ *www.dukeswaikiki.com.*

Genius Lounge Sake Bar & Grill. Removed from the tourist traps along Kalakaua Avenue, the Genius Lounge is tucked away on the third floor of a former apartment building on Lewers Street. The extensive drink menu offers beer and wine, cocktails, house-made sangria, and, of course, sake. Locally inspired dishes are also available. Though small, the space, furnished with dark woods and lit by candles, makes an intimate setting for small gatherings and Friday-night dates. The crowd is mostly Asian visitors and transplants, but a daily happy hour (6–8 pm) lures office workers and pre-club prowlers. ⊠ *346 Lewers St., 3rd fl., Waikiki* ☎ *808/626–5362* ⊕ *www.geniusloungehawaii.com.*

Hideout. The Hideout is a mini-oasis on the outdoor lobby level of the Laylow Hotel, one of Waikiki's newer hotels. Technically, it's not a rooftop bar, but with a fire pit (surrounded by sand), tiki torches, comfy couches, and palm trees swaying overhead, it certainly exudes rooftop vibes. The Hideout has a full menu, but it's best to come here for some pre- or postdinner drinks and pupu. And with a daily happy hour from 4:30 to 6:30 pm, it's easier on your wallet, too. Get the Lime in the Coconut, made with Old Lahaina rum, lime, coconut, and mango boba at the bottom of the martini glass. ⊠ *Laylow Hotel, 2299 Kuhio Ave., Waikiki* ☎ *808/628–3060* ⊕ *www.hideoutwaikiki.com.*

Fodor's Choice
★
Lewers Lounge. A great spot for predinner drinks or post-sunset cocktails, Lewers Lounge offers a relaxed but chic atmosphere in the middle of Waikiki. There are classic and contemporary cocktails. Some standouts include Chocolate Dreams (made with Van Gogh Dutch Chocolate Vodka) and the Lost Passion (featuring a rich blend of tequila, Cointreau, and fresh juices topped with champagne). Enjoy your libation with nightly live jazz and tempting desserts, such as the hotel's famous coconut cake. Or just sit back and relax in the grand setting of the luxurious lounge, which is decked in dramatic drapes and cozy banquettes. ⊠ *Halekulani Hotel, 2199 Kalia Rd., Waikiki* ☎ *808/923–2311* ⊕ *www.halekulani.com.*

Lulu's Waikiki. Even if you're not a surfer, you'll love this place's retro vibe and the unobstructed second-floor view of Waikiki Beach. The open-air setting, casual dining menu, and tropical drinks are all you need to help you settle into your vacation. The venue transforms from a nice spot for breakfast, lunch, or dinner (happy hour is 3 to 5 pm) to a bustling, high-energy club with live music lasting into the wee hours. ⊠ *Park Shore Waikiki Hotel, 2586 Kalakaua Ave., Waikiki* ☎ *808/926–5222* ⊕ *www.luluswaikiki.com.*

Fodor's Choice
★
Mai Tai Bar at the Royal Hawaiian. The bartenders here sure know how to mix up a killer mai tai. This is, after all, *the* establishment that first made the famous drink in the Islands. The umbrella-shaded tables at the outdoor bar are front-row seating for sunsets and also have an unobstructed view of Diamond Head. Contemporary Hawaiian musicians hold jam sessions onstage nightly. ⊠ *Royal Hawaiian Hotel, 2259 Kalakaua Ave., Waikiki* ☎ *808/923–7311* ⊕ *www.royal-hawaiian.com.*

Maui Brewing Co. Maui Brewing Co. has been a longtime Hawaii craft beer favorite. And while you can get the Lahaina-made beer in local grocery stores and restaurants, it's best to head straight to the source. Thankfully, you don't have to island-hop since the brewery opened a brewpub in Waikiki. (Even better—Maui Brewing is opening a second Oahu location in Kailua.) Ask the staff about Maui Brewing's limited-release drafts, to imbibe the brand's hidden gems. Maui Brewing strives to source local ingredients for its beer and food, so it's likely what you order was grown and harvested here. There's the poke bowl with locally caught tuna, kale salad with Waianae-based Naked Cow Dairy feta, and a Brewmaster pizza made with Honolulu-based Kukui sausage. ⊠ *Holiday Inn Resort Waikiki Beachcomber, 2300 Kalakaua Ave., 2nd Fl., Waikiki* ☎ *808/843–2739* ⊕ *www.mauibrewingco.com/waikiki.*

Moana Terrace. Three floors up from Waikiki Beach, this is a casual, open-air terrace where some of Hawaii's finest musicians play every evening. Order a drink served in a fresh pineapple and watch the sun dip into the Pacific Ocean. ⊠ *Waikiki Beach Marriott Resort, 2552 Kalakaua Ave., Waikiki* ☎ *808/922–6611* ⊕ *www.marriott.com.*

RumFire. Locals and visitors head here for the convivial atmosphere, trendy decor, and the million-dollar view of Waikiki Beach and Diamond Head. Come early to get a seat for happy hour (3–5 pm daily). If you're feeling peckish, there's a menu of Asian-influenced dishes. RumFire also features original cocktails, signature shots, and daily live music. On Friday and Saturday, the bar gets even livelier once local DJs start spinning at 9:30. ⊠ *Sheraton Waikiki, 2255 Kalakaua Ave., Waikiki* ☎ *808/922–4422* ⊕ *www.rumfirewaikiki.com.*

> **MAI TAIS**
>
> Hard to believe, but the cocktail known around the world as the mai tai has been around for more than 50 years. Although the recipe has changed slightly over the years, the original formula, created by bar owner Victor J. "Trader Vic" Bergeron, included 2 ounces of 17-year-old J. Wray & Nephew rum over shaved ice, ½ ounce Holland Dekuyper orange curaçao, ¼ ounce Trader Vic's rock candy syrup, ½ ounce French Garier orgeat syrup, and the juice of one fresh lime. Done the right way, this tropical drink still lives up to the name "mai tai!," meaning "out of this world!"

The Study. It's tricky to find the Study at the Modern Honolulu—it's behind a huge, revolving bookcase in the lobby behind the registration desk. It's an überchic space, with intimate alcoves and oversize sofas that are both hip and inviting. The bar features literary-themed cocktails, like the Huckleberry Finn and the War and Peace. ⊠ *The Modern Honolulu, 1775 Ala Moana Blvd., Waikiki* ☎ *808/450–3396* ⊕ *www.themodernhonolulu.com/the-study.*

Tiki's Grill & Bar. Tiki torches light the way to this restaurant and bar overlooking Kuhio Beach. A mix of locals and visitors head here on the weekend to get their fill of kitschy cool. There's nightly entertainment featuring contemporary Hawaiian musicians. Don't leave without sipping on the Lava Flow, or noshing on the famous coconut shrimp. ⊠ *Aston Waikiki Beach Hotel, 2570 Kalakaua Ave., Waikiki* ☎ *808/923–8454* ⊕ *www.tikisgrill.com.*

Waiolu Ocean View Lounge. Hawaiian bars should have two things: stellar views of the sunset over the ocean and equally awesome mai tais. Both are on offer at the Waiolu Ocean View Lounge at the posh Trump International Hotel. And on Fridays, take in the Waikiki evening fireworks show from here. There's live music, ranging from contemporary to Hawaiian, Thursday through Sunday nights, with an attractive crowd showing up around 8 pm. It's busy but not suffocating, and seats are scarce once the music starts at 6:30 pm, so reserve a table in advance. ⊠ *Trump International Hotel, 223 Saratoga Rd., Waikiki* ☎ *808/683–7456* ⊕ *www.trumpwaikikihotel.com.*

Wang Chung's Karaoke Bar. Dubbed the "Friendliest Bar in Waikiki," this charming karaoke bar is a must-see on any trip to the island. The positive vibe comes from owner Dan Chang, who personally welcomes his guests. (He might even hug you.) The bar is located in the lobby of the Stay Hotel and has a full kitchen cranking out Asian- and Latin-inspired dishes. The cocktails are innovative, and the list of karaoke songs is extensive. Don't be surprised if the entire bar starts singing along. ⊠ *Stay Hotel Waikiki, 2424 Koa Ave., Waikiki* ☏ *808/201–6369* ⊕ *www.wangchungs.com.*

CLUBS
Addiction Nightclub. Traditional banquettes offer intimate seating for VIP tables, and bottle service lends a New York City nightclub feel at The Modern Honolulu. Red-velvet ropes guide you to the entrance; once inside you can dance to house and hip-hop music under a stunning ceiling installation of 40,000 round lights. But Addiction comes with a price: there's a hefty cover for men, less for women (if you're not on the guest list), and drinks aren't cheap. ⊠ *The Modern Honolulu, 1775 Ala Moana Blvd., Waikiki* ☏ *888/244–9925 For reservations* ⊕ *www. addictionnightclub.com.*

Hula's Bar and Lei Stand. Hawaii's oldest and best-known gay-friendly nightspot offers panoramic views of Diamond Head by day and high-energy club music by night. Patrons have included Elton John, Adam Lambert, and Dolly Parton. ⊠ *Waikiki Grand Hotel, 134 Kapahulu Ave., 2nd fl., Waikiki* ☏ *808/923–0669* ⊕ *www.hulas.com.*

Sky Waikiki. This may just be the club Oahu has been waiting for. Sky Waikiki sits 19 stories above the city, just below Top of Waikiki, the strip's iconic revolving restaurant (and is managed by the same company). From the couches on the welcoming open-air lanai, you are treated to nearly 360-degree scenic views of Diamond Head, the Waikiki beaches, and the classic coral Royal Hawaiian hotel. It's one of the best spots to take in a Waikiki sunset. The club inside exudes contemporary-LA chic every night, and resident DJs spin on Friday and Saturday nights. ⊠ *Waikiki Trade Center, 2270 Kalakaua Ave., Waikiki* ☏ *808/979–7590* ⊕ *www.skywaikiki.com.*

DOWNTOWN HONOLULU
BARS
Fodor'sChoice **Bar Leather Apron.** The bar at this intimate cocktail spot on the mezza-
★ nine of a downtown Honolulu office building seats only six, so you'll want to make reservations to enjoy bespoke cocktails that utilize only the finest liquors and ingredients. Owners Tom Park and Justin Park (no relation) have cultivated a reputation for their E Ho'o Pau Mai Tai made with raisin-infused, five-year-old El Dorado rum, 12-year-old El Dorado, coconut water syrup, spiced orgeat, ohia blossom honey, lime, and absinthe. The bar is closed on Sunday and Monday. ⊠ *Topa Financial Center, 745 Fort St., Mezzanine Level, Ste. 127A, Downtown* ☏ *808/524–0808* ⊕ *www.barleatherapron.com.*

Gordon Biersch. This outdoor bar flanks Honolulu Harbor. Live bands serenade patrons with everything from funk to jazz to rock and roll. Those who feel inspired can strut their stuff in front of the stage, while others can enjoy a pint of the restaurant's own brew and nice views. ✉ *Aloha Tower Marketplace, 1 Aloha Tower Dr., Suite 1123, Downtown* ☎ *808/599–4877* ⊕ *www.gordonbiersch.com.*

Murphy's Bar & Grill. On the edge of Chinatown, this bar has served drinks to such locals and visitors as King Kalakaua and Robert Louis Stevenson since the late 1800s. The kind of Irish pub you'd find in Boston, Murphy's is a break from all the tropical, fruit-garnished drinks found in Waikiki, and it's definitely the place to be on St. Patrick's Day. Its block-party fund-raiser on that day is one of the most popular on the island. On Friday it serves some of the best homemade fruit pies around; they're so good, they sell out during lunch. ✉ *2 Merchant St., Downtown* ☎ *808/531–0422* ⊕ *www.murphyshawaii.com.*

Nocturna Lounge. This is Hawaii's first self-described NextGen lounge, a stylish and sophisticated karaoke and gaming lounge at the Waterfront Plaza. It boasts a full bar, four private suites with state-of-the-art karaoke, and video game consoles around the lounge featuring the latest in social gaming. Play Street Fighter in the open lounge, perfect your moves in Dance Central on the Xbox Kinect in a side room, or wander through the noisy club while sipping one of Nocturna's creative cocktails with names like Princess Peach and Falcon Punch. The crowd isn't as young as you'd expect at a club outfitted with video game consoles—in fact, you must to be at least 21 to enter. ✉ *Waterfront Plaza, 500 Ala Moana Blvd., No. 5D, Downtown* ☎ *808/521–1555* ⊕ *www. nocturnalounge.com.*

CHINATOWN
BARS

Downbeat Lounge. This dimly lit but welcoming lounge is the soulful little sister of the trendy all-night Downbeat Diner next door, and owned by the same people. There's live music most nights, so it's a great place to catch one of Oahu's local acts. And it's a diverse lineup, from punk, ska, and indie rock, to bluegrass and folk. The lounge serves craft and draft beers as well as creative cocktails focusing on whiskey and moonshine, such as the Oke Punch made with Okolehau Hawaiian Moonshine. If your late-night Chinatown partying has you hankering for a hamburger, you can also order from the diner's menu. The lounge is closed on Sunday. ✉ *42 N. Hotel St., Chinatown* ☎ *808/533–2328* ⊕ *www.downbeatdiner.com.*

Encore Saloon. Hawaii isn't a hotbed for quality Mexican cuisine, so when Encore opened in 2016, it was a welcome addition to Chinatown's already buzzing bar and restaurant scene. The mezcal-focused bar also serves good Mexican-inspired food, but its drinks menu is most impressive, offering more than 50 varieties of tequila and mezcal, both of which are distilled from agave. You can also get a traditional margarita here, as well as wine and canned beer. If you're hungry, order the pork carnitas or the chicken mole street-style tacos, which come in sets of two. The bar is closed Sunday. ✉ *10 North Hotel St., Chinatown* ☎ *808/367–1656* ⊕ *www.encoresaloon.com.*

6

Fodor's Choice
★

J.J. Dolan's. This place bills itself as an "Irish pub with New York pizza from two guys in Chinatown." Those two guys are J.J. and Dolan, respectively, the pub's owners. And they know how to make a killer pie. The classics are always on the menu, but J.J. Dolan's daily specials are toothsome and inventive, like its white pie generously topped with smoked salmon, Maui sweet onions, capers, roasted red peppers, and feta. From downtown professionals to local families, these pies are crowd pleasers. The drinks are just as popular as the pizza and reasonably priced by Honolulu standards, making it a favorite among locals. Don't be surprised if you have to put your name on the waiting list come 5 pm. It's closed on Sunday. ⊠ *1147 Bethel St., Chinatown* ☎ *808/537–4992* ⊕ *www.jjdolans.com.*

Manifest. With exposed red brick, big skylights, and rotating exhibitions every three months from local photographers and painters, Manifest Hawaii has an artist's loft feel to it. Indeed, graphic designers, artists, and writers who have offices nearby are known regulars. The bar handcrafts quality cocktails such as the Love of My Life (Espolon tequila, Vieux Pontarlier absinthe, orgeat, lemon, and Peychaud bitters) and mules made with vodka, tequila, gin, whiskey, bourbon, or even absinthe. It's even a good "coffice" (coffee shop–office); by day Manifest serves coffee and tea and has free Wi-Fi. ⊠ *32 N. Hotel St., Chinatown* ⊕ *www.manifesthawaii.com.*

The Tchin Tchin! Bar This chill Chinatown bar gets its name from the Chinese expression "qing, qing" (which means "please please"), often used as a toast; soldiers returning from the Chinese Opium Wars introduced it in France and throughout Europe. With 45 wines by the glass, another 150 more by the bottle, plus a selection of single malt bourbon, whiskey, and scotch, it's an ideal spot for a drink or even a meal (there's also a tapas-style food menu). The bar's open-air rooftop lanai is the best place to sit, romantically lit with string lights and featuring a large living wall flourishing with ferns. The bar is closed on Sunday and Monday. ⊠ *39 North Hotel St., Chinatown* ☎ *808/528–1888* ⊕ *www. thetchintchinbar.com.*

CLUBS
The Dragon Upstairs. In the heart of Chinatown, this cool club—formerly a tattoo parlor, hence the dragon mural—serves up classic cocktails along with loungy jazz performances most nights of the week. You'll hear local vocalists, as well as small combos, in this unique venue upstairs from Hank's Cafe Honolulu. ⊠ *1038 Nuuanu Ave., Chinatown* ☎ *808/526–1411* ⊕ *thedragonupstairs.com.*

ALA MOANA
BARS
Mai Tai Bar. After a long day of shopping at Ala Moana Center, the fourth-floor Mai Tai Bar is a perfect spot to relax. There's live entertainment and happy hour specials for both food and drink. There's never a cover charge and no dress code. To avoid waiting in line, get here before 9 pm. ⊠ *Ala Moana Center, 1450 Ala Moana Blvd., Ala Moana* ☎ *808/947–2900* ⊕ *www.maitaibar.com.*

KAKAAKO

BARS

Aloha Beer Co. At this cool brewpub, you order everything at the counter and then pick a spot to sit in either the industrial indoor taproom or the casual outdoor area. (There's also an upstairs space, complete with its own speakeasy-style entrance.) With 11 beers on draft, including the Hop Lei IPA, Waimanalo Farmhouse, and Portlock Porter, you can find something to your taste. If you're hungry, there's hearty sandwiches, some made with Oahu-based Pono Pork. ⊠ *700 Queen St., Kakaako* ☎ *808/544–1605* ⊕ *www.alohabeer.com.*

Fodor's Choice ★ **Bevy.** Tucked at the end of a row of new boutiques in Kakaako, Bevy is urban, modern, and furnished with up-cycled materials; its benches are upholstered in denim jeans and the table tops feature flattened wine boxes. But locals in the know go for artisan cocktails created by owner and award-winning mixologist Christian Self, who deftly concocts libations utilizing ingredients such as rye whiskey and Italian green walnut. One happy hour (4–7 pm) bright spot is the $1.50 oyster shooters. The bar is closed on Sunday. (Next door is Bevy Market, Self's foray into the gourmet food market; it's open for lunch.) ⊠ *675 Auahi St., Kakaako* ☎ *808/594–7445* ⊕ *www.bevyhawaii.com.*

The Brewseum. This brewpub is a must-visit for imbibers who like a little history with their beer. The charming spot wonderfully combines World War II memorabilia with small-craft brews. On the walls hang 1940s-era telephones that transmit actual archival radio transmissions through their receivers. Overhead, a model freight train chugs around the room, while model bomber planes fly over on a pulley system. There's even an army jeep parked inside—everyone loves to have their photo taken in it. The bar is owned and operated by the Tomlinson family, who treat each patron like *ohana*. The Brewseum has its own label, Home of the Brave Brewing. Each pint comes with complimentary popcorn, or you can order a soft pretzel or a personal pizza. It's closed Sunday and Monday. ⊠ *901 Waimanu St., Kakaako* ☎ *808/396–8112* ⊕ *www.brewseums.com.*

Fodor's Choice ★ **Honolulu Beerworks.** Oahu's brewing scene has erupted in Kakaako's industrial neighborhood, and one brewpub in particular has led the charge: Honolulu Beerworks. In a converted warehouse, this is a beer connoisseur's paradise. Owner Geoff Seideman and his crew brew nine beers—in addition to limited releases—such as the Pia Mahiai Saison, made with locally grown oranges, tangerines, lemons, limes, lemongrass, and Big Island honey, and the rich South Shore Stout. When you need some *ono* grinds (delicious food) to go along with your local brew, order the bar's ahi dip. It's a regular spot for many locals, particularly on the weekends. You might just make new friends sitting at one of the bar's long picnic tables, made from reclaimed wood. It's closed Sunday. ⊠ *328 Cooke St., Kakaako* ☎ *808/589–2337* ⊕ *www. honolulubeerworks.com.*

Fodor's Choice ★ **Waikiki Brewing Company.** This company not only brews its own quality craft beer but also serves delicious food. Although the original is still operational in Waikiki at 1945 Kalakaua Ave., this second location

6

opened in 2017. The brewery always offers nine beers on tap, including the Skinny Jeans IPA and the Hana Hou Hefe, in which sweet orange peel and strawberry puree are added before fermentation. You can also buy six-packs at the bar to go. What makes this location unique is that the chef smokes meat in-house using local kiawe wood, resulting in tender beef brisket, flavorful pulled pork, juicy bratwursts, and herb-crusted chicken. Any of these would be the perfect pairing for your beer. ⊠ *831 Queen St., Kakaako* ☎ *808/591–0387* ⊕ *www.waikikibrewing.com.*

MOILIILI

BARS

Anna O'Brien's. Generations of college students have spent more than an evening or two at this legendary two-story, smoky dive near the University of Hawaii campus. A living-room atmosphere makes it a comfortable place to hang out and drink a cheap beer. Here, the music is fresh, loud, and sometimes experimental. Live music usually happens at the end of the week. ⊠ *2440 S. Beretania St., Moiliili* ☎ *808/946–5190* ⊕ *www.annaobriens.com.*

Fodor'sChoice
★
Pint + Jigger. This spot has cultivated a regular following with nearby college students and thirtysomethings since its opening by doing two simple, but essential things: making a high-quality cocktail and dishing up polished pub fare. It doesn't hurt that the bar also boasts a rotation of 20 beers, plus one cocktail on tap. Its Scotch egg and stout burger are consistent, while drinks such as the Talventi (rye whiskey, Campari, and cold-brewed coffee topped with house-made vanilla cream) are refreshing and inventive. After your meal, head to the back of the bar for a friendly game of shuffleboard. ⊠ *1936 S. King St., Moiliili* ☎ *808/744–9593* ⊕ *www.pintandjigger.com.*

KAIMUKI

BARS

BREW'd Craft Pub. The Kaimuki night scene got a bit livelier when BREW'd Craft Pub opened in 2014 (it was particularly welcomed by the neighborhood's craft beer lovers). After all, this local pub stays open until 2 am. It's a small place—you have to squeeze between nearby dining companions to get in and out of your table—but the wait staff are friendly and knowledgeable about the pub's 150-plus beer menu. BREW'd also offers better versions of the standard pub fare than you'll find at some places in town, including a good braised beef poutine. It's closed Sunday. ⊠ *3441 Waialae Ave., Suite A, Kaimuki* ⊕ *Corner of 9th and Waialae Aves.* ☎ *808/732–2337* ⊕ *www.brewdcraftpub.com.*

SOUTHEAST OAHU

BARS

Kona Brewing Co. This massive restaurant and bar on the docks of Koko Marina has long been a hot spot in east Honolulu. In addition to serving the company's signature brews, this authentic pub offers live music on Friday, Saturday, and Sunday nights. It's a lively spot, especially on the weekends when it's standing-room only at the bar. ⊠ *Koko Marina Center, 7192 Kalanianiole Hwy., Honolulu* ☎ *808/396–5662* ⊕ *www.konabrewingco.com.*

WINDWARD OAHU

BARS

Boardrider's Bar & Grill. Tucked away in Kailua Town, Boardrider's has long been the place for local bands to strut their stuff. Look for live music—reggae to rock and roll—every Friday and Saturday night. The space includes a pool table, dartboards, and eight TVs for watching the game. ⊠ *201-A Hamakua Dr., Kailua* ☎ *808/261–4600.*

THE NORTH SHORE

BARS

Surfer, the Bar. This laid-back bar is located in the Turtle Bay Resort and is a partnership between the hotel and *Surfer* magazine. It's a hip spot for the bar's namesake crowd to unwind, as well as meandering hotel guests. There's live music and Talk Story sessions, where Hawaii's surfing legends regale bar goers with their gnarliest experiences out on the waves. ⊠ *Turtle Bay Resort, 57-091 Kamehameha Hwy., Kahuku* ☎ *808/293–6000* ⊕ *www.surferthebar.com.*

PERFORMING ARTS

DANCE

Ballet Hawaii. Established in 1975, Ballet Hawaii is a local company active throughout the year. Its annual production of *The Nutcracker* is usually held at the nearby **Blaisdell Concert Hall** (777 Ward Ave.) during Christmas week and is a local holiday tradition. Other performances can be seen at the **Hawaii Theatre** (1130 Bethel St.) in Chinatown. ⊠ *Honolulu* ☎ *808/521–8600* ⊕ *www.ballethawaii.org* 🎫 *From $30.*

DINNER CRUISES AND SHOWS

Dinner cruises depart either from the piers adjacent to the Aloha Tower Marketplace in downtown Honolulu or from Kewalo Basin, near Ala Moana Beach Park, and head along the coast toward Diamond Head. There's usually a buffet-style dinner with a local flavor, dancing, drinks, and a sensational sunset. Except as noted, dinner cruises cost approximately $80 to $200, cocktail cruises $40 to $55. Some cruises offer discounts for online reservations. Most major credit cards are accepted. In all cases, reservations are essential. Check the websites for savings of up to 15%.

Atlantis Cruises. The sleekly high-tech *Majestic,* designed to sail smoothly in rough waters, powers farther along Waikiki's coastline than its competitors, sailing past Diamond Head. Enjoy sunset dinners or moonlight cruises aboard the 400-passenger boat, feasting on garlic shiitake teriyaki chicken and the catch of the day. ⊠ *Aloha Tower Marketplace, 1 Aloha Tower Rd., Pier 6, Honolulu* ☎ *808/973–1311, 800/381–0237* ⊕ *www.atlantisadventures.com* 🎫 *From $79.*

Ha: Breath of Life. The Polynesian Cultural Center's long-running nightly show, *Ha: Breath of Life*, is a story of love, respect, and responsibility. *Ha,* which means "breath" in Hawaiian, follows the central character of Mana from his birth to the birth of his own child. The performances highlight ancient Hawaiian, Polynesian, Samoan, and Tahitian culture, music, and dance, including fire-knife dancers, and with more than 100 performers. Performances are Monday–Saturday at 7:30 pm. ✉ *Polynesian Cultural Center, 55-370 Kamehameha Hwy., Laie* ☎ *800/367–7060* ⊕ *www.habreathoflife.com* ☞ *From $89.95.*

Magic of Polynesia. Hawaii's top illusionist, John Hirokawa, displays mystifying sleight of hand in this highly entertaining show, which incorporates contemporary hula and Islands music into its acts. It's held in the Waikiki Beachcomber by Outrigger's $7.5-million showroom. Reservations are required for dinner and the show. Dinner choices range from a ginger sesame glazed chicken dinner to a deluxe steak-and-lobster combo. Walk-ins are permitted if you just want the entertainment. Nightly dinner begins at 5:45, the show at 7 pm. ✉ *Holiday Inn Waikiki Beachcomber Hotel, 2300 Kalakaua Ave., Waikiki* ☎ *808/539-9400* ⊕ *www.robertshawaii.com* ☞ *Show from $52; show and dinner from $91.*

Star of Honolulu Cruises. The award-winning 1,500-passenger *Star of Honolulu* boasts four sunset dinner-cruise packages, from a roast beef buffet and Polynesian show to a romantic seven-course fine-dining excursion with live jazz. The company also runs whale-watching cruises. ✉ *Aloha Tower Marketplace, 1 Aloha Tower Dr., Pier 8, Downtown* ☎ *808/983-7827* ⊕ *www.starofhonolulu.com* ☞ *From $97.*

LUAU

The luau is an experience that everyone, both local and tourist, should have. Today's luau still offer traditional foods and entertainment, but there's often a fun, contemporary flair. With many, you can watch the roasted pig being carried out of its *imu,* a hole in the ground used for cooking food with heated stones.

Luau average around $100 per person—some are cheaper, others twice that amount—and are held around the island, not just in Waikiki. Reservations—and a camera—are a must.

Chief's Luau at Wet 'n' Wild Hawaii. Chief Sielu and his *ohana* (family) perform at Wet 'n' Wild Hawaii waterpark. It's a top-rated luau with everything you'd expect from this island tradition: good food, rhythmic music, and interactive performances. The show ends with a high-energy fire-knife dance. The chef also heads the Fia Fia Luau at the Marriott in Ko Olina. ✉ *Wet 'n' Wild Hawaii, 400 Farrington Hwy., Kapolei* ☎ *877/357-2480* ⊕ *www.chiefsluau.com* ☞ *From $95.*

Fia Fia Luau. Just after sunset at the Marriott Ko Olina Beach Club, the charismatic Chief Sielu Avea leads the Samoan-based Fia Fia, an entertaining show that takes guests on the journey through the South Pacific. Every show is different and unscripted, but always a good look at Polynesian culture. It's the only recurring show with eight fire-knife dancers in a blazing finale. It's held on Tuesday at 4:30. Admission includes a buffet dinner. ✉ *92-161 Waipahe Pl., Ko Olina* ☎ *808/679–4700,* ⊕ *www.marriott.com/hotels/hotel-information/restaurant/hnlko-marriotts-ko-olina-beach-club* ✍ *From $105.*

Germaine's Luau. More than 3 million visitors have come to this luau, held about 45 minutes west of Waikiki in light traffic. Widely considered one of the most folksy and laid-back, Germaine's offers a tasty, multicourse, all-you-can-eat buffet. Admission includes the buffet and one drink to three drinks (depending on the package). It's held Tuesday to Sunday at 6. ✉ *91-119 Olai St., Kapolei* ☎ *808/202–2528* ⊕ *www.germainesluau.com* ✍ *From $85, transportation from $16.*

Paradise Cove Luau. One of the largest shows on Oahu, the lively Paradise Cove Luau is held in the Ko Olina resort area, about 45 minutes from Waikiki (if there's light traffic). Drink in hand, you can stroll through the authentic village, learn traditional arts and crafts, and play local games. The stage show includes a fire-knife dancer, singing emcee, and both traditional and contemporary hula and other Polynesian dances. A finale dance features participation from the audience. Admission includes the buffet, activities, and the show. You pay extra for table service, box seating, and shuttle transport to and from Waikiki—the stunning sunsets are free. It starts daily at 5. ✉ *92-1089 Alii Nui Dr., Ko Olina* ☎ *808/842–5911* ⊕ *www.paradisecove.com* ✍ *From $97* ☞ *Round-trip Waikiki transportation, $16.*

Fodor'sChoice
★ **Polynesian Cultural Center Alii Luau.** Although this elaborate luau has the sharpest production values, there is no booze allowed (it's a Mormon-owned facility in the heart of Laie—Mormon country). It's held amid the seven re-created villages at the Polynesian Cultural Center in the North Shore town of Laie, about a 1½-hour drive from Honolulu. The luau—considered one of the most authentic on the island—includes the *Ha: Breath of Life* show that has long been popular with both residents and visitors. Rates vary depending on activities and amenities that are included (personalized tours, reserved seats, or table service, for example). Waikiki transport is available. It's held Monday–Saturday at 5. ✉ *Polynesian Cultural Center, 55-370 Kamehameha Hwy., Laie* ☎ *808/293–3333, 800/367–7060* ⊕ *www.polynesia.com* ✍ *From $119.95.*

Waikiki Starlight Luau. This Waikiki luau is done spectacularly on the rooftop of the Hilton Hawaiian Village. There isn't an imu ceremony, but the live entertainment is top-notch, and the views are unparalleled. Prices vary depending on your age and where you want to sit. The event also includes traditional activities, such as hula lessons and conch blowing. It's held Sunday–Thursday at 5. ✉ *Hilton Hawaiian Village, 2005 Kalia Rd., Waikiki* ☎ *808/941–5828* ⊕ *www.hiltonhawaiianvillage.com* ✍ *From $116.23.*

6

MUSIC

Chamber Music Hawaii. This group, consisting of four ensembles, has been around for decades and performs 20 to 25 concerts a year at the Honolulu Museum of Arts' Doris Duke Theatre (900 S. Beretania St., Honolulu), the Paliku Theatre at Windward Community College (45-720 Keaahala Rd., Kaneohe), the UH West Oahu library (*91-1001 Farrington Hwy., Kapolei*), and other locations around the island. Seasons run from fall through spring. ✉ *Honolulu* ☎ *808/489–5038* ⊕ *www.chambermusichawaii.org.*

First Friday. Rain or shine, on the first Friday of every month, the downtown Honolulu and Chinatown districts come alive. The more family-friendly early evening art tours evolve into an adults-only club atmosphere. Art galleries and restaurants stay open late, and local musicians and DJs provide the sound track for the evening. ✉ *Downtown* ⊕ *www.firstfridayhawaii.com* 🎫 *Free entrance to galleries; cover charge for nightclubs.*

Hawaii Opera Theatre. Locals refer to it as "HOT," probably because the Hawaii Opera Theatre has been turning the opera-challenged into opera lovers since 1960. All operas are sung in their original language with a projected English translation. ✉ *Neal S. Blaisdell Center Concert Hall, 777 Ward Ave., Honolulu* ☎ *808/596–7372, 800/836–7372* ⊕ *www.hawaiiopera.org.*

Hawaii Symphony Orchestra. The Hawaii Symphony Orchestra is the latest incarnation of the now-defunct century-old Honolulu Symphony, with the mission to bring international talent to a Hawaiian audience of any age. The orchestra performs at the Neil Blaisdell Concert Hall under the advisement of the internationally acclaimed conductor JoAnn Falletta, and features guest conductors and soloists. Ticket prices vary. ✉ *Honolulu* ☎ *808/380–7784* ⊕ *www.hawaiisymphonyorchestra.org.*

Honolulu Zoo Concerts. Since the early 1980s the Honolulu Zoo Society has sponsored hourlong evening concerts branded the "Wildest Show in Town." They're held at 6 pm on Wednesday, June–August. Listen to local legends play everything from Hawaiian to jazz to Latin music. Take a brisk walk through the zoo, or join in the family activities. This is an alcohol-free event, and there's food for those who haven't brought their own picnic supplies. Gates open at 4:35. ■TIP→ This is one of the best deals in town. ✉ *Honolulu Zoo, 151 Kapahulu Ave., Waikiki* ☎ *808/971–7171* ⊕ *www.honoluluzoo.org* 🎫 *$5.*

Ke Kani O Ke Kai. Every other Thursday evening June–August, the Waikiki Aquarium holds an ocean-side concert series called Ke Kani O Ke Kai. You can listen to top performers while enjoying food from local restaurants. The aquarium stays open throughout the night, so you can see the marine life in a new light. Bring your own beach chairs or blankets. Proceeds support the aquarium, the third-oldest in the United States. Doors open at 5:30 pm; concerts start at 7 pm. ✉ *Waikiki Aquarium, 2777 Kalakaua Ave., Waikiki* ☎ *808/923–9741* ⊕ *www.waikikiaquarium.org* 🎫 *$50.*

SHOPS AND SPAS

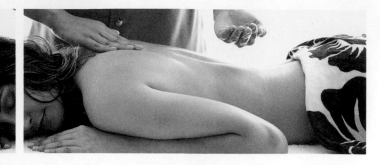

Updated by
Chris Oliver

Eastern and Western traditions meet on Oahu, where savvy shoppers find luxury goods at high-end malls and scout tiny boutiques and galleries filled with pottery, blown glass, woodwork, and Hawaiian-print clothing by local artists. This blend of cultures is pervasive in the wide selection of spas as well. Hawaiian *lomilomi* and hot-stone massages are as omnipresent as the orchid and plumeria flowers decorating every treatment room.

Exploring downtown Honolulu, Kailua on the windward side, and the North Shore often yields the most original merchandise. Some of the small stores carry imported clothes and gifts from around the world— a reminder that, on this island halfway between Asia and the United States, shopping is a multicultural experience.

If you're getting a massage at a spa, there's a spiritual element to the *lomilomi* that calms the soul while the muscles release tension. During a hot-stone massage, smooth rocks, taken from the earth with permission from Pele, the goddess of volcanoes, are heated and placed at focal points on the body. Others are covered in oil and rubbed over tired limbs, feeling like powerful fingers. For an alternative, refresh skin with mango scrubs so fragrant they seem edible. Savor the unusual sensation of bamboo tapped against the arches of the feet. Indulge in a scalp massage that makes the entire body tingle. Day spas provide additional options to the self-indulgent services offered in almost every major hotel on the island.

SHOPS

HONOLULU

There are two distinct types of shopping experiences for visitors: vast malls with the customary department stores and tiny boutiques with specialty items. Three malls in Honolulu provide a combination of the standard department stores and interesting shops showcasing original paintings and woodwork from local artists and craftsmen. Shoppers who know where to look in Honolulu will find everything from designer merchandise to unusual Asian imports.

Possibilities are endless, but a bit of scouting is usually required to get past the items you'll find in your own hometown. Industrious bargain hunters can detect the perfect gift in the sale bin of a slightly hidden store at every mall.

You'll find that shops stay open fairly late in Waikiki. Stores open at around 9 am and many don't close until 10 or even 11 pm.

WAIKIKI

Most hotels and shops are clustered along a relatively short strip in Waikiki, which can be convenient or overwhelming, depending on your sensibilities. Clothing, jewelry, and handbags from Europe's top designers sit next to Hawaii's ABC Stores, a chain of convenience stores that sell groceries as well as tourist items and souvenirs. It's possible to find interesting items at reasonable prices in Waikiki, but shoppers have to be willing to search beyond the $4,000 purses and the tacky wooden tikis to find innovation and quality.

CLOTHING

Blue Ginger. Look inside this little shop across from The Yardhouse for beach-casual clothing, bags, jewelry, and accessories in soft cotton and rayon aloha prints for adults and children. ⊠ *227 Lewers St, Waikiki* ☎ *808/924–7900* ⊕ *www.blueginger.com.*

Newt at the Royal. Newt is known for high-quality, handwoven Panama hats and tropical sportswear for men and women. ⊠ *The Royal Hawaiian Hotel, 2259 Kalakaua Ave., Waikiki* ☎ *808/923–4332* ⊕ *www.newtattheroyal.com.*

GALLERIES

Na Hoku Gallery. This is a smaller version of the designer and island-lifestyle jewelry store whose original is located in the Ala Moana Shopping Center. ⊠ *Outrigger Waikiki, 2335 Kalakaua Ave., Waikiki* ☎ *808/922–0556* ⊕ *www.nahoku.com.*

FOOD

Honolulu Chocolate Company. To really impress those back home, pick up a box of gourmet chocolates here. Choose from dozens of flavors of Hawaii, from Kona coffee to macadamia nuts, dipped in fine chocolate. ⊠ *Sheraton Waikiki, 2255 Kalakaua Ave., Ala Moana* ☎ *808/931–8937.*

GIFTS

Sand People. This little shop stocks beach-inspired, easy-to-carry gifts, such as fish-shaped Christmas ornaments, Hawaiian-style notepads, frames, charms in the shape of flip-flops (known locally as "slippahs"), soaps, kitchen accessories, and ceramic clocks. There's another branch in the Waikiki Sheraton, one in Kailua, as well as three each on Kauai and Maui. ⊠ *Moana Surfrider, 2369 Kalakaua, Waikiki* ☎ *808/924–6773.*

JEWELRY

Philip Rickard. The heirloom design collection of this famed jeweler features custom Hawaiian jewelry, particularly its Wedding Collection often sought by various celebrities. The jewelry is made in many different gold colors and platinum, which feature the scrolling patterns, enameled names, and inlays of traditional Hawaiian jewelry. ⊠ *International Market Place, 2330 Kalakaua Ave., Level 1, Banyan Court, #105, Waikiki* ☎ *808/924–7972* ⊕ *www.philiprickard.com.*

SHOPPING CENTERS

Royal Hawaiian Center. An open and inviting facade has made this three-block-long shopping center a garden of Hawaiian shops. There are more than 110 stores and restaurants, including local gems such as Fighting Eel, Honolulu Home Collection, and Koi Honolulu. Check out tropical Panama hats at Hawaiian Island Arts or offerings at Island Soap & Candleworks, while Royal Hawaiian Quilt offers handmade Hawaiian quilts, pillow covers, kitchen accessories, and more. Nine restaurants round out the dining options, along with the Paina Lanai Food Court, complimentary cultural classes, plus a theater and nightly outdoor entertainment. ⊠ *2201 Kalakaua Ave., Waikiki* ☎ *808/922–0588* ⊕ *www.royalhawaiiancenter.com.*

T Galleria Hawaii. Hermès, Cartier, Michael Kors, Dior, and Marc Jacobs are among the shops on the Waikiki Luxury Walk in this enclosed mall, as well as Hawaii's largest beauty and cosmetic store. The third floor caters to duty-free shoppers only and features an exclusive Watch Shop. ⊠ *330 Royal Hawaiian Ave., Waikiki* ☎ *808/931–2700* ⊕ *www.dfs. com/en/tgalleria-hawaii.*

2100 Kalakaua. Tenants of this elegant, town house–style center known as Luxury Row include Chanel, Coach, Tiffany & Co., Yves Saint Laurent, Bottega Veneta, Gucci, Hugo Boss, Miu Miu, and Montcler. ⊠ *2100 Kalakaua Ave., Waikiki* ☎ *808/922–2246* ⊕ *www.luxuryrow.com.*

Waikiki Beach Walk. This open-air shopping center greets visitors at the west end of Waikiki's Kalakaua Avenue with 70 locally owned stores and restaurants. Get reasonably priced, fashionable resort wear for yourself at Mahina; find unique pieces by local artists at Under the Koa Tree; or buy local delicacies from the Poke Bar. Or you can browse Koa and sandalwood gifts at Martin & MacArthur in the nearby Outrigger Reef Hotel. The mall also features free local entertainment on the outdoor-fountain stage at least once a week. ⊠ *226 Lewers St., Waikiki* ☎ *808/931–3591* ⊕ *www.waikikibeachwalk.com.*

DOWNTOWN HONOLULU

Downtown shopping is an entirely different, constantly changing experience from what you'll find elsewhere in Honolulu. Focus on the small galleries—which are earning the area a strong reputation for its arts and culture renaissance—and the burgeoning array of hip, home-decor stores tucked between ethnic restaurants. ■TIP➔ Don't miss the festive atmosphere on the first Friday of every month, when stores, restaurants, and galleries stay open 5–9 pm for the Downtown Gallery Walk.

HOME DECOR

Robyn Buntin Galleries. Chinese antiques, Japanese art, Buddhist sculptures, and important works by Hawaiian artists are among the international pieces sold here as well as jewelry and an extensive selection of prints. The gallery has more than 7,000 items available online. ✉ *Robyn Buntin Gallery, 848 S. Beretania St., Downtown* ☎ *808/523-5913* ⊕ *www.robynbuntin.com.*

CHINATOWN

Chinatown offers the typical mix of the tacky and unique, depending on individual taste, but it is an experience not to be missed. The vital, bright colors of fresh fruits and vegetables blend with the distinct scent of recently killed pigs and poultry. Tucked in between are authentic shops with Asian silk clothing at reasonable prices. The bustling, ethnic atmosphere adds to the excitement. If you're hungry for a local experience, you should at least walk through the area, even if you don't plan to purchase the mysterious herbs in the glass jars lining the shelves.

Curio shops sell everything from porcelain statues to woks, ginseng to Mao shoes. Visit the Hong Kong Supermarket in the Wo Fat Chop Sui building (at the corner of N. Hotel and Maunakea) for fresh fruit, crack seed (Chinese dried fruit popular for snacking), and row upon row of boxed, tinned delicacies with indecipherable names.

Chinatown Cultural Plaza offers fine-quality jade. Chinatown is also Honolulu's lei center, with shops strung along Beretania and Maunakea; the locals have favorite shops where they're greeted by name. In spring look for gardenia nosegays wrapped in ti leaves.

GALLERIES

Louis Pohl Gallery. Stop in this gallery to browse modern works from some of Hawaii's finest artists. In addition to pieces by resident artists, there are monthly exhibitions by local and visiting artists. ✉ *1142 Bethel St., Chinatown* ☎ *808/521-1812* ⊕ *www.louispohlgallery.com.*

BUYING TROPICAL FLOWERS AND FRUIT

You can bring home fresh pineapple, papaya, or coconut to share with friends and family. Orchids also will brighten your home and remind you of your trip to the Islands. By law, all fresh fruit and plant products must be inspected by the Department of Agriculture before export. Ask at the shop about Department of Agriculture rules so a surprise confiscation doesn't spoil your departure. Shipping to your home usually is best.

7

HOME DECOR

Place. This design studio/workshop is known for its sophisticated assemblage of carefully chosen home items in all price ranges. You'll find a global collection of fine lighting, furniture, and textiles, as well as art by local artists and artisans. Occasional hands-on workshops give shoppers a glimpse of how owner and interior designer Mary Philpotts McGrath creates a Hawaiian sense of place. ⊠ *54 S. School St., Chinatown* ☎ *808/275–3075* ⊕ *www.placehawaii.com.*

KAKAAKO

CLOTHING

Anne Namba Designs. This designer combines the beauty of classic kimonos with contemporary styles to make unique pieces for career and evening. In addition to women's apparel, she designs a men's line and a wedding couture line. ⊠ *324 Kamani St., Kakaako* ☎ *808/589–1135* ⊕ *www.annenamba.com.*

HOME DECOR

fishcake. A place to find unusual art, fishcake is a gallery for designers that hosts changing exhibitions and events by favorite artists near and far. Plus, you'll find a unique collection of small and large home items you won't find anywhere else in Honolulu. Morning Glass Coffee kiosk serves juices, teas, coffee, and pastries. ⊠ *307c Kamani St., Kakaako* ☎ *808/593–1231* ⊕ *www.fishcake.us.*

SPORTING GOODS

Boca Hawaii. This triathlon shop near the Bike Factory offers training gear and bike rentals ($40 per day with a two-day minimum, $200 per week), aerial yoga and capoeira classes, and nutritional products. ■TIP→ Inquire directly about the latest schedule of classes at the store, which is owned and operated by top athletes. ⊠ *330 Cooke St., Kakaako* ☎ *808/591–9839* ⊕ *www.bocahawaii.com.*

ALA MOANA

Getting to the Ala Moana shopping centers from Waikiki is quick and inexpensive thanks to TheBus and the Waikiki Trolley.

BOOKS

Na Mea Hawaii. In addition to Islands-style clothing for adults and children, Hawaiian cultural items, and unusual artwork such as Niihau-shell necklaces, this boutique's book selection covers Hawaiian history and language, and offers children's books set in the Islands. ⊠ *Ward Village, 1200 Ala Moana Blvd., Ste. 270, Ala Moana* ☎ *808/596–8885* ⊕ *www.nameahawaii.com.*

CLOTHING

Reyn Spooner. This clothing store is a good place to buy the aloha-print fashions residents wear. Look for the limited-edition Christmas shirt, a collector's item manufactured each holiday season. Reyn Spooner has eight locations statewide and offers styles for both men and children. ⊠ *Ala Moana Shopping Center, 1450 Ala Moana Blvd., Ala Moana* ☎ *808/949–5929* ⊕ *www.reynspooner.com.*

INEXPENSIVE LOCAL SOUVENIRS

Hawaii can be an expensive place. If you are looking to bring someone a gift, consider the following, which can be found all over the island:

Try the coconut peanut butter from **North Shore Goodies**. Just when you thought peanut butter couldn't get any better, someone added coconut to it and made it even more delicious.

If you are a fan of plate lunches, **Rainbow Drive In** has T-shirts with regular orders—"All rice," "Gravy all over," "Boneless"—printed on them. They come packed in an iconic plate lunch box.

Relive your memories of tea on the Veranda by purchasing Island Essence Tea, created by the **Moana Surfrider**.

Harvested from a salt farm on Molokai, **Hawaii Traditional Salts** come in a variety of flavors, including black lava, Cabernet, balsamic, and classic. They're colored to match their flavor, so they are beautiful as well as tasty.

Foodland makes insulated cooler bags that are decorated with uniquely local designs that go beyond tropical flowers and coconuts. Look for the pidgin or poke designs.

Made with all-natural, local ingredients, like kukui-nut oil, local flowers, herbs, even seaweed, indigenous bar soap is available online or in stores, like **Blue Hawaii Lifestyle**.

CRAFTS

Hawaiian Quilt Collection. Traditional island comforters, wall hangings, pillows, bags, and other Hawaiian-print quilt accessories are the specialty here. There are also two locations in Waikiki hotels and one on Waikiki Beach Walk. ⊠ *Ala Moana Shopping Center, 1450 Ala Moana Blvd., Ala Moana* ☎ *808/946–2233* ⊕ *www.hawaiian-quilts.com.*

Na Hoku. If you look at the wrists of *kamaaina* (local) women, you might see Hawaiian heirloom bracelets fashioned in either gold or silver and engraved in a number of Islands-inspired designs. Na Hoku sells traditional and modern jewelry in designs that capture the heart of the Hawaiian lifestyle in all its elegant diversity. ⊠ *Ala Moana Center, 1450 Ala Moana Blvd., Ala Moana* ☎ *808/946–2100* ⊕ *www.nahoku.com.*

FOOD

Honolulu Cookie Co. Hugely popular with Islands residents and visitors, these pineapple-shaped shortbread cookies half-dipped in milk or dark chocolate come in an assortment of flavors from macadamia nut to mango and lilikoi. Made locally in Kalihi, these gourmet cookies come in boxes and tins of varying sizes at 10 locations in Ala Moana and Waikiki. ⊠ *Ala Moana Shopping Center, 1450 Ala Moana Blvd., Ala Moana* ☎ *808/945-0787* ⊕ *www.honolulucookie.com.*

Longs Drugs. For gift items in bulk, try one of the many outposts of Longs, the perfect place to stock up on chocolate-covered macadamia nuts—at reasonable prices—to carry home. ⊠ *Ala Moana Shopping Center, 1450 Ala Moana Blvd., 2nd level, Ala Moana* ☎ *808/941–4433* ⊕ *www.alamoanacenter.com/en/directory/longs-drugs-789.html.*

GIFTS

Blue Hawaii Lifestyle. The Ala Moana store carries a large selection of locally made products, including soaps, honey, tea, salt, chocolates, art, and CDs. Every item, in fact, is carefully selected from various Hawaiian companies, artisans, and farms, from the salt fields of Molokai to the lavender farms on Maui to the single-estate chocolate on Oahu's North Shore. A café in the store serves healthy smoothies, panini, tea,

> **KOA KEEPSAKES**
>
> Items handcrafted from native Hawaiian wood make beautiful gifts. Koa and milo have a distinct color and grain. The scarcity of koa forests makes the wood extremely valuable. That's why you'll notice a large price gap between koa-wood-veneer products and the real thing.

and espresso. ⊠ *Ala Moana Shopping Center, 1450 Ala Moana Blvd., Ala Moana* 🕾 *808/949–0808* ⊕ *www.bluehawaiilifestyle.com.*

SHOPPING CENTERS

Ala Moana Shopping Center. The world's largest open-air shopping mall is five minutes from Waikiki by bus. More than 350 stores and 60 restaurants make up this 50-acre complex, which is a unique mix of national and international chains as well as smaller, locally owned shops and eateries—and everything in between. Thirty-five luxury boutiques in residence include Gucci, Louis Vuitton, Christian Dior, and Emporio Armani. All of Hawaii's major department stores are here, including the state's only Neiman Marcus and Nordstrom, plus Macy's, Target, and Bloomingdales. To get to the mall from Waikiki, catch TheBus line 8, 19, 20, 23, 24 or 42; a one-way ride is $2.50. Or hop aboard the Waikiki Trolley's Pink Line for $2 each way; it comes through the area every 10 minutes. ⊠ *1450 Ala Moana Blvd., Ala Moana* 🕾 *808/955–9517* ⊕ *www.alamoanacenter.com.*

Ward Village. Heading west from Waikiki toward downtown Honolulu, you'll run into a section of town with five distinct shopping-complex areas; there are more than 135 specialty shops and 40 eateries here. The Ward Entertainment Center features 16 movie theaters, including a state-of-the-art, 3-D, big-screen auditorium. For distinctive Hawaiian gifts, such as locally made muumuu, koa-wood products, and Niihau shell necklaces, visit Martin & MacArthur and Na Mea Hawaii. Twin Islands sells clothing for adults and children representing the laid-back lifestyle of Hawaii. Take TheBus line 19, 20, or 42; fare is $2.50 one-way. Or hop on the Waikiki Trolley Red Line; it comes through the area every 40 minutes. There also is free parking nearby and a valet service. ⊠ *1050-1200 Ala Moana Blvd., Ala Moana* 🕾 *808/591–8411* ⊕ *www.wardvillageshops.com.*

MOILIILI

This neighborhood, although considered separate from the University of Hawaii's Manoa campus, has a distinct college-town feel. About 3 miles from Waikiki, the area is extremely tired in some sections and needs updating. Nevertheless, a look past the exterior reveals a haven for excellent family-owned restaurants, health food stores, and shops that have a loyal following in the residential community.

JEWELRY

Maui Divers Design Center. For a look into the harvesting and design of coral and black pearl jewelry, visit this shop and take a free tour at its adjacent factory near the Ala Moana Shopping Center. ✉ *1520 Liona St., Moiliili* ☎ *808/946–7979* ⊕ *www.mauidivers.com.*

IWILEI

GIFTS

Indich Collection. Bring home some aloha you can sink your bare feet into. Designs from this exclusive Hawaiian rug collection depict Hawaiian petroglyphs, banana leaves, heliconia, and other tropical plants or scenery. ✉ *550 Ward Ave., Kakaako* ☎ *808/596–7333* ⊕ *www. indichcollectionhawaii.net.*

KAPAHULU

Kapahulu, like many older neighborhoods, should not be judged at first glance. It begins at the Diamond Head end of Waikiki and continues up to the H1 freeway and is full of variety; shops and restaurants are located primarily on Kapahulu Avenue.

CLOTHING

Bailey's Antiques & Aloha Shirts. Vintage aloha shirts are the specialty at this kitschy store. Prices range from $3.99 to several hundred dollars for the 15,000 shirts in stock; thousands of them are used while others come from top designers. The tight space and musty smell are part of the thrift-shop atmosphere. ■**TIP→** Antiques hunters can also buy old-fashioned postcards, Hawaiian LPs, authentic military clothing, funky hats, and denim jeans from the 1950s. ✉ *517 Kapahulu Ave., Kapahulu* ☎ *808/734–7628* ⊕ *www.alohashirts.com.*

SPORTING GOODS

Island Paddler. Fashionable beach footwear, clothing, bathing suits, fun beach bags, and rash guards supplement a huge selection of canoe paddles and paddling accessories. A second store at 350 Hahani Street in Kailua (☎ *808/262–4866*), where paddling out to offshore islands is a popular activity, serves the windward side of the island. ■**TIP→** Check out the wooden decorative paddles: they become works of art when mounted on the wall at home. ✉ *716 Kapahulu Ave., Kapahulu* ☎ *808/737–4854* ⊕ *www.islandpaddlerhawaii.com.*

Island Triathlon & Bike. Another source for bikes, sports bathing suits, water bottles, and active clothing. The store also rents bicycles and organizes group bike rides around Honolulu. ✉ *569 Kapahulu Ave., Kapahulu* ☎ *808/732–7227* ⊕ *www.itbhawaii.com.*

TAKE HOME A TASTE OF OAHU

You don't necessarily have to buy a whole pineapple to enjoy Hawaii's fruit flavors back home. Jams are easy to pack and don't spoil. They come in flavors such as poha, passion fruit, and guava. Coffee is another option. Kona- and Oahu-grown Waialua coffee beans have an international following. There are also dried-food products such as saimin, haupia, and teriyaki barbecue sauce. All kinds of cookies are available, as well as exotic teas, drink mixes, and pancake syrups. And don't forget the macadamia nuts, from plain to chocolate-covered and brittled.

7

Snorkel Bob's. The chain, popular throughout the Islands, sells or rents necessary gear, including fins, snorkels, wet suits, and beach chairs, and schedules ocean activities with other suppliers. This is a good place to seek advice about the best snorkeling beaches and conditions, which vary considerably with the season. ⊠ *702 Kapahulu Ave., Kapahulu* ☎ *808/735-7944* ⊕ *www.snorkelbob.com.*

KAIMUKI
FLOWERS AND PLANTS
Kawamoto Orchid Nursery. Kawamoto grows all flowers on its three-acre orchid farm near downtown Honolulu. Their specialty is the Cattleya, a favorite for Mother's Day, but they also grow hundreds of hybrids. The nursery now does the bulk of its business online, and they have decades of experience shipping temperamental orchids to the mainland. ⊠ *Kawamoto Orchid Nursery, 2630 Waiomao Rd., Kaimuki* ☎ *808/732-5808* ⊕ *www.kawamotoorchids.com.*

SPORTING GOODS
Downing Hawaii. Look for old-style Birdwell surf trunks here, along with popular labels such as Quiksilver, Roxy, DaKine, and Billabong, which supplement Downing's own line of surf wear and surfboards. ⊠ *3021 Waialae Ave., Kaimuki* ☎ *808/737-9696* ⊕ *www.downingsurf.com.*

KAHALA
The upscale residential neighborhood of Kahala, near the slopes of Diamond Head, is 10 minutes by car from Waikiki and has a shopping mall and some gift stores.

SHOPPING CENTERS
Kahala Mall. The upscale residential neighborhood of Kahala, near the slopes of Diamond Head, is 10 minutes by car from Waikiki. The only shopping of note in the area is located at the indoor mall, which has more than 100 stores and restaurants, including Macy's, Reyn Spooner, an Apple store, Island Sole footwear, and T&C Surf. Shops include local and national retailers. Don't miss fashionable boutiques such as **Ohelo Road** (☎ *808/735-5525*), where contemporary clothing for all occasions fills the racks. You can also browse local foods and products at Whole Foods. Eight movie theaters provide post-shopping entertainment. ⊠ *4211 Waialae Ave., Kahala* ☎ *808/732-7736* ⊕ *www.kahalamallcenter.com.*

WINDWARD OAHU

Shopping on the windward side is one of Oahu's best-kept secrets. The trip here takes a half hour by car or about an hour on TheBus. The real treats lie in the small boutiques and galleries in the heart of Kailua—the perfect place to gather unique gifts. After shopping, enjoy the outdoors in one of the most beautiful beach towns in the world. Kailua is the best place to rent kayaks and paddle out to the Mokulua Islands with a guide, take a windsurfing lesson, or watch the expert kiteboarders sailing across the bay. ■ TIP➔ Stop by Kalapawai Market at Kailua Beach near the entrance to Lanikai—for sandwiches and cold drinks and souvenirs, and finish the day relaxing on a sparsely populated white-sand beach. The surf here is minimal, making it a perfect picnic spot with the kids, but not the place to learn to ride waves. Save that for Waikiki.

BOOKS

Fodor's Choice ★ **Bookends.** The perfect place to shop for gifts, or just take a break with the family, this independent bookstore feels more like a small-town library, welcoming browsers to linger for hours. Selling new and secondhand books, the large children's section is filled with toys and books to read. ⊠ *600 Kailua Rd., Kailua* ☎ *808/261–1996.*

CLOTHING

Fodor's Choice ★ **Global Village.** Tucked into a tiny strip mall near Maui Tacos, this boutique features jewelry, clothing, accessories, gifts, and handcrafted jewelry from the islands and around the globe. ⊠ *Kailua Village Shops, 539 Kailua Rd., No. 104, Kailua* ☎ *808/262–8183* ⊕ *www.globalvillagehawaii.com.*

HEALTH AND BEAUTY PRODUCTS

Lanikai Bath and Body. Take home the fragrances of the Islands with these organic body lotions, hand creams, soaps, sprays, bath salts, and scrubs. Botanical extracts such as papaya, mango, sea kelp, and calendula are combined with essential oils including macadamia and kukui nuts to produce fine bath and body products. Try Naupaka, a blend of coconut, lime, and verbena that suits both men and women. ⊠ *Kailua Shopping Center, 600 Kailua Rd., Kailua* ☎ *808/262–3260* ⊕ *www.lanikaibathandbody.com.*

HOME DECOR

Jeff Chang Pottery & Fine Crafts. This family-owned and operated gallery offers the artist's functional and decorative pottery as well as the works of approximately 200 other American artisans. Jeff has worked with clay for more than 40 years and his wife, Karon, operates the gallery and selects other works including jewelry, glass, metal sculpture, wall art, wood, musical instruments, chimes, suncatchers, sand globes and pictures, holiday decor, and ornaments. ⊠ *Windward Mall, 46-056 Kamehameha Hwy., 2nd Floor, Theatre Wing, Kaneohe* ☎ *808/235–5150* ⊕ *www.windwardmall.com/stores/jeff-chang-pottery.*

Fodor's Choice ★ **Under a Hula Moon.** Exclusive tabletop items and Pacific home decor, such as shell wreaths, shell night-lights, Hawaiian beach sheets, frames, and unique one-of-a-kind gifts with an Islands influence, define this eclectic shop. ⊠ *Kailua Shopping Center, 600 Kailua Rd., Kailua* ☎ *808/261–4252.*

THE NORTH SHORE

A drive to the North Shore takes about one hour from Waikiki, but allot a full day to explore the beaches and Haleiwa, a burgeoning destination that has managed to retain its surf-town charm. The occasional makeshift stand selling delicious fruit or shrimp beside the road adds character to the beach, farm, and artist-colony atmosphere. Eclectic shops are the best place to find skin-care products made on the North Shore, Hawaiian music CDs, sea glass and shell mobiles, coffee grown in the Islands, and clothing items unavailable anywhere else. Be sure to chat with the owners in each shop. North Shore residents are an animated, friendly bunch with multiple talents. Stop in for coffee and the shop's owner might reveal a little about his or her passion for creating distinguished pieces of artwork.

SHOPPING CENTERS

Haleiwa Store Lots. In 2015 the North Shore town debuted a shiny new complex, the Haleiwa Store Lots. Its most notable tenant is the legendary Matsumoto Shave Ice. (You'll know it by the long line of people.) The open-air shopping center has several locally owned stores such as Global Creations and the casual beach-chic boutique Guava Shop, and it's also home to surf photographer's Clark Little's art gallery. ⊠ *66-111 Kamehameha Hwy., Haleiwa* ⊕ *www.haleiwastorelots.com.*

North Shore Marketplace. While playing on the North Shore, check out this open-air plaza that includes art galleries, clothing, gelato, and jewelry stores. And don't miss the Silver Moon Emporium for eclectic Islands fashions. People drive out of their way for the Coffee Gallery, or for happy hour at Cholo's Homestyle Mexican Restaurant. ⊠ *66-250 Kamehameha Hwy., Haleiwa* ☎ *808/637–4416* ⊕ *www.northshoremarketplacehawaii.com.*

CLOTHING

The Growing Keiki. Frequent visitors return to this store year after year for a fresh supply of unique, locally made Hawaiian-style clothing for youngsters. ⊠ *66-051 Kamehameha Hwy., Haleiwa* ☎ *808/637–4544* ⊕ *www.thegrowingkeiki.com.*

Fodor'sChoice **Silver Moon Emporium.** The small boutique carries everything from
★ Brighton jewelry and European designer wear to fashionable T-shirts, shoes, and handbags. Shoppers get attentive yet casual and personalized service. The stock changes frequently, and there's always something wonderful on sale. No matter what your taste, you'll find something for everyday wear or special occasions. ⊠ *North Shore Marketplace, 66-250 Kamehameha Hwy., Haleiwa* ☎ *808/637–7710* ⊕ *silvermoonhawaii.blogspot.com.*

FOOD

Tropical Fruits Distributors of Hawaii. Avoid the hassle of airport inspections. This company specializes in packing inspected pineapple and papaya; they will deliver to your hotel and to the airport check-in counter, or ship to the mainland U.S. and Canada. Think about ordering online. ⊠ *Dole Plantation, 64-1550 Kamehameha Hwy., Haleiwa* ☎ *808/621–8408* ⊕ *www.dolefruithawaii.com.*

GIFTS

Global Creations Interiors. Look for Hawaiian bath products, pikake perfume, locally made jewelry, island bedding, and a carefully chosen selection of Hawaiian music CDs. Popular gifts include Hawaiian sarongs and Islands-inspired kitchen items. ⊠ *66-111 Kamehameha Hwy., No. 901, Haleiwa* ☎ *808/637–1780* ⊕ *www.globalcreationshaleiwa.com.*

Island X Hawaii. This eclectic store in a section of the old Waialua Sugar Mill carries gifts, clothes, and local food items—especially coffee and chocolate that is grown in Waialua. Visitors get a short unofficial tour of the coffee and chocolate trees and the roasting area just outside. ⊠ *Waialua Sugar Mill, 67-106 Kealohanui St., Waialua* ☎ *808/637–2624* ⊕ *www.islandxhawaii.com.*

North Shore Soap Factory. Housed in a converted silo in the historic Waialua Sugar Mill, this is a working factory where you can watch the soap as it's made. The soaps are all natural and use as many local ingredients as possible. The factory also sells lotions and essential oils, gift sets, and T-shirts. ⊠ *Waialua Sugar Mill, 67-106 Kealohanui St., Waialua* ☎ *808/637–8400* ⊕ *www.northshoresoapfactory.com.*

SPORTING GOODS

Surf 'N Sea. A North Shore water-sports store with everything you need for an active vacation under one roof. Purchase rash guards, swimwear, T-shirts, footwear, hats, and shorts. Book scuba-diving tours and lessons, rent kayaks, snorkeling or scuba gear, spears for free diving, windsurfing equipment, surfboards, stand-up paddleboards, and bodyboards. Experienced surfing instructors will take beginners to the small breaks on the notoriously huge (winter) or flat (summer) North Shore beaches. Warning to fishing enthusiasts: a fishing pole is the one ocean apparatus they don't carry. ⊠ *62-595 Kamehameha Hwy., Haleiwa* ☎ *800/899–7873* ⊕ *www.surfnsea.com.*

WEST (LEEWARD) OAHU

Shopping on this part of the island is at two extremes—an outdoor market that literally sells everything under the sun, and a high-end shopping outlet with many of the big designer names.

SHOPPING CENTERS

Aloha Stadium Swap Meet & Marketplace. This thrice-weekly outdoor bazaar attracts hundreds of vendors and even more bargain hunters. Every Hawaiian souvenir imaginable can be found here, from coral shell necklaces to bikinis, as well as a variety of ethnic wares, from Chinese brocaded dresses to Japanese pottery. There are also ethnic foods, silk flowers, and luggage in aloha floral prints. Shoppers must wade through the typical sprinkling of used and stolen goods to find value. Wear comfortable shoes, use sunscreen, and bring bottled water. The flea market takes place in the Aloha Stadium parking lot Wednesday and Saturday 8–3, Sunday 6:30–3. Admission is $1 per person ages 12 and up.

Several shuttle companies serve Aloha Stadium for the swap meet for those tourists who don't rent a car, including VIP Shuttle (☎ *808/839–0911*), Reliable Shuttle (☎ *808/924–9292*), and Hawaii Super Transit (☎ *808/841–2928*), with a cost of $20 or less round-trip. The Waikiki Trolley Purple Line also stops at the Swap Meet. For a cheaper but slower ride, take TheBus (⊕ *www.thebus.org*). ⊠ *Aloha Stadium, 99-500 Salt Lake Blvd., Aiea* ☎ *808/486–6704* ⊕ *www.alohastadium-swapmeet.net.*

Waikele Premium Outlets. AIX Armani Exchange, Calvin Klein, Coach, and Saks Fifth Avenue outlets anchor this discount destination of around 50 stores. You can take a shuttle from Waikiki for the 30-minute ride to the outlets for $18 round-trip, but the companies do change frequently. Reservations are recommended. ✉ *94-790 Lumiaina St., Waipahu* ☎ *808/676-5656* ⊕ *www.premiumoutlets.com/outlet/waikele.*

SPORTING GOODS

Hawaiian Fire. Honolulu firefighters no longer offer surfing lessons, but proceeds from their Hawaiian Firefighter–inspired clothing and accessories store on the southwest side of Oahu help to sponsor island athletic teams and organizations. If you are heading to the less-crowded beaches on the southwest side, check out the store for T-shirts, hats, and beach accessories. ✉ *92-1047 Olani St., Ko Olina* ☎ *808/492–1939* ⊕ *www. hawaiianfire.com.*

SPAS

Excellent day and resort spas can be found throughout Oahu, primarily in the resorts of Waikiki but also downtown and on the North Shore. Individual treatments and day packages offer a wide choice of rejuvenating therapies, some of which are unique to the Islands. Try the popular *lomilomi* massage with kukui-nut oil (*lomi* meaning to rub, knead, and massage using palms, forearms, fingers, knuckles, elbows, knees, feet, even sticks). Add heated *pohaku* (stones) placed on the back to relieve sore muscles, or choose a facial using natural ingredients such as coconut, mango, papaya, ti leaf, Hawaiian honey, or ginger. Many full-service spas offer couples' private treatment rooms, fitness suites, yoga, and hydrotherapy pools.

HONOLULU

WAIKIKI

Abhasa Spa. Natural organic skin and body treatments are the highlights at this spa tucked away in the Royal Hawaiian Hotel's coconut grove. Vegetarian-lifestyle spa therapies, color-light therapy, a facial fusing invigorating lomilomi technique with pohaku are all available. You can choose to have your treatment in any of Abhasa's eight indoor rooms or in one of its three garden cabanas. ✉ *Royal Hawaiian Hotel, 2259 Kalakaua Ave., Waikiki* ☎ *808/922–8200* ⊕ *www.abhasa.com.*

LaaKea Spa Hawaii. Only steps off the beach, this renovated Aveda Concept spa provides aromatherapy treatments, massages, and facials. Each room is extra spacious not just to give therapists area to move, but to accommodate handicapped guests as well. Signature massages include a stress-fix body massage that relieves jet lag and stiffness from traveling and a massage using lomi techniques and pohaku. ■**TIP➜ Book the last appointment of the day—usually 4, 5, or 6 pm—so you can watch the sunset as you're finishing your massage treatment.** ✉ *Outrigger Reef on the Beach, 2169 Kalia Rd., Waikiki* ☎ *808/926–2882, 866/926–2882* ⊕ *www.laakeaspahawaii.com.*

Mandara Spa at the Hilton Hawaiian Village Beach Resort & Spa. From its perch in the Kalia Tower, Mandara Spa, an outpost of the chain that originated in Bali, overlooks the mountains, ocean, and downtown Honolulu. Fresh Hawaiian ingredients and traditional techniques headline an array of treatments. Try an exotic upgrade, such as reflexology or a Balinese body polish. Or relieve achy muscles with a traditional Thai poultice massage. The delicately scented, candlelit foyer can fill up quickly with robe-clad conventioneers, so be sure to make a reservation. There are spa suites for couples, a private infinity pool, and a boutique. ✉ *Hilton Hawaiian Village Beach Resort & Spa, 2005 Kalia Rd., 3rd & 4th fl., Kalia Tower, Waikiki* ☎ *808/945–7721* ⊕ *www.mandaraspa.com.*

Na Hoola Spa at the Hyatt Regency Waikiki Resort & Spa. Na Hoola is the premier resort spa in Waikiki, with 16 treatment rooms sprawling across 10,000 square feet and two floors of the Hyatt on Kalakaua Avenue. Arrive early for your treatment to enjoy the postcard views of Waikiki Beach. Four packages identified by Hawaii's native healing plants—noni, kukui, awa, and kalo—combine various body, face, and hair treatments; the spa also has luxurious packages that last three to six hours. The Kele Kele body wrap employs a self-heating mud wrap to release tension and stress. The small exercise room is for use by hotel guests only. ✉ *Hyatt Regency Waikiki Resort & Spa, 2424 Kalakaua Ave., Waikiki* ☎ *808/923–1234, 808/237–6330 for reservations* ⊕ *www.nahoolaspawaikiki.com.*

Royal Kaila Spa. The Marriott's spa, which faces Waikiki Beach, uses nature-based Aveda products in all their treatments. Linger with a cup of tea between treatments and gaze through 75-foot-high windows at the activity outside. Lush Hawaiian foliage, sleek Balinese teak furnishings, and a mist of ylang-ylang and nutmeg in the air inspire relaxation. Treatments incorporate natural minerals and sea salts as well as the healing power of plant essences. ✉ *Waikiki Beach Marriott Resort & Spa, 2552 Kalakaua Ave., Waikiki* ☎ *808/369–8088* ⊕ *www.royalkaila-spa.com.*

The Spa at Trump Waikiki. The Spa at Trump offers private changing and showering areas for each room, creating an environment of uninterrupted relaxation. No matter what treatment you choose, it is inspired by "personal intention," such as purify, balance, heal, revitalize, or calm, to elevate the senses throughout your time there. Don't miss the signature gemstone treatments, which feature products by Shiffa; or treat yourself to a Naturally Yours facial to emerge with younger-looking skin. The Healing Hawaiian Ocean Ritual is one of the most popular massages to begin—or end—your day. ✉ *Trump International Hotel Waikiki, 223 Saratoga Rd., Waikiki* ☎ *808/683–7466* ⊕ *www.trumpwaikikihotel.com.*

Fodor's Choice **SpaHalekulani.** SpaHalekulani mines the traditions and cultures of the
★ Pacific Islands with massages and body and facial therapies. Try the Samoan Nonu, which uses warm stones and healing nonu gel to relieve muscle tension. The exclusive line of bath and body products is scented by maile, lavender orchid, or coconut passion. Facilities are specific to treatment but may include Japanese furo bath or steam shower. ✉ *Halekulani Hotel, 2199 Kalia Rd., Waikiki* ☎ *808/931–5322* ⊕ *www.halekulani.com/living/spahalekulani.*

ALA MOANA

Hoala Salon and Spa. This Aveda concept spa has everything from Vichy showers to hydrotherapy rooms to customized aromatherapy. Ladies, they'll even touch up your makeup for free before you leave. ⊠ *Ala Moana Shopping Center, 3rd fl., 1450 Ala Moana Blvd., Ala Moana* ☎ *808/947–6141* ⊕ *www.hoalasalonspa.com.*

KAHALA

The Kahala Spa. Escape the hustle and bustle of metro Honolulu at the elegant yet homey Kahala property favored by celebrities and U.S. presidents. The two-story spa suites feature wooden floors, handmade Hawaiian quilts, Kohler infinity-edged whirlpool tubs, private vanity areas, and private gardens where clients can relax with a green tea extract infused with various fruits. Custom treatments merge Hawaiian, Asian, and traditional therapies. "Romance packages" are also available. ⊠ *The Kahala Hotel & Resort, 5000 Kahala Ave., Kahala* ☎ *808/739–8938* ⊕ *www.kahalaresort.com.*

THE NORTH SHORE

Nalu Kinetic Spa at Turtle Bay Resort. Luxuriate at the ocean's edge in this renovated spa on Oahu's North Shore. Try one of the spa's body wraps, including the lilikoi citrus polish using Hawaiian cane sugar and organic lehua honey in its Vichy shower treatment room. Or book a shiatsu massage, which utilizes foot pressure to release soft tissue constrictions and improve circulation. There are private spa suites, an outdoor treatment cabana that overlooks the surf, an outdoor exercise studio, and a lounge area and juice bar. ⊠ *Turtle Bay Resort, 57-091 Kamehameha Hwy., Kahuku* ☎ *808/447–6868* ⊕ *www.nalukineticspa.com.*

WEST (LEEWARD) OAHU

Laniwai Spa at Aulani, A Disney Resort & Spa. At this spa, every staff member—or "cast member," as they call themselves—is extensively trained in Hawaiian culture and history to ensure they are projecting the right *mana*, or energy, in their work. To begin each treatment, you select a special pohaku with words of intent, then cast it into a reflective pool. Choose from about 150 spa therapies, and indulge in Kulu Wai, the only outdoor hydrotherapy garden on Oahu—with private vitality pools, co-ed mineral baths, six different "rain" showers, whirlpool jet spas, and more. ⊠ *Aulani, A Disney Resort & Spa, 92-1185 Aliinui Dr., Ko Olina* ☎ *808/674–6300* ⊕ *disneyaulani.com/spa-fitness.*

WATER SPORTS AND TOURS

Updated by
Trina Kudlacek

From snorkeling on the North Shore to kayaking to small islands off Kailua Beach to stand-up paddleboarding in Waikiki—when you're on Oahu, there's always a reason to get wet. You can swim with native fish in a protected bay, surf waves in an outrigger canoe, take to the skies in a parasail above Diamond Head, or enjoy panoramic views of Waikiki aboard a 45-foot catamaran. Diving into the ocean—whether in a boat, on a board, or with your own finned feet—is a great way to experience Oahu.

But, as with any physical activity, heed the warnings. The ocean is unpredictable and unforgiving, and it can be as dangerous as it can be awe-inspiring. But if you respect it, it can offer you the kind of memories that last well after your vacation.

ANIMAL ENCOUNTERS

Pods of dolphins surround the Islands, and spotting them can be as easy as just getting yourself out in the ocean. They are wild animals, of course, and do not follow a schedule, but a catamaran sail off Waikiki will usually net you a sighting. Dolphins also generally make appearances shortly after sunrise on the West Shore and can be clearly observed from beaches like Makua and Makaha. And while they won't have the peppy music of Sea World in the background, their jumping and spinning is even more awe-inspiring when you realize they are just doing it as a natural part of their lives rather than for a reward.

Some tour operators offer opportunities to swim with dolphins, but keep in mind that these are federally protected marine mammals, so you should always follow the instructions given by the tour operator if you take one of these trips. The National Oceanographic and Atmospheric Administration (NOAA) provides specific guidelines for tour operators encountering dolphins through their Dolphin Safe program.

The cost for dolphin encounters can be pricey and ranges from $130 for a chance to swim with wild dolphins on a snorkel cruise to $700 for getting in the pool with them as trainer-for-a-day. ⇨ *Both Sea Life Park in Waimanolo and Dolphin Quest at The Kahala offer opportunities to view and interact with captive dolphins; for more information, see Chapter 2, Exploring Oahu.*

Similarly, you can also swim with sharks, though you do so in a protective cage.

FAMILY **Dolphin Excursions Hawaii.** For those who are a little timid about entering these waters, this outfitter provides a tour with a naturalist guide to help alleviate your fears and provide great information about marine life. The company's three-hour Dolphin Adventure departs from Waianae Boat Harbor and includes round-trip transportation from Waikiki and Ko Olina. ✉ *Waianae Boat Harbor, 85-491 Farrington Hwy., Waianae ✛ Check in at Spinners Café* ☏ *808/239–5579, 877/257–5579* ⊕ *www. dolphinexcursions.com* 💲 *From $130.*

Dolphin Quest at The Kahala Hotel & Resort. This worldwide dolphin-encounter group has an Oahu location in the Kahala Hotel & Resort, where trained Atlantic bottlenose dolphins hold court in an enclosed lagoon at the center of the hotel. The Kid's Aquatic Adventure is a 90-minute session of feeding and interacting with sting rays and dolphins. For the adults, there is more variety starting with a 15-minute encounter and going up to the "Trainer for a Week" experience. ✉ *The Kahala Hotel & Resort, 5000 Kahala Ave., Kahala* ☏ *808/739–8918* ⊕ *www.kahalaresort.com/Experiences/Dolphin-Quest* 💲 *From $189 for a 15-min encounter.*

North Shore Shark Adventures. "You go in the cage, cage goes in the water, you go in the water, shark's in the water." You remember this line from *Jaws,* and now you get to play the role of Richard Dreyfus, as North Shore Shark Adventures provides you with an interactive experience out of your worst nightmare. The tour allows you to swim and snorkel in a cage as dozens of sharks lurk just feet from you in the open ocean off the North Shore. They'll provide transportation from Waikiki for an additional charge. Discounts are available if you book online. ■ TIP➔ **If you go, go early: the sea is more calm and clear in the morning.** ✉ *Haleiwa Small Boat Harbor, 66-105 Haleiwa Rd., Haleiwa ✛ Check in at the Shark Shack in the harbor* ☏ *808/228–5900* ⊕ *www.sharktourshawaii. com* 💲 *From $96.*

8

BOAT TOURS AND CHARTERS

Being on the water can be the best way to enjoy the Islands. Whether you want to see the fish in action or experience how they taste, there is a tour for you.

For a sailing experience in Oahu, you need go no farther than the beach in front of your hotel in Waikiki. Strung along the sand are several beach catamarans that will provide you with one-hour rides during the day and 90-minute sunset sails. Look for $35 for day sails and $49–$120 for sunset rides. ■ TIP➔ **Feel free to haggle, especially with**

Sail around the island to spot wildlife and deserted beaches.

the smaller boats. Some provide drinks for free, some charge for them, and some let you pack your own, so keep that in mind when pricing the ride. Or choose to go the ultraluxe route and charter a boat for a day or week. These run from less than $100 per person per day to over $1,000. *(see Deep-Sea Fishing).*

FAMILY **Hawaii Duck Tours.** These unique tours in amphibious vehicles take advantage of the ducks' dual means of travel by navigating the streets of Waikiki and then gliding into the waters of Waikiki Harbor. The tour starts in Waikiki and then travels on land to Kapiolani Park, Diamond Head, and the Ala Wai Canal. Then it's out to sea for views of Waikiki's famous beaches and landmarks from the water. Tours last approximately 75 minutes and run throughout the day and at sunset. On Friday nights there's a special evening fireworks tour. All tours start at the Ilikai Hotel. ⊠ *Illikai Hotel, 1777 Ala Moana Blvd., Waikiki* ☎ *808/988–3825* ⊕ *www.hawaiiducktours.com* ⊠ *From $35.*

Hawaii Nautical. With two locations in Waikiki and one on the Waianae Coast, this outfit offers a wide variety of cruise options including guaranteed-sighting dolphin and whale-watching (in season), gourmet dinners, lunches, snorkeling, scuba diving, and sunset viewing. Three-hour cruises, including lunch and two drinks, depart from the Kewalo Basin Harbor just outside Waikiki. (The company's Port Waikiki Cruises sail from the Hilton Pier off the Hilton Hawaiian Village in Waikiki.) For those interested in leaving from the Waianae Coast, snorkel tours are available from the Waianae Boat Harbor on Farrington Highway (85-471 Farrington Hwy.). Prices include all gear, food, and two alcoholic beverages. The dock in the Waianae Boat Harbor is a little more out of the way, but this is a much more luxurious option than what is offered in Waikiki. Both morning and afternoon snorkel tours include stops for observing dolphins from the boat and visit to a snorkel spot well populated with fish. All gear, snacks, sandwiches, and two alcoholic beverages make for a more complete experience. Pickup in Ko Olina is free. ⊠ *Kewalo Basin Harbor, 1125 Ala Moana Blvd., Waikiki* ☎ *808/234–7245* ⊕ *www.hawaiinautical.com* ⊠ *From $97.*

Honolulu Sailing Company. With a small fleet of mono- and multihull sail and power boats, the Honolulu Sailing Company combines boat charters with sailing instruction opportunities. Itineraries include private chartered day or sunset sails or powerboating around Oahu as well as multiday interisland cruises. Nevertheless, these are all full-ship charters, so you need at least a small group to make them affordable. ⊠ *Kewalo Basin Harbor, 1125 Ala Moana Blvd., Honolulu* ☎ *808/239–3900* ⊕ *www.honsail.com* ⊠ *From $350.*

Maitai Catamaran. Taking off from the stretch of sand behind the Sheraton Waikiki, this 44-foot cat is the fastest and sleekest on the beach. There are a variety of tours to choose from, including a sunset sail and a snorkel excursion. If you have a need for speed and enjoy a little more upscale experience, this is the boat for you. ⊠ *Sheraton Waikiki, 2255 Kalakaua Ave., Waikiki* ✛ *On the beach behind the hotel* ☎ *808/922–5665, 800/462–7975* ⊕ *www.maitaicatamaran.net* ⊠ *From $39.*

Makani Catamaran. This 65-foot *Makani* is the top catamaran in Hawaii for luxury, from its Bose stereo system to its LCD TVs to its freshwater bathrooms. It sails out of Kewalo Basin four times daily, offering snorkel cruises that include lunch, afternoon "fun" sails, "Honolulu City Lights/Sunset" dinner cruises, and Friday night fireworks-viewing cruises. ⊠ *Kewalo Basin Harbor, 1125 Ala Moana Blvd., Ala Moana* ☎ *808/591–9000* ⊕ *www.sailmakani.com* ⊠ *From $75.*

FAMILY **Star of Honolulu Cruises.** Founded in 1957, this company's fleet includes two family-friendly vessels. The 232-foot *Star of Honolulu,* which casts off at Pier 8 in the **Aloha Tower harbor** (*1 Aloha Tower Drive, downtown Honolulu*) offers seasonal whale-watching as well as sunset gourmet dinner cruises with live entertainment. Some cruises even teach you how to string lei, play ukulele, or dance hula. Moored at the **Waianai Boat Harbor** (*85-491 Farrington Hwy., Waianae* ⊕ *www.dolphin-star. com*), the 65-foot *Dolphin Star* catamaran, offers either dolphin-viewing or snorkeling cruises with optional barbecue lunches. Because of its size, this cat provides a comfortable way for three generations of family members to enjoy the water together. Transportation from all hotels on the island can be arranged. ⊠ *Honolulu* ☎ *808/983–7827, 800/334–6191* ⊕ *www.starofhonolulu.com* ⊠ *From $34.*

Tradewind Charters. This company's half-day private excursions can include sailing, snorkeling, reef fishing, sunset dinner cruises, or whale-watching excursions and can accommodate from two to 49 people. Traveling on these luxury yachts not only gets you away from the crowds but also gives you the opportunity to take the helm if you wish. The cruises may include snorkeling at an exclusive anchorage, as well as hands-on snorkeling and sailing instruction. All charters are

8

for the full ship. ✉ *Kewalo Basin Harbor, 1125 Ala Moana Blvd., Ala Moana* ☏ *808/227–4956, 800/829–4899* ⊕ *www.tradewindcharters. com* ✉ *From $495.*

BODYBOARDING AND BODYSURFING

Bodyboarding (or sponging) has long been a popular alternative to surfing for a couple of reasons. First, the start-up cost is much less—a usable board can be purchased for $30–$40 or can be rented on the beach for $5 an hour. Second, it's a whole lot easier to ride a bodyboard than to tame a surfboard. All you have to do is paddle out to the waves, then turn toward the beach as the wave approaches and kick like crazy.

Most grocery and convenience stores sell bodyboards. Though these boards don't compare to what the pros use, beginners won't notice a difference in their handling on smaller waves.

Though they are not absolutely necessary for bodyboarding, fins do give you a tremendous advantage when you're paddling. If you plan to go out into bigger surf, we would also suggest getting a leash, which reduces the chance you'll lose your board. The smaller, sturdier versions of dive fins used for bodyboarding sell for $25–$60 at surf and sporting-goods stores. Most beach stands don't rent fins with the boards, so if you want them you'll probably need to buy them.

Bodysurfing requires far less equipment—just a pair of swim fins with heel straps—but it can be a lot more challenging to master. Typically, surf breaks that are good for bodyboarding are good for bodysurfing.

If the direction of the current or dangers of the break are not readily apparent to you, don't hesitate to ask a lifeguard for advice.

BEST SPOTS

Bodyboarding and bodysurfing can be done anywhere there are waves, but due to the paddling advantage surfers have over spongers, it's usually more fun to go to surf breaks exclusively for bodyboarding. ⇨ *For more information on Oahu beaches, see Chapter 3, Beaches.*

Bellows Beach. On Oahu's windward side, Bellows Field Beach has shallow waters and a consistent break that makes it an ideal spot for bodyboarders and bodysurfers. (Surfing isn't allowed between the two lifeguard towers.) But take note: the Portuguese man-of-war, a blue jellyfishlike invertebrate that delivers painful and powerful stings, is often seen here. ✉ *41-043 Kalanianaole Hwy., Waimanalo.*

Kuhio Beach Park. This beach is an easy spot for first-timers to check out the action. The Wall, a break near the large pedestrian walkway called Kapahulu Groin, is the quintessential bodyboarding spot. The soft, rolling waves make it perfect for beginners. Even during summer's south swells, it's relatively tame because of the outer reefs. ✉ *Waikiki Beach, between the Sheraton Moana Surfrider Hotel and the Kapahulu Groin, Honolulu.*

The windward side has many good spots for bodyboarding.

Makapuu Beach. With its extended waves, Makapuu Beach is a sponger's dream. If you're a little more timid, go to the far end of the beach to **Keiki's**, where the waves are mellowed by Makapuu Point. Although the main break at Makapuu is much less dangerous than Sandy's, check out the ocean floor—the sands are always shifting, sometimes exposing coral heads and rocks. Always check (or ask lifeguards about) the currents, which can get pretty strong. ⊠ *41-095 Kalanianaole Hwy., across from Sea Life Park.*

Sandy Beach. The best spot—and arguably one of the most dangerous—on the island for advanced bodyboarding is Sandy Beach, located on Oahu's eastern shore. Dubbed one of the most treacherous shore breaks in the nation, the break can be extremely dangerous even when it's small. As lifeguards will attest, there are more neck injuries suffered here than at any other surf break in the United States. It's awesome for the advanced, but know its danger before paddling out. ⊠ *8800 Kalanianaole Hwy., 2 miles east of Hanauma Bay, Honolulu.*

Waimanalo Beach Park. With the longest sand beach on Oahu's windward side, Waimanalo Bay has a shallow sandbar at the water's edge that provides good waves for bodyboarding and bodysurfing. It's an ideal break for novices because of its soft waves. Like Walls in Waikiki, this area is protected by an outer reef. And like Bellows, it's favored by the dangerous Portuguese man-of-war. ⊠ *Aloiloi St., Waimanalo.*

EQUIPMENT

There are more than 30 rental spots along Waikiki Beach, all offering basically the same prices. But if you plan to bodyboard for more than just an hour, we would suggest buying an inexpensive board for $20–$40 at an ABC Store—there are more than 30 in the Waikiki area—and giving it to a kid at the end of your vacation. It will be more cost-effective for you, and you'll be passing along some aloha spirit in the process.

DEEP-SEA FISHING

Fishing isn't just a sport in Hawaii, it's a way of life. A number of charter boats with experienced crews can take you on a sportfishing adventure throughout the year. Sure, the bigger yellowfin tuna (ahi) are generally caught in summer, and the coveted spearfish are more frequent in winter, but you can still hook them any day of the year. You can also find dolphinfish (mahimahi), wahoo (ono), skipjacks, and the king—Pacific blue marlin—ripe for the picking on any given day. The largest marlin ever caught, weighing in at 1,805 pounds, was reeled in along Oahu's coast.

When choosing a fishing boat in the Islands, keep in mind the immensity of the surrounding ocean. Look for veteran captains who have decades of experience. Better yet, find those who care about Hawaii's fragile marine environment. Many captains now tag and release their catches to preserve the state's fishing grounds.

The general rule for the catch is an even split with the crew. Unfortunately, there are no "freeze-and-ship" providers in the state, so unless you plan to eat the fish while you're here, you'll probably want to leave it with the boat. Most boats do offer mounting services for trophy fish; ask your captain.

Prices vary greatly, but expect to pay from around $65 per person for a spot on a boat with more than 20 people to $2,000 for an overnight trip for up to 6 people. Besides the gift of fish, a gratuity of 10%–20% is standard, but use your own discretion depending on how you feel about the overall experience.

BOATS AND CHARTERS

Maggie Joe Sport Fishing. The oldest sportfishing company on Oahu boasts landing one of the largest marlins ever caught out of Kewalo Basin. With a fleet of three boats including the 53-foot custom *Maggie Joe* (which can hold up to 15 anglers and has air-conditioned cabins, hot showers, and cutting-edge fishing equipment), they can offer a variety of offshore fishing packages. A marine taxidermist can mount the monster you reel in. Half-day exclusives on the 41-foot *Sea Hawk* or the 38-foot *Ruckus* can accommodate up to six people and are the cheapest options for daytime fishing. Charters on the larger *Maggie Joe* can start at a three-quarter day or a full day (but not a half day). ⊠ *Kewalo Basin, 1025 Ala Moana Blvd., Ala Moana* ☎ *808/591–8888, 877/806–3474* ⊕ *www.maggiejoe.com* ⊠ *From $190.*

Magic Sportfishing. This 50-foot Pacifica fishing yacht, aptly named *Magic*, boasts a slew of sportfishing records, including some of the largest marlins caught in local tournaments and the most mahimahi hooked during a one-day charter. This yacht is very comfortable, with twin diesel engines that provide a smooth ride, air-conditioning, and a cozy seating area. The boat can accommodate up to six passengers and offers both shared and full charters. ⊠ *Kewalo Basin Harbor, 1125 Ala Moana Blvd., Slip G, Ala Moana* 🕿 *808/596–2998* ⊕ *www.magicsportfishing.com* ✉ *From $220 per person for a shared charter; from $1,095 for a private charter.*

Sashimi Fun Fishing. With a luxury 74-foot boat for sport fishing, a 65-footer for bottom fishing, and a 100-foot double-decker boat for dinner cruises, Sashimi Fun Fishing offers a variety of water activities. Choose a midnight shark hunt, head out in search of marlin, bottom fish near shore, or relax and enjoy live entertainment on the *Prince Kuhio's* sunset steak and seafood dinner cruise. Rates can include hotel transportation. ⊠ *Kewalo Basin Harbor, 1025 Ala Moana Blvd., Ala Moana* 🕿 *808/955–3474* ⊕ *www.808955fish.com or princekuhiocruises.com* ✉ *From $63 per person for shared trips; $69 for dinner cruises.*

JET SKIING AND WATERSKIING

Aloha Jet Ski. Skip across the surface of the immense Keehi Lagoon from Friday through Monday as planes from Honolulu International Airport soar above you. After an instructional safety course, you can try your hand at navigating the buoyed course. Waverunners can either be operated tandem or solo. Reservations are required. ⊠ *Keehi Lagoon, Sand Island Access Rd., Honolulu* 🕿 *888/538–6248, 808/721–1754* ⊕ *www.alohajetski.com* ✉ *From $65 per person for a tandem trip, from $82 for a solo trip.*

FAMILY **Hawaii Water Sports Center.** This company transforms Maunalua Bay into a water park with activities for all ages. You can bounce around in a bumper tube, zoom around on Jet Skis, wakeboard, scuba dive, or ride the six-person banana boats. Jet Ski rentals can be as short as 30 minutes. ⊠ *Koko Marina Center, 7192 Kalanianaole Hwy., Honolulu* 🕿 *808/395–3773* ⊕ *www.hawaiiwatersportscenter.com* ✉ *From $39.*

FAMILY **H2O Sports Hawaii.** Parasailing, banana boats, bumper boats, jetskiing, snorkeling, and scuba diving: this company offers a wide variety of tours and activities on the water. But the Jet Pack is H2O's most famous program. Pumping 1,000 gallons of seawater per minute through the pack gets you airborne like a character in a sci-fi film. With a 90% success rate for first-time flyers, this safety-conscious outfitter allows you to rocket into the air or walk on water. Launches for first-timers last 15 minutes and depart from a floating platform in Maunalua Bay near Hawaii Kai. ◼TIP➔ **Make your reservations early, as flights book up more than a week in advance, and note that the Jet Pack is only available on weekdays.** ⊠ *Hawaii Kai Shopping Center, 377 Keahole St., near Longs Drugs, Hawaii Kai* 🕿 *808/396–0100* ⊕ *www.h2osportshawaii.com* ✉ *From $199.*

KAYAKING

Kayaking is an easy way to explore the ocean—and Oahu's natural beauty—without much effort or skill. It offers a vantage point not afforded by swimming or surfing, and a workout you won't get lounging on a catamaran. Even novices can get in a kayak and enjoy the island's scenery.

The ability to travel long distances can also get you into trouble. ■ TIP→ **Experts agree that rookies should stay on the windward side.** Their reasoning is simple: if you get tired, break or lose an oar, or just plain pass out, the onshore winds will eventually blow you back to the beach. The same cannot be said for the offshore breezes of the North Shore and West Oahu.

Kayaks are specialized: some are better suited for riding waves while others are designed for traveling long distances. Your outfitter can address your needs depending on your skill level. Sharing your plans with your outfitter can lead to a more enjoyable—and safer—experience. Expect to pay from $35 for a half-day single rental to $139 for a guided kayak tour with lunch. Some kayaking outfitters also rent stand-up paddleboards (⇨ *see Stand-Up Paddleboarding*).

BEST SPOTS

If you want to try your hand at surfing kayaks, **Bellows Field Beach** (near Waimanalo Town Center, entrance on Kalanianaole Highway) on the windward side and **Mokuleia Beach** (across from Dillingham Airfield) on the North Shore are two great spots. Hard-to-reach breaks, the ones that surfers exhaust themselves trying to reach, are easily accessed by kayak. The buoyancy of the kayak also allows you to catch the wave earlier and get out in front of the white wash. One reminder on these spots: if you're a little green, stick to Bellows Field Beach with those onshore winds. Generally speaking, you don't want to be catching waves where surfers are; in Waikiki, however, pretty much anything goes.

The perennial favorite of kayakers is **Lanikai Beach,** on the island's windward side. Tucked away in an upscale residential area, this award-winning beach has become a popular spot for amateur kayakers because of its calm waters and onshore winds. More adventurous paddlers can head to the Mokulua Islands, two islets less than 1 mile from the beach. You can land on Moku Nui, which has surf breaks and small beaches great for picnicking. Take a dip in Queen's Bath, a small saltwater swimming hole.

For something a little different, try the Kahana River on the island's windward side, which empties into the ocean at **Kahana Bay Beach Park.** The river may not have the blue water of the ocean, but the majestic Koolau Mountains, with waterfalls during rainy months, make for a picturesque backdrop. It's a short jaunt, about 2 miles round-trip from the beach, but it's tranquil and packed with rain-forest foliage. Bring mosquito repellent. ⇨ *For more information on this and other beaches in Oahu, see Chapter 3.*

DID YOU KNOW?

Waikiki was once a swampy marsh until the Ala Wai Canal was built in the 1920s to drain the land for redevelopment.

EQUIPMENT, LESSONS, AND TOURS

Go Bananas. Staffers make sure that you rent the appropriate kayak for your abilities, and can also outfit your rental car with soft racks to transport your boat to the beach. (Racks are included in the rental fee.) You can rent either a single or double kayak. The store also carries clothing and kayaking accessories and rents stand-up paddleboards. (There's a second location in Aiea, which is closer to the North Shore.) ✉ *799 Kapahulu Ave., Kapahulu* ☎ *808/737–9514* ⊕ *www.gobananaskayaks.com* 🛒 *From $35.*

FAMILY **Hawaiian Water Sports.** With an emphasis on teaching ocean safety, this multifaceted outfitter offers guided tours with instruction on tours to the Mokes and Flat Island. Fully guided 90-minute and 3-hour tours include instruction and equipment rental. Experienced paddlers can also rent a kayak and venture out on their own on either a single or double kayak. The company also rents windsurfing equipment, surf and bodyboards, snorkel equipment, and stand-up paddleboards. Discounts are available if you reserve online. ✉ *171 Hamakua Dr., Kailua* ☎ *808/262–5483* ⊕ *www.hawaiianwatersports.com* 🛒 *Rentals from $29, tours from $74.*

Kailua Beach Adventures. One of the best places for beginners to rent kayaks is Kailua Beach, and Kailua Beach Adventures has an ideal location just across the street. The company offers two- and five-hour guided kayak tours (the longer tour includes lunch, time for kayaking, and time for the beach). More adventurous visitors can rent a kayak (double or single for a half or full day) and venture to the Mokulua Islands off Lanikai. You can also rent snorkeling equipment, stand-up paddleboards, and bikes. (Discounts are given if booked online.) ✉ *Kailua Beach Shopping Center, 130 Kailua Rd., Kailua* ☎ *808/262–2555* ⊕ *www.kailuasailboards.com* 🛒 *From $59 for rental; $139 for tours.*

Surf 'N Sea. This outfitter is located in a rustic wooden building on the beach, so in minutes you can start paddling on a single or double kayak. ■TIP➔ **Keep in mind that these plastic boats are great from spring to fall, but winter weather can be hazardous for even veteran kayakers.** Their proximity to a protected stream makes kayaking in any sea conditions possible. This company also offers just about any surf-related activity you can imagine on the North Shore in addition to kayaking. ✉ *62-595 Kamehameha Hwy., Haleiwa* ☎ *800/899–7873* ⊕ *www.surfnsea.com* 🛒 *From $60 for a full-day rental.*

KAYAKING TO THE MOKES

The Mokulua Islands—commonly referred to as The Mokes—are two islets off Lanikai Beach. The larger of the islands, Moku Nui, is a perfect kayaking destination and a popular place for picnics. The islands are state-protected bird sanctuaries, and sometimes you can catch a glimpse of one of the 11 different kinds of seabirds that nest there. Some outfitters offer guided tours. But since the water between the islets and Lanikai is typically calm and as it would be impossible to miss them, spend your money on sunscreen and snacks instead, and enjoy the paddle.

Twogood Kayaks Hawaii. The outfitter offers kayak rentals (single or double), lessons, and guided tours. Guides are trained in the history, geology, and birds of the area. Fully guided kayak excursions are either 2½ or 5 hours and include lunch, snorkeling gear, and transportation to and from Waikiki. For those who want to create their own itinerary, owner Bob Twogood also offers custom "Elite" tours. ✉ *134B Hamakua Dr., Kailua* ☎ *808/262–5656* ⊕ *www.twogoodkayaks.com* ✉ *Rentals from $60, tours from $115.*

SCUBA DIVING

Not all of Hawaii's beauty is above water. What lurks below can be just as magnificent.

Although snorkeling provides adequate access to this underwater world, nothing gives you the freedom—or depth, quite literally—as scuba.

The diving on Oahu is comparable with any you might do in the tropics, but its uniqueness comes from the isolated environment of the Islands. There are literally hundreds of species of fish and marine life that you can find only in this chain. In fact, about 25% of Hawaii's marine life can be seen here only—nowhere else in the world. Adding to the singularity of diving off Oahu is the human history of the region. Military activities and tragedies of the 20th century filled the waters surrounding Oahu with wreckage that the ocean creatures have since turned into their homes.

Although instructors certified to license you in scuba are plentiful in the Islands, we suggest that you get your PADI certification before coming, as a week of classes may be a bit of a commitment on a short vacation. Expect to pay around $100 for a two-tank boat dive (provided that you are certified). ■TIP➜ You can go on short, shallow introductory dives without the certification, but the best dives require it and cost a bit more.

8

BEST SPOTS

Hanauma Bay Nature Preserve. On Oahu's southeast shore, about 30 minutes drive east of Waikiki, Hanauma Bay Nature Preserve is home to more than 250 different species of fish, of which a quarter can be found nowhere else in the world. This has made this volcanic crater bay one of the most popular dive sites in the state. It's a long walk from the parking lot to the beach—even longer lugging equipment—so consider hooking up with a licensed dive-tour operator. Preservation efforts have aided the bay's delicate ecosystem, so expect to see various butterfly fish, surgeonfish, tangs, parrot fish, and endangered Hawaiian sea turtles. ✉ *7455 Kalanianaole Hwy., Hawaii Kai* ☎ *808/396–4229* $7.50 per person and $1 parking.

Hundred Foot Hole. Once an ancient Hawaiian fishing ground reserved for royalty, the Hundred Foot Hole is a cluster of volcanic boulders that have created ledges, caves, and a large open-ended cavern perfect for diving. Accessible from shore, this spot near Diamond Head attracts octopus, manta rays, and the occasional white-tip shark. ✉ *Off Diamond Head, Honolulu.*

Mahi Waianae. Hawaii's waters are littered with shipwrecks, but one of the most intact and accessible is the *Mahi Waianae,* a 165-foot mine-sweeper that was sunk in 1982 off the Waianae Coast. It lies upright in about 90 feet of calm and clear water, encrusted in coral and patrolled by white spotted eagle rays and millet seed butterfly fish. The wreck serves as an artificial reef for such Hawaii aquatic residents as blue-striped snappers, puffer fish, lionfish, moray eels, and octopus. Visibility averages about 100 feet, making this one of the most popular dives on the island. ⊠ *Waianae.*

Maunalua Bay. The bay stretches about 7 miles, from Portlock Point to Black Point on Oahu's southeastern shore. Teeming with marine life, this spot has several accessible dive sites of varying difficulty. The shallow-water Turtle Canyon is home to endangered Hawaiian green sea turtles. Fantasy Reef is another shallow dive with three plateaus of volcanic rock lined with coral that is home to fish, eels, and sea turtles. In about 85 feet of water, *Baby Barge* is an easy-to-penetrate sunken vessel encrusted in coral. An advanced dive, the wreck of a Vought F4U Corsair gives you a close-up look at garden eels and stingrays. ⊠ *Southeast Oahu.*

Sharks Cove. Oahu's best shore dive is accessible only during the summer months. Sharks Cove, on Oahu's North Shore, churns with monster surf during the winter, making this popular snorkeling and diving spot extremely dangerous. In summer, the cavernous lava tubes and tunnels are great for both novices and experienced divers. Some dive-tour companies offer round-trip transportation from Waikiki. ⊠ *Haleiwa.*

Three Tables. A short walk from Sharks Cove is Three Tables, named for a trio of flat rocks running perpendicular to shore. There are lava tubes to the right of these rocks that break the surface and then extend out about 50 feet. Although this area isn't as active as Sharks Cove, you can still spot octopus, moray eels, parrot fish, green sea turtles, and the occasional shark. ⊠ *Haleiwa.*

EQUIPMENT, LESSONS, AND TOURS

Aaron's Dive Shop. Whether you're diving for the first time or a master diver, this friendly and well-equipped dive shop caters to everyone. Take an "introductory" dive if you're not certified; get certified; or sign up for an offshore day or night dive excursion if you're experienced. In addition to organized group dives, the company's "Dive Concierge" can arrange private charters for those who want a completely customized experience. Snorkelers can go along on many dives as well. ⊠ *307 Hahani St., Kailua* ☎ *808/262–2333* ⊕ *aaronsdiveshop.com* ⊠ *From $120 for 2-tank dive.*

Surf 'N Sea. The North Shore headquarters for all things water-related is also great for diving. One interesting perk: upon request, their dive guides can shoot a video of you diving. It's hard to see facial expressions under the water, but it still might be fun for those who want to prove that they took the plunge. Two-tank shore dives are the most economical choice (prices for noncertified divers are higher), but the company also offers boat dives, and in the summer, night dives are available for only slightly more. ⊠ *62-595 Kamehameha Hwy., Haleiwa* ☎ *800/899–7873* ⊕ *www.surfnsea.com* ⊠ *From $100 (2-tank shore dives).*

Here in the warm waters off the coast of Oahu, there's a good chance you'll find yourself swimming alongside a green sea turtle.

SNORKELING

If you can swim, you can snorkel. And you don't need any formal training, either.

Snorkeling is a favorite pastime for both visitors and residents and can be done anywhere there's enough water to stick your face in. You can pick up a mask and snorkel at a corner ABC store for around $35, including fins, and get going on your own or pay up to $175 for a luxurious snorkel cruise including lunch and drinks. Each spot will have its great days depending on the weather and time of year, so consult with the purveyor of your gear for tips on where the best viewing is that day. Keep in mind that the North Shore should be attempted only when the waves are calm, namely in the summertime.

Make sure you put plenty of sunscreen on your back (or better yet, wear a T-shirt) because once you start gazing below, your head may not come back up for hours.

BEST SPOTS

Electric Beach. On the western side of the island, directly across from the electricity plant—hence the name—Electric Beach is a haven for tropical fish, making it a great snorkeling spot. The expulsion of hot water from the plant raises the temperature of the ocean, attracting Hawaiian green sea turtles, spotted moray eels, and spinner dolphins. Although visibility is not always the best, the crowds are small and the fish are guaranteed. ⌧ *Farrington Hwy., 1 mile west of Ko Olina Resort, Kapolei.*

Hanauma Bay Nature Preserve. What Waimea Bay is to surfing, Hanauma Bay in Southeast Oahu is to snorkeling. Easily the most popular snorkeling spot on the island, it's home to more than 250 different species of marine life. Due to the protection of the narrow mouth of the cove and the prodigious reef, you will be hard-pressed to find a place you will feel safer while snorkeling. ⊠ *7455 Kalanianaole Hwy., Honolulu* ☎ *808/396–4229 $7.50 per person and $1 parking.*

Queen's Surf Beach. On the edge of Waikiki, Queen's Surf is a marine reserve located between Kapahulu Groin and the Waikiki Aquarium. It's not as chock-full of fish as Hanauma Bay, but it has its share of colorful reef fish and the occasional Hawaiian green sea turtle. Just yards from shore, it's a great spot for an escape if you're stuck in Waikiki and have grown weary of watching the surfers. ⊠ *Kalakaua Ave., Honolulu.*

Sharks Cove. Great shallows protected by a huge reef make Sharks Cove on the North Shore a prime spot for snorkelers, even young ones, in the summer. You'll find a plethora of critters, from crabs to octopus, in water that's no more than waist deep. When the winter swells come, this area can turn treacherous. ⊠ *Kamehameha Hwy., across from Foodland, Haleiwa.*

EQUIPMENT AND TOURS

FAMILY **Hanauma Bay Rental Stand.** You can rent masks, fins, and snorkels here.
Fodor'sChoice The stand also has small lockers available right at the park that are large
★ enough for your valuables. Bring ID or car keys as deposit for rental. ⊠ *Hanauma Bay Nature Preserve, 7455 Kalanianaole Hwy., Hawaii Kai* ☎ *808/396–3483* 🖱 *Rentals from $9, lockers from $8.*

Hanauma Bay Snorkeling Excursions. If you're going to Hanauma Bay, you have three options: take a chance with limited parking spaces at the park, take TheBus, or contact Hanauma Bay Snorkeling Excursions. They provide transportation to and from Waikiki hotels, equipment, and instruction on how to use the equipment for a reasonable price that does not include the $7.50 park entrance fee. ☎ *808/306–3393* ⊕ *www.hanaumabaysnorkel.com* 🖱 *From $25.*

Snorkel Bob's. This place has all the stuff you'll need—and more—to make your water adventures more enjoyable. Bob makes his own gear and is active in protecting reef fish species. Feel free to ask the staff about good snorkeling spots, as the best ones can vary with weather and the seasons. You can either rent or buy gear (and reserve it in advance online). ⊠ *700 Kapahulu Ave., Kapahulu* ☎ *808/735–7944, 800/262–7725* ⊕ *www.snorkelbob.com* 🖱 *Rentals from $38 per wk.*

SUBMARINE TOURS

Atlantis Submarines. This is the underwater adventure for the unadventurous. Not fond of swimming, but want to see what you've been missing? Board this high-tech 64-passenger vessel for a ride past shipwrecks, turtle breeding grounds, and coral reefs. The tours, which depart from the pier at the Hilton Hawaiian Village, are available in several languages.

DID YOU KNOW?

Sharks Cove is a wonderful place for young snorkelers to spend time exploring the ocean's bottom in shallow waters, as the area is protected by a huge reef just offshore.

A smaller 48-passenger semisubmersible boat with underwater viewing windows is a bit cheaper than the submarine trip. (Discounts are available if booked online.) ✉ *Hilton Hawaiian Village Beach Resort & Spa, 2005 Kalia Rd., Honolulu* ☎ *808/973–9800, 800/381–0237 for reservations* ⊕ *www.atlantisadventures.com* ⊠ *From $119.*

STAND-UP PADDLEBOARDING

From the lakes of Wisconsin to the coast of Lima, Peru, stand-up paddleboarding (or SUP, for short) is taking the sport of surfing to the most unexpected places. Still, the sport remains firmly rooted in the Hawaiian Islands.

Back in the 1960s, Waikiki beach boys would paddle out on their longboards using a modified canoe paddle. It was longer than a traditional paddle, enabling them to stand up and stroke. It was easier this way to survey the ocean and snap photos of tourists learning how to surf. Eventually it became a sport unto itself, with professional contests at world-class surf breaks and long-distance races across treacherous waters.

Stand-up paddleboarding is easy to learn—though riding waves takes some practice—and most outfitters on Oahu offer lessons for all skill levels starting at about $55. It's also a great workout; you can burn off yesterday's dinner buffet, strengthen your core, and experience the natural beauty of the island's coastlines all at once. Once you're ready to head out on your own, half-day rentals start at $50.

If you're looking to learn, go where there's already a SUP presence. Avoid popular surf breaks, unless you're an experienced stand-up paddle surfer, and be wary of ocean and wind conditions. You'll want to find a spot with calm waters, easy access in and out of the ocean, and a friendly crowd that doesn't mind the occasional stand-up paddleboarder.

BEST SPOTS

Ala Moana Beach Park. About a mile west of Waikiki, Ala Moana is the most SUP-friendly spot on the island. In fact, the state installed a series of buoys in the flat-water lagoon to separate stand-up paddlers and swimmers. There are no waves here, making it a great spot to learn, but beware of strong trade winds, which can push you into the reef.

Anahulu Stream. Outfitters on the North Shore like to take SUP beginners to Anahulu Stream, which empties into Waialua Bay near the Haleiwa Boat Harbor. This area is calm and protected from winds, plus there's parking at the harbor, and surf shops nearby rent boards.

Waikiki. There are a number of outfitters on Oahu's South Shore that take beginners into the waters off Waikiki. **Canoes**, the surf break fronting the Duke Kahanamoku statue, and the channels between breaks are often suitable for people learning how to maneuver their boards in not-so-flat conditions. But south swells here can be deceptively menacing, and ocean conditions can change quickly. Check with lifeguards before paddling out and be mindful of other surfers in the water.

White Plains. If you've got a car with racks, you might want to venture to White Plains, a fairly uncrowded beach about 27 miles west of Waikiki. It's a long, sandy beach with lots of breaks, and plenty of room for everyone. There are lifeguards, restrooms, and lots of parking, making this a great spot for beginners and those just getting comfortable in small waves.

EQUIPMENT AND LESSONS

Hans Hedemann Surf School. Get professional instruction in stand-up paddleboarding right in Waikiki, where the sport originated. This school offers group lessons, semiprivate lessons, and private training. Lessons are also offered through locations at the Park Shore Hotel in Waikiki and Turtle Bay Resort in Kahuku. ⊠ *Park Shore Waikiki, 2586 Kalakaua Ave., Honolulu* ☎ *808/924–7778, 808/447–6755* ⊕ *www. hhsurf.com* ⊠ *From $75.*

FAMILY **Hawaiian Watersports.** Paddle off the shore of picturesque Kailua Beach. This safety-conscious outfitter offers both equipment rentals and 90-minute and 3-hour group or individual lessons. A one-stop shop for water sports, they also offer kiteboarding, surfing, and windsurfing lessons as well as kayak tours and equipment rentals. Discounts are available online if you book ahead. ⊠ *171 Hamakua Dr., Kailua* ☎ *808/262–5483* ⊕ *www.hawaiianwatersports.com* ⊠ *Rentals from $29, lessons from $74.*

Paddle Core Fitness. Paddling is a way of life for Reid Inouye, who now shares his passion for the sport with students. (He's also the publisher of *Standup Paddle Magazine.*) His company offers introductory classes as well as fitness programs for serious paddlers. Lessons and workout programs are held in the flat waters of Ala Moana Beach, where there's a designated area for paddling, and you can have either group or private lessons. ⊠ *Ala Moana Beach Park, Ala Moana Blvd., Ala Moana* ☎ *808/200–0574* ⊕ *www.paddlecorefitness.com* ⊠ *Workout programs from $25, lessons from $75.*

Rainbow Watersports Adventures. When you spot this company's colorful Rainbow Watersports van at the bay near Haleiwa Beach Park, you'll know you're in the right place. You can get a two-hour private or group lesson on Oahu's North Shore. All lessons are held in a spot popular with the resident green sea turtles. The company also offers a 3½-hour coastal eco-adventure trip including snorkeling and lunch. Their Twilight Glow Paddle lets you glide through calm waters illuminated by lights mounted to your board. ⊠ *Haleiwa Beach Park, Kamehameha Hwy., Haleiwa* ☎ *800/470–4964, 808/372–9304* ⊕ *www.rainbowwatersports.com* ⊠ *Lessons from $69.*

FAMILY **Surf 'N Sea.** With stand-up paddleboarding lessons for every skill level, Surf 'N Sea is a great place to start. Beginners can take the introductory lesson to learn proper paddling technique. A one-hour session focuses on honing your skills. More advanced paddlers can book surf trips that take you out to several North Shore breaks. ⊠ *62-595 Kamehameha Hwy., Haleiwa* ☎ *808/637–3008, 800/899–7873* ⊕ *www.surfnsea.com* ⊠ *Rentals from $20; lessons from $55.*

SURFING

Perhaps no word is more associated with Hawaii than surfing. Every year the best of the best gather on Oahu's North Shore to compete in their version of the Super Bowl: the prestigious Vans Triple Crown of Surfing. The pros dominate the waves for a month, but the rest of the year belongs to folks just trying to have fun.

Oahu is unique because it has so many famous spots: Banzai Pipeline, Waimea Bay, Kaiser Bowls, and Sunset Beach. These spots, however, require experience. Nonetheless, with most dependable sets and access to lessons, Waikiki is still a great place for beginners to learn or for novice surfers to catch predictable waves. Group lessons on Waikiki Beach start at $50, but if you really want to fine-tune your skills, you can pay up to $500 for a daylong private outing with a former pro.

The island also has miles of coastline with surf spots that are perfect for everyday surfers. But remember this surfer's credo: when in doubt, don't go out. If you're unsure about conditions, stay on the beach and talk to locals to get more info about surf breaks before trying yourself.

⚠ **If you don't want to run the risk of a confrontation with local surfers, who can be very territorial about their favorite breaks, try some of the alternate spots listed below. They may not have the name recognition, but the waves can be just as great.**

BEST SPOTS

Makaha Beach Park. If you like to ride waves, try Makaha Beach on Oahu's west side. It has legendary, interminable rights that allow riders to perform all manner of stunts: from six-man canoes with everyone doing headstands to Bullyboards (oversize bodyboards) with whole families along for the ride. Mainly known as a longboarding spot, it's predominantly local but respectful to outsiders. Use caution in winter, as the surf can get huge. It's not called Makaha—which means "fierce"—for nothing. ✉ *84-369 Farrington Hwy., Waianae.*

Sunset Beach. If you want to impress your surfing buddies back home, catch a wave at the famous Sunset Beach on Oahu's North Shore. Two of the more manageable breaks are **Kammie Land** (or Kammie's) and **Sunset Point.** For the daring, Sunset is part of the Vans Triple Crown of Surfing for a reason. Thick waves and long rides await, but you're going to want to have a thick board and a thicker skull. Surf etiquette here is a must, as it's mostly local. ✉ *59-104 Kamehameha Hwy., 1 mile north of Ehukai Beach Park, Haleiwa.*

Ulukou Beach. In Waikiki you can paddle out to **Populars**, a break at Ulukou Beach. Nice and easy, Populars—or Pops—never breaks too hard and is friendly to both newbies and veterans. It's one of the best places to surf during pumping south swells, as this thick wave breaks in open ocean, making it more rideable. The only downside

This surfer is doing a stellar job of riding the infamous Banzai Pipeline on Oahu's North Shore.

is the long paddle out to the break from Kuhio Beach, but that keeps the crowds manageable. ⊠ *Waikiki Beach, in front of the Sheraton Waikiki hotel, Honolulu.*

White Plains Beach. Known among locals as "mini Waikiki," the surf at White Plains breaks in numerous spots, preventing the logjams that are inevitable at many of Oahu's more popular spots. It's a great break for novice to intermediate surfers, though you do have to keep a lookout for wayward boards. From the H1, take the Makakilo exit. ⊠ *Off H1, Kapolei.*

EQUIPMENT AND LESSONS

Aloha Beach Services. It may sound like a cliché, but there's no better way to learn to surf than from a beach boy in Waikiki. And there's no one better than Harry "Didi" Robello, a second-generation beach boy and owner of Aloha Beach Services. Learn to surf in an hour-long group lesson, a semiprivate lesson, or with just you and an instructor. You can also rent a board here. ⊠ *2365 Kalakaua Ave., on beach near Moana Surfrider, Waikiki* ☎ *808/922–3111* ⊕ *www.alohabeachservices.com* ⊡ *Lessons from $50, board rentals from $20.*

Faith Surf School. Professional surfer Tony Moniz started his own surf school in 2000, and since then he and his wife, Tammy, have helped thousands of people catch their first waves in Waikiki. The 90-minute group lessons include all equipment and are the cheapest option. You can pay more (sometimes a lot more) for semiprivate lessons with up

SURF SMART

A few things to remember when surfing in Oahu:

■ The waves switch with the seasons—they're big in the south in summer and loom large in the north in winter. If you're not experienced, it's best to go where the waves are small. There will be smaller crowds, and your chances of injury will dramatically decrease.

■ Always wear a leash. It may not look the coolest, but when your board gets swept away from you

and you're swimming a half mile after it, you'll remember this advice.

■ Watch where you're going. Take a few minutes and scan the surf from the shore. Observe how big it is, where it's breaking, and how quickly the sets are coming. This will allow you to get in and out more easily and to spend more time riding waves and less time paddling.

■ Ask a local before going out: they're your best bet for specifics about surf breaks.

to three people or for private lessons. You can also book an all-day surf tour with Moniz, riding waves with him at his favorite breaks. ⊠ *Outrigger Waikiki Beach Resort, 2335 Kalakua Ave., Waikiki* ☎ *808/931–6262* ⊕ *www.faithsurfschool.com* ⊠ *Lessons from $65; board rental from $20.*

Hans Hedemann Surf School. Hans Hedemann spent 17 years on the professional surfing circuit. He and his staff offer surfing, bodysurfing, and stand-up paddleboarding instruction, multiday intensive surf camps, and fine-tuning courses with Hedemann himself. Two-hour group lessons are the cheapest option, but private lessons are also available. There are also locations at Turtle Bay Resort in Kahuku and at Kahala Hotel & Resort in Kahala. ⊠ *Park Shore Waiki, 2586 Kalakaua Ave., Waikiki* ☎ *808/924–7778 for Park Shore Waikiki, 808/447–6755 for Turtle Bay Resort* ⊕ *www.hhsurf.com* ⊠ *From $78.*

FAMILY **Hawaiian Water Sports.** Although the shop is located in Kailua, this jack-of-all-trades outfitter conducts surf lessons on storied Waikiki Beach. Choose from a 1½- or 3-hour group or private lesson. There are discounts if you book online in advance. This safety-conscious company also offers windsurfing, stand-up paddleboarding, kayaking, and kitesurfing lessons and equipment rental. ⊠ *171 Hamakua Dr., Kailua* ☎ *808/262–5483* ⊕ *www.hawaiianwatersports.com* ⊠ *Group lessons from $15.*

Surf 'N Sea. This is a one-stop shop for surfers (and other water-sports enthusiasts) on the North Shore. Rent a short or long board by the hour or for a full day. Two-hour group lessons are offered, as well as surf safaris for experienced surfers, which can last between four and five hours. ⊠ *62-595 Kamehameha Hwy., Haleiwa* ☎ *800/899–7873* ⊕ *www.surfnsea.com* ⊠ *Lessons from $85, rentals from $5 per hr.*

WHALE-WATCHING

December is marked by the arrival of snow in much of America, but in Hawaii it marks the return of the humpback whale. These migrating behemoths move south from their North Pacific homes during the winter months for courtship and calving, and they put on quite a show. Watching males and females alike throwing themselves out of the ocean and into the sunset awes even the saltiest of sailors. Newborn calves riding gently next to their 2-ton mothers will stir you to your core. These gentle giants can be seen from the shore as they make a splash, but there is nothing like having your boat rocking beneath you in the wake of a whale's breach.

FAMILY **Atlantis Majestic Cruises.** The 150-foot cruise vessel *Majestic* bills itself as the smoothest whale-watching tour on Oahu and guarantees a whale sighting. Because of the boat's size—it has three decks—you can choose from indoor or outdoor viewing while listening to Hawaiian music and an onboard naturalist who provides information as you search for the leviathans. Included among the offerings are 2½-hour lunch cruises. Departures are from the historic Aloha Tower Marketplace at Pier 6. Transportation from Waikiki can be arranged. ■TIP→ Check-in begins 30 minutes before departure. Arrive early to get a table near a window for the best views while you dine. ⊠ *Aloha Tower Marketplace, 1 Aloha Tower Dr., Pier 6, Downtown* ☎ *800/381–0237* ⊕ *www.atlantisadventures.com* ⊠ *From $69.*

Wild Side Specialty Tours. Boasting a marine-biologist/naturalist crew, this company takes you to undisturbed snorkeling areas. Along the way you may see dolphins and turtles. The company promises a sighting of migrating whales year-round on some itineraries. Tours may depart as early as 8 am from Waianae, so it's important to plan ahead. The three-hour deluxe wildlife tour is the most popular option. ⊠ *Waianae Boat Harbor, 85-471 Farrington Hwy., Waianae* ☎ *808/306–7273* ⊕ *www.sailhawaii.com* ⊠ *From $175.*

8

WINDSURFING AND KITEBOARDING

Those who call windsurfing and kiteboarding cheating because they require no paddling have never tried hanging on to a sail or kite. It will turn your arms to spaghetti quicker than paddling ever could, and the speeds you generate earn these sports the label of "extreme."

Windsurfing was born here in the Islands. For amateurs, the windward side is best because the onshore breezes will bring you back to land even if you're not a pro. The newer sport of kiteboarding is tougher but more exhilarating, as the kite will sometimes take you in the air for hundreds of feet. ■TIP→ Recent changes to local laws restrict lessons on the beach, so outfitters offering lessons are few and far between.

Hawaiian Water Sports. Learn to kiteboard, windsurf, kayak, surf, or ride a stand-up paddleboard with this multifaceted outfitter. This is the only shop to offer kiteboarding and windsurfing lessons on Oahu, and the location of your lessons—off Kailua Beach—is one of the best and most beautiful on the island. The company also offers windsurfing, stand-up paddleboard, surf and boogie board, snorkeling, and kayak equipment rentals. (For experienced kitesurfers, kitesurfing equipment rental is available.) You'll get a discount by booking your rental or lessons online in advance. ⊠ *171 Hamakua Dr., Kailua* ☎ *808/262–5483* ⊕ *www.hawaiianwatersports.com* ✉ *Group lessons from $120, equipment rental from $100.*

EQUIPMENT AND LESSONS

Naish Hawaii. Although they don't offer lessons, Naish Hawaii offers windsurfing and kiteboarding equipment rentals for those who are already proficient. You can rent for a half day or for 24 hours. The company also rents stand-up paddleboards by the half day or for 24 hours. ⊠ *155A Hamakua Dr., Kailua* ☎ *808/262–6068* ⊕ *www. naish.com* ✉ *Windsurfers from $55, kiteboards from $25, paddleboards from $45.*

GOLF, HIKING, AND OUTDOOR ACTIVITIES

Updated by Cheryl Crabtree

Although much is written about the water surrounding this little rock known as Oahu, there is as much to be said for the rock itself. It's a wonder of nature, thrust from the ocean floor thousands of millennia ago by a volcanic hot spot that is still spitting out islands today. Hawaii is the most remote island chain on Earth, and there are creatures and plants that can be seen here and nowhere else. And there are dozens of ways for you to check them all out.

From the air you can peer down into nooks and crannies in the mountains—where cars cannot reach and hikers don't dare. Whether flitting here and there amid a helicopter's rush and roar, or sailing by in the silence of a glider's reverie, you glimpse sights that few have experienced. Or, if you would rather, take a step back in time and take off from the waters of Keehi Lagoon in a World War II–era seaplane. Follow the flight path flown by the Japanese Zeros as they attempted to destroy Pearl Harbor and the American spirit.

Would you prefer the ground tour, where you and gravity are no longer at odds? Oahu is covered in hiking trails that vary from tropical rain forest to arid desert. Even when in the bustling city of Honolulu, you are but minutes from hidden waterfalls and bamboo forests. Out west you can wander a dusty path that has long since given up its ability to accommodate cars but is perfect for hikers. You can splash in tidal pools, admire sea arches, and gape at caves opened by the rock slides that closed the road. You can camp out on many of these treks and beaches.

If somewhat less rugged and less vigorous exploration is more your style, how about letting horses do your dirty work? You can ride them on the beaches and in the valleys, checking out ancient holy sites, movie sets, and brilliant vistas.

Finally, there is the ancient sport of Scotland. Why merely hike into the rain forest when you can slice a 280-yard drive through it and then

Take a helicopter tour for a unique perspective of the island.

hunt for your Titleist in the bushy leaves instead? Almost 40 courses cover this tiny expanse, ranging from the target jungle golf of the Royal Hawaiian Golf Club to the pro-style links of Turtle Bay. There is no off-season in the tropics, and no one here knows your real handicap.

AERIAL TOURS

Taking an aerial tour of the Islands opens up a world of perspective. Look down from the sky at the outline of the USS *Arizona,* where it lies in its final resting place below the waters of Pearl Harbor, or get a glimpse of the vast carved expanse of a volcanic crater—here are views only seen by an "eye in the sky." Don't forget your camera.

Blue Hawaiian Helicopters. This company stakes its claim as Hawaii's largest helicopter company, with tours on all the major Islands and more than two-dozen choppers in its fleet. The 45-minute Oahu tour seats up to six passengers and includes narration from your friendly pilot along with sweeping views of Waikiki, the beautiful Windward Coast, and the North Shore. If you like to see the world from above or are just pinched for time and want to get a quick overview of the whole island without renting a car, this is the way to go. Discounts are available if you book online in advance. ⊠ *99 Kaulele Pl., Honolulu* ☎ *808/831–8800, 800/745–2583* ⊕ *www.bluehawaiian.com* 🖃 *From $259.*

Island Seaplane Service. Harking back to the days of the earliest air visitors to Hawaii, the seaplane has always had a special spot in island lore. The only seaplane service still operating in Hawaii takes off from Keehi Lagoon. (It was featured in the film *50 First Dates.*) Flight options are either a twenty-minute or half-hour southern and eastern Oahu shoreline tour or an hour-long island circle tour. Groups can opt for a catered dinner on a floating dock in the lagoon. The Pan Am Clipper may be gone, but you can revisit the experience with this company. ⊠ *85 Lagoon Dr., Airport Area* ☎ *808/836–6273* ⊕ *www. islandseaplane.com* ✉ *From $99.*

Makani Kai Helicopters. This may be the best—if not the only—way to see the beautiful Sacred Falls on the windward side of the island, as the park around the falls was closed to hikers after a deadly 1999 rock slide. Makani Kai flies the helicopter over the pristine waterfall to show you the once-favorite trail that leads to it. Tours can last either a half hour, 45 minutes, or a full hour. Or the more adventurous can book the 50-minute Doors Off tour in the MD-500, the iconic helicopter from the *Magnum PI* TV series. Customized private charters are available for up to six passengers. ⊠ *130 Iolana Pl., Honolulu* ☎ *808/834–5813, 877/255–8532* ⊕ *www.makanikai.com* ✉ *From $170.*

The Original Glider Rides. "Mr. Bill" has been offering piloted glider (sailplane) rides over the northwest end of Oahu's North Shore since 1970. Choose from piloted scenic rides for one or two passengers in sleek, bubble-top, motorless aircraft with aerial views of mountains, shoreline, coral pools, windsurfing sails, and, in winter, humpback whales. Seeking more thrills? You can also take a more acrobatic ride or take control yourself in a mini lesson. Flights run 15–60 minutes long and depart continuously, daily 10–5. Reservations are requested. ⊠ *Dillingham Airfield, 69-132 Farrington Hwy., Waialua* ☎ *808/637–0207* ⊕ *www. honolulusoaring.com* ✉ *From $85.*

Paradise Helicopters. A certified Hawaii Ecotourism Association operator, Paradise offers tours on several islands. On Oahu, the tours depart from two helipads: Kalaeloa (at the Ko Olina resorts on the west side) and Turtle Bay Resort on the North Shore. Kalaeloa options range from a one-hour scenic tour over Diamond Head to a two-hour island circle (daytime and sunset) to specialized trips that focus on WW II history. Turtle Bay choices include several one- to one-and-a half-hour North Shore adventures. ☎ *808/969–7392* ⊕ *paradisecopters.com* ✉ *From $189.*

BIKING

Oahu's coastal roads are flat, well-paved, and, unfortunately, awash in vehicular traffic. Frankly, biking is no fun in either Waikiki or Honolulu, but things are a bit better outside the city. Your best bet is to cycle early in the morning or get off the road to check out the island's bike trails.

BEST SPOTS

Kaena Point Trail. If going up a mountain is not your idea of mountain biking, then perhaps Kaena Point Trail is better suited to your needs. A longer ride (10 miles) but much flatter, this trail takes you oceanside around the westernmost point on the island. You pass sea arches and a mini-blowhole, then finish up with some motocross jumps right before you turn around. There's no drinking water available on this ride, but

Kaena Point in the northwestern corner of the island is windy and dry, and it's where rare, native Hawaiian plants grow.

at least at the end you have the Yokohama Beach showers to cool you off. ✉ *69-385 Farrington Hwy., Waialua.*

Maunawili Demonstration Trail. Locals favor biking this 10-mile trail that has breathtaking views as you descend into Waimanalo. There are many flat portions but also some uneven ground to negotiate unless you're willing to carry your bike for small stretches. The main trailhead is at the Pali Lookout on the blacktop of Old Pali Rd. ✉ *Nuuanu Pali Dr., at Pali Lookout, Honolulu.*

North Shore Bike Park. Wind around 12 miles of trails plus seven professionally designed, single-track loops at the North Shore's Turtle Bay Resort. Trails lead to protected wildlife areas and ancient Hawaiian sites, a WW II pillbox, a giant banyan tree, and secluded beaches and bays. Purchase day passes at the Hele Huli Adventure Center. ✉ *57-091 Kuilima Dr., Kahuku* ☎ 808/293-6024 ⊕ *northshoreexplorers. com/northshorebikepark* 🎫 *Day pass $10.*

West Kaunala Trail. Biking the North Shore may sound like a great idea, but the two-lane road is narrow and traffic-heavy. We suggest you try the West Kaunala Trail. It's a little tricky at times, but with the rain-forest surroundings and beautiful ocean vistas you'll hardly notice your legs burning on the steep ascent at the end. It's about 5½ miles round-trip. Bring water because there's none on the trail unless it comes from the sky. ✉ *59-777 Pupukea Rd., at the end of Pupukea Rd., Haleiwa* ✣ *Pupukea Rd. is next to Foodland, the only grocery store on the North Shore.*

9

EQUIPMENT AND TOURS

Bike Hawaii. Whether it's road tours of the North Shore or muddy off-road adventures in the Koolau Mountains, this is the company to get you there. There are combination packages that pair cycling with snorkeling, sailing, or hiking. They also offer guided hikes combined with kayaking, sailing, and/or snorkeling. The company offers both three-hour road tours and a six-hour mountain-biking foray. Tours include equipment, transportation, and water; some also include lunch. The company will pick you up at central locations in Waikiki. ☎ *808/734–4214* ⊕ *www.bikehawaii.com* ✉ *From $60.*

Biki. In late 2017 nonprofit Bikeshare Hawaii launched a Honolulu bike-sharing system equipped with 1,000 bicycles at 100 solar-powered, self-service stops between Chinatown and Diamond Head. The comfortable, easy-to-maneuver bikes are designed to accommodate riders of all sizes. The procedure is easy: pay at the kiosk, hop on the bike, and dock it at the kiosk closest to your destination. ✉ *Honolulu* ☎ *888/340–2454* ⊕ *gobiki.org* ✉ *$3.50 single ride, $20 for 300 minutes, $15 for month of unlimited 30-minute rides, $30 for month of unlimited 60-minute rides.*

Hawaii Bicycling League. Don't want to go cycling by yourself? Visit this shop online, and you can get connected with rides and contests. ☎ *808/735–5756* ⊕ *www.hbl.org.*

North Shore Explorers. Rent cruisers, fat tire bikes, mountain bikes, or mopeds at this outfitter's three North Shore and Laie locations: Hele Huli Adventure Center at Turtle Bay Resort, Polynesian Cultural Center, and the Courtyard Marriott hotel. The company also runs an array of guided adventure tours, plus disc and foot golf, tennis, and mountain bike lessons. ✉ *Kahuku* ☎ *808/293–6024* ⊕ *northshoreexplorers.com* ✉ *bike rentals from $20 per hour.*

GOLF

Unlike on the other Hawaiian Islands, the majority of Oahu's golf courses are not associated with hotels and resorts. In fact, of the island's three dozen–plus courses, only five are tied to lodging; none is in the tourist hub of Waikiki.

Municipal courses are a good choice for budget-conscious golfers but are more crowded and are not always maintained to the same standard as the private courses. Your best bet is to call the day you want to play and inquire about walk-on availability. Greens fees are standard at city courses: walking rate $66 for visitors, riding cart $20 for 18 holes, pull carts $4.

Greens fees listed here are the highest course rates per round on weekdays and weekends for U.S. residents. (Some courses charge non–U.S. residents higher prices.) Discounts are often available for resort guests and for those who book tee times online. Twilight fees are usually offered; call individual courses for information.

CLOSE UP

Camping in Oahu

If you are looking for a more rugged escape from the resorts of Waikiki, consider pitching a tent on the beach or in the mountains, where you have easy access to hiking trails and the island's natural features.
■ **TIP→ Camping here is not as highly organized as it is on the mainland: expect few marked sites, scarce electrical outlets, and nary a ranger station.** What you find instead are unblemished spots in the woods and on the beach. Both the Division of Forestry and Wildlife and the State Park Service offer recreation areas at which you can camp, both

in the mountains and on the beach. All state park and Division of Forestry and Wildlife campsites can now be reserved up to a year in advance online at ⊕ *www.hawaiistateparks.org.* The fee is $18 per night per campsite for up to six people. As for the county spots, there are 17 currently available and all require a permit. The good news is that the permits are only $32 for three nights over the weekend or $52 for five days at the site. They are also easy to obtain, as long as you're not trying to go on a holiday weekend. Visit ⊕ *camping.honolulu. gov* for more information.

HONOLULU

There is only one spot to golf near Waikiki and it is the busiest course in America. Although not a very imaginative layout, the price is right and the advantage of walking from your hotel to the course is not to be overlooked. Unless you make a reservation, make sure you bring a newspaper because it will be a little while before you tee off.

Ala Wai Municipal Golf Course. Just across the Ala Wai Canal from Waikiki, this municipal golf course is said to host more rounds than any other U.S. course—up to 500 per day. Not that it's a great course, just really convenient. The best bet for a visitor is to show up and expect to wait at least an hour or call up to three days in advance for a tee-time reservation. When reserving, the automated system will ask for an ID code—simply enter your phone number and give that number and your tee time when checking in. The course itself is flat; Robin Nelson did some redesign work in the 1990s, adding mounding, trees, and a lake. The Ala Wai Canal comes into play on several holes on the back nine, including the treacherous 18th. There's also an on-site restaurant and bar. ⊠ *404 Kapahulu Ave., Waikiki* ☎ *808/733–7387 for starter's office, 808/738–4652 for pro shop, 808/296–2000 for reservations only* ⊕ *www.honolulu.gov/des/golf/alawai.htm* ⛳ *$66* ⛳ *18 holes, 5861 yards, par 70.*

Moanalua Golf Club. Said to be (not without dispute) the oldest golf club west of the Rockies, this 9-holer is semiprivate, allowing public play except on weekend and holiday mornings. Near Pearl Harbor and nestled in the hardwoods, this course will remind you more of golf in Pennsylvania than in the tropics, but it offers the lowest greens fees in the area, and by the time you get here, you'll probably be over the whole palm tree theme anyway. The course is a bit quirky, but the final two holes, a par 3 off a cliff to a smallish tree-rimmed green and a par

9

TIPS FOR THE GREEN

Before you head out to the first tee, there are a few things you should know about golf in Hawaii:

■ All resort courses and many daily-fee courses provide rental clubs. In many cases, they're the latest lines from Titleist, Ping, Callaway, and the like. This is true for both men and women, as well as for left-handers, which means you don't have to schlep clubs across the Pacific.

■ Most courses offer deals varying from twilight deep-discount rates to frequent-visitor discounts, even for tourists. Ask questions when calling pro shops, and don't just accept the first quote—deals abound if you persist.

■ Pro shops at most courses are well stocked with balls, tees, and other accoutrements, so even if you bring your own bag, it needn't weigh a ton.

■ Come spikeless—very few Hawaii courses still permit metal spikes.

■ Sunscreen. Buy it, apply it (minimum 30 SPF). The subtropical rays of the sun are intense, even in December.

■ Resort courses, in particular, offer more than the usual three sets of tees, sometimes four or five. So bite off as much or little challenge as you can chew. Tee it up from the tips and you'll end up playing a few 600-yard par 5s and see a few 250-yard forced carries.

■ In theory, you can play golf in Hawaii 365 days a year. But there's a reason the Hawaiian Islands are so green. Better to bring an umbrella and light jacket and not use them than not to bring them and get soaked.

■ Unless you play a muni or certain daily-fee courses, plan on taking a cart. Riding carts are mandatory at most courses and are included in greens fees.

4 with an approach to a green set snugly between stream and jungle, are classic. Although carts are not required, they are recommended, as this course is a bit steep in places. ⊠ *1250 Ala Aolani St., Salt Lake* ☎ *808/839–2411 for starter's office, 808/839–2311 for pro shop and clubhouse* ⌸ *$30–$45 for 9 holes; $45–$55 for 18 holes* 🏌 *9 holes, 2972 yards, par 36.*

SOUTHEAST OAHU

Prepare to keep your ball down on this windy corner of Oahu. You'll get beautiful ocean vistas, but you may need them to soothe you once your perfect drive gets blown 40 yards off course by a gusting trade wind.

Hawaii Kai Golf Course. The **Championship Golf Course** (William F. Bell, 1973) winds through a Honolulu suburb at the foot of Koko Crater. Homes (and the liability of a broken window) come into play on many holes, but they are offset by views of the nearby Pacific and a crafty routing of holes. With several lakes, lots of trees, and bunkers in all the wrong places, Hawaii Kai really is a "championship" golf course, especially when the trade winds howl. Greens fees for this course include mandatory cart. The **Executive Course** (1962), a par-54 track, is the first of only three courses in Hawaii built by Robert Trent Jones Sr. Although a few changes have been made to his original design, you can find the usual Jones attributes, including raised greens and lots of risk-reward options. You may walk or use a cart on this course for an additional fee. ⊠ *8902 Kalanianaole Hwy., Hawaii Kai* ☎ *808/395–2358* ⊕ *hawaiikaigolf.com* ⊠ *Championship Course $150, Executive Course $50* ⚑. *Championship Course: 18 holes, 6207 yards, par 72. Executive Course: 18 holes, 2196 yards, par 54.*

WINDWARD OAHU

Windward Oahu is what you expect when you think of golfing in the Islands. Lush, tropical foliage will surround you, with towering mountains framing one shot and the crystal-blue Pacific framing the next. Although it's a bit more expensive to golf on this side, and a good deal wetter, the memories and pictures you take on these courses will last a lifetime.

Koolau Golf Club. Koolau Golf Club is marketed as the toughest golf course in Hawaii and one of the most challenging in the country. Dick Nugent and Jack Tuthill (1992) routed 10 holes over jungle ravines that require at least a 110-yard carry. The par-4 18th may be the most difficult closing hole in golf. The tee shot from this hole's regular tees must carry 200 yards of ravine, 250 from the blue tees. The approach shot is back across the ravine, 200 yards to a well-bunkered green. Set at the windward base of the Koolau Mountains, the course is as much beauty as beast. Kaneohe Bay is visible from most holes, orchids and yellow ginger bloom, the shama thrush (Hawaii's best singer since Don Ho) chirps, and waterfalls flute down the sheer, green mountains above. The greens fee includes a (required) cart. ⊠ *45-550 Kionaole Rd., Kaneohe* ☎ *808/236–4653* ⊕ *www.koolaugolfclub.com* ⊠ *$155* ⚑. *18 holes, 7310 yards, par 72.*

9

Olomana Golf Links. Bob and Robert L. Baldock are the architects of record for this layout, but so much has changed since it opened in 1969 that they would recognize little of it. A turf specialist was brought in to improve fairways and greens, tees were rebuilt, new bunkers added, and mangroves cut back to make better use of natural wetlands. But what really puts Olomana on the map is that this is where wunderkind Michelle Wie learned the game. A cart is required at this course and is included in the greens fee. ⊠ *41-1801 Kalanianaole Hwy., Waimanalo* ☎ *808/259–7926* ⊕ *olomana.golf* ⊠ *$50 for 9 holes, $89 for 18 holes* ⚑. *18 holes, 6306 yards, par 72.*

Pali Golf Course. Panoramic views of the Koolau Mountains and Kaneohe Bay enhance the many challenges at this popular municipal course between Kaneohe and Kailua. ⊠ *45-050 Kamehameha Hwy., Kaneohe* ☎ *808/266–7612 starter's office, 808/262–2911 pro shop* ⊕ *www.honolulu.gov/des/golf/pali.html* ⊠ *$66* ⚑. *18 holes, 6524 yards, par 72.*

Fodor's Choice **Royal Hawaiian Golf Club.** In the cool, lush Maunawili Valley, Pete and
★ Perry Dye created what can only be called target jungle golf. In other words, the rough is usually dense jungle, and you may not hit a driver on three of the four par 5s, or several par 4s, including the perilous

18th that plays off a cliff to a narrow green protected by a creek. Mt. Olomana's twin peaks tower over the course. ■ TIP→ The back nine wanders deep into the valley, and includes an island green (par-3 11th) and perhaps the loveliest inland hole in Hawaii (par-4 12th). ⊠ 770 *Auloa Rd., at Luana Hills Rd., Kailua* ☎ *808/262–2139* ⊕ *royalhawaiiangc.com* ✉ *$160* ⚐ *18 holes, 5541 yards, par 72.*

NORTH SHORE

The North Shore has both the cheapest and the most expensive courses on the island. You can play nine holes in your bare feet, and you can chunk up the course played by both the LPGA and Champions Tour here, too. Don't try to go the barefoot route on the LPGA course, or the only course in the Islands you may be allowed on will be the Kahuku muni.

Kahuku Municipal Golf Course. The only true links course in Hawaii, this 9-hole municipal course is not for everyone. Maintenance is an ongoing issue, and in summer it can look a bit like the Serengeti. It's walking-only (a few pull-carts are available for rent); there's no pro shop, just a starter who sells lost-and-found balls; and the 19th hole is a soda machine and a covered picnic bench. And yet the course stretches out along the blue Pacific where surf crashes on the shore, the turf underfoot is spongy, sea mist drifts across the links, and wildflowers bloom in the rough. ⊠ *56-501 Kamehameha Hwy., Kahuku* ☎ *808/293–5842* ⊕ *www.honolulu.gov/des/golf/kahuku.html* ✉ *$19* ⚐ *9 holes, 2699 yds, par 35.*

Turtle Bay Resort & Spa. When the Lazarus of golf courses, the **Fazio Course** (George Fazio, 1971), rose from the dead in 2002, Turtle Bay on Oahu's rugged North Shore became a premier golf destination. Two holes had been plowed under when the **Palmer Course** (Arnold Palmer and Ed Seay, 1992) was built, while the other seven lay fallow, and the front nine remained open. Then new owners came along and re-created holes 13 and 14 using Fazio's original plans, and the Fazio became whole again. It's a terrific track with 90 bunkers. The gem at Turtle Bay, though, is the Palmer. The front nine is mostly open as it skirts Punahoolapa Marsh, a nature sanctuary, while the back nine plunges into the wetlands and winds along the coast. The short par-4 17th runs along the rocky shore, with a diabolical string of bunkers cutting diagonally across the fairway from tee to green. Carts are required for both courses and are included in the greens fee. ⊠ *57-049 Kuilima Dr., Kahuku* ☎ *808/293–8574* ⊕ *www.turtlebaygolf.com* ✉ *Fazio Course: $115 for 18 holes, $65 for 9 holes. Palmer Course: $165 for 18 holes, $95 for 9 holes* ⚐ *Fazio Course: 18 holes, 6600 yards, par 72. Palmer Course: 18 holes, 7200 yards, par 72.*

CENTRAL OAHU

Golf courses are densest here in Central Oahu, where plantations morphed into tract housing and golf courses were added to anchor communities. The vegetation is much sparser, but some of the best

The North Shore's Turtle Bay Resort attracts golfers who come for the prized Palmer Course.

greens around can be found here. Play early to avoid the hot afternoons, but if you can handle the heat, note that most courses offer substantial discounts for twilight hours.

Hawaii Country Club. Also known as Kunia—but not to be confused with Royal Kunia a few miles away—this course is in the middle of former sugarcane fields and dates to plantation times. Several par 4s are drivable, including the 9th and 18th holes. This is a fun course, but it's a bit rough around the edges. You can walk the course on weekdays only. ✉ *94-1211 Kunia Rd., Waipahu* ☎ *808/621–5654* 💲 *$50* 🏌 *18 holes, 5910 yards, par 71.*

Mililani Golf Course. Located on Oahu's central plain, Mililani is usually a few degrees cooler than downtown, 25 minutes away. The eucalyptus trees through which the course plays add to the cool factor, and stands of Norfolk pines give Mililani a "mainland course" feel. Bob and Robert L. Baldock (1966) make good use of an old irrigation ditch reminiscent of a Scottish burn. Carts are required and are included in the greens fee. ✉ *95-176 Kuahelani Ave., Mililani* ☎ *808/623–2222* ⊕ *www.mililanigolf.com* 💲 *$160* 🏌 *18 holes, 6274 yards, par 72.*

Pearl Country Club. Carved in the hillside high above Pearl Harbor, the 18 holes here are really two courses. The front nine rambles out along gently sloping terrain, while the back nine zigzags up and down a steeper portion of the slope as it rises into the Koolau Mountains. The views of Pearl Harbor are breathtaking. Carts are required and are included in the greens fee. ✉ *98-535 Kaonohi St., Aiea* ☎ *808/487–3802* ⊕ *www.pearlcc.com* 💲 *$55 for 9 holes, $150 for 18 holes* 🏌 *18 holes, 6232 yards, par 72.*

Royal Kunia Country Club. At one time, the PGA Tour considered buying the Royal Kunia Country Club and hosting the Sony Open here. It's that good. ■ TIP➔ **Every hole offers fabulous views from Diamond Head to Pearl Harbor to the nearby Waianae Mountains.** Robin Nelson's eye for natural sight lines and his dexterity with water features add to the visual pleasure. Carts are required and are included in the greens fee. ⊠ 94-1509 Anonui St., Waipahu ☎ 808/688–9222 ⊕ www.royalkuniacc.com ✉ $60 for 9 holes, $150 for 18 holes ⚑ 18 holes, 6507 yards, par 72.

Ted Makalena Golf Course. The flat layout of this bare-bones municipal course with Bermuda grass fairways appeals to all levels of players, but especially those just starting to learn the sport. ⊠ 93-059 Waipio Point Access Rd., Waipahu ☎ 808/675–6052 ⊕ www.honolulu.gov/des/golf/makalena.html ✉ $30 for 9 holes; $66 for 18 holes ⚑ 18 holes, 5976 yards, par 71.

Waikele Country Club. Outlet stores are not the only bargain at Waikele. The adjacent golf course is a daily-fee course that offers a private club–like atmosphere and a terrific Ted Robinson (1992) layout. Robinson's water features are less distinctive here but define the short par-4 4th hole, with a lake running down the left side of the fairway and guarding the green; and the par-3 17th, which plays across a lake. The par-4 18th is a terrific closing hole, with a lake lurking on the right side of the green. Carts are required and are included in the greens fee. ⊠ 94-200 Paioa Pl., Waipahu ☎ 808/676–9000 ⊕ www.golfwaikele.com ✉ $170 ⚑ 18 holes, 6261 yards, par 72.

WEST (LEEWARD) OAHU

On the leeward side of the mountains, shielded from the rains that drench the Kaneohe side, West Oahu is arid and sunny and has a unique kind of beauty. The Ewa area is dotted with golf courses and new development, so you'll have your pick of a number of different options—golfers generally choose courses in Ewa and Kapolei because they provide a totally different landscape from Waikiki or the North Shore. The resort courses on the west side are a long drive from town, but the beaches are magnificent and you can find deals if you're combining a room with a round or two on the greens.

Coral Creek Golf Course. On the Ewa Plain, 4 miles inland, Coral Creek is cut from ancient coral left from when this area was still underwater. Robin Nelson (1999) did some of his best work in making use of the coral—and of some dynamite, blasting out portions to create dramatic lakes and tee and green sites. They could just as easily call it Coral Cliffs, because of the 30- to 40-foot cliffs Nelson created. They include the par-3 10th green's grotto and waterfall, and the vertical drop-off on the right side of the par-4 18th green. An ancient creek meanders across the course, but there's not much water, just enough to be a babbling nuisance. Carts are required and are included in the greens fee. ⊠ 91-1111 Geiger Rd., Ewa Beach ☎ 808/441–4653 ⊕ www.coralcreekgolfhawaii.com ✉ $70 for 9 holes, $140 for 18 holes ⚑ 18 holes, 6347 yards, par 72.

Ewa Beach Golf Club. A private course open to the public, Ewa is one of the delightful products of the too-brief collaboration of Robin Nelson and Rodney Wright (1992). Trees are very much part of the character here, but there are also elements of links golf, such as a double green shared by the 2nd and 16th holes. Carts are required and are included in the greens fee. ✉ *91-050 Fort Weaver Rd., Ewa Beach* ☎ *808/689–6565* ⊕ *www.ewabeachgc.com* ✉ *$165* ♨ *18 holes, 5861 yards, par 72.*

Hawaii Prince Golf Course. Affiliated with the Hawaii Prince Hotel in Waikiki, the Hawaii Prince Golf Course (not to be confused with the Prince Course at Princeville, Kauai) has a links feel to it, and it is popular with local-charity fund-raiser golf tournaments. Arnold Palmer and Ed Seay (1991) took what had been flat, featureless sugarcane fields and sculpted 27 challenging, varied holes. Mounding breaks up the landscape, as do 10 lakes. Water comes into play on six holes of the A course, three of B, and seven of C. The most difficult combination is A and C (A and B from the forward tees). Carts are required and are included in the greens fee. ✉ *91-1200 Fort Weaver Rd., Ewa Beach* ☎ *808/944–4567* ⊕ *www.hawaiiprincegolf.com* ✉ *$87 for 9 holes, $170 for 18 holes* ♨ *A Course: 9 holes, 3138 yards, par 36. B Course: 9 holes, 3099 yards, par 36. C Course: 9 holes, 3076 yards, par 36.*

Kapolei Golf Course. This is a Ted Robinson water wonderland with waterfalls and four lakes—three so big they have names—coming into play on 10 holes. Set on rolling terrain, Kapolei is a serious golf course, especially when the wind blows. Carts are required and are included in the greens fee. ✉ *91-701 Farrington Hwy., Kapolei* ☎ *808/674–2227* ⊕ *www.kapoleigolf.com* ✉ *$185* ♨ *18 holes, 6586 yards, par 72.*

Ko Olina Golf Club. Hawaii's golden age of golf-course architecture came to Oahu when Ko Olina Golf Club opened in 1989. Ted Robinson, king of the water features, went splash-happy here, creating nine lakes that come into play on eight holes, including the par-3 12th, where you reach the tee by driving behind a Disney-like waterfall. Tactically, though, the most dramatic is the par-4 18th, where the approach is a minimum 120 yards across a lake to a two-tiered green guarded on the left by a cascading waterfall. Today Ko Olina has matured into one of Hawaii's top courses. You can niggle about routing issues—the first three holes play into the trade winds (and the morning sun), as do two consecutive par 5s on the back nine play—but Robinson does enough solid design to make those of passing concern. ■**TIP**➔ **The course provides free transportation from Waikiki hotels.** ✉ *92 1220 Aliinui Dr., Ko Olina* ☎ *808/676–5300* ⊕ *www.koolinagolf.com* ✉ *$115 for 9 holes, $225 for 18 holes* ♨ *18 holes, 6432 yards, par 72.*

Makaha Valley Country Club. This course (William F. Bell, 1968), known locally as Makaha East, is indeed a valley course, taking great advantage of the steep valley walls and natural terrain. The double-dogleg, downhill-uphill, par-5 18th is a doozy of a closer. Carts are required and are included in the greens fee. ✉ *84-627 Makaha Valley Rd., Waianae* ☎ *808/695–7111* ⊕ *www.pacificlinks.com/makahaeast* ✉ *$42 for 9 holes, $97 for 18 holes* ♨ *18 holes, 6260 yards, par 71.*

9

West Loch Municipal Golf Course. The best of Honolulu's municipal courses, this Robin Nelson (1991) design plays along Pearl Harbor's West Loch. In the process of building the course, wetlands were actually expanded, increasing bird habitat. ✉ *91-1126 Okupe St., Ewa Beach* ☎ *808/675–6076* ⊕ *www.honolulu.gov/des/golf/westloch.html* ⛳ *$66* 🏌️ *18 holes, 6335 yds, par 72.*

HIKING

The trails of Oahu cover a full spectrum of environments: desert walks through cactus, slippery paths through bamboo-filled rain forest, and scrambling rock climbs up ancient volcanic calderas. The only thing you won't find is an overnighter, as even the longest of hikes won't take you more than half a day. In addition to being short in length, many of the prime hikes are within 10 minutes of downtown Waikiki, meaning that you won't have to spend your whole day getting back to nature.

Hawaii State Department of Land and Natural Resources. Go to the website for information on all major hiking trails on Oahu. You can also obtain camping permits for state parks here. ✉ *1151 Punchbowl St., Room 310, Honolulu* ☎ *808/587–0300* ⊕ *dlnr.hawaii.gov/dsp/hiking/oahu.*

Na Ala Hele Trails and Access. Contact the Na Ala Hele ("Trails to Go On") folks for a free hiking-safety guide and trail information. The interactive website has maps and information about the current status of trails on all of the Islands. You can also stop in their office for free printed maps and information. ✉ *1151 Punchbowl St., Room 325, Downtown* ☎ *808/587–0166* ⊕ *hawaiitrails.hawaii.gov.*

BEST SPOTS

Aiea Loop Trail. This 4.8-mile loop begins and ends in the Keaiwa Heiau State Recreation Area, running along the ridge on the west side of Halawa Valley. It's a fairly easy hike that lasts about 2½ to 3 hours and brings many rewards, including views of the southern coastline of Oahu from Pearl Harbor and the Waianae Range to Honolulu and Diamond Head. Foresters replanted this area with various trees in the 1920s, so scents of lemon eucalyptus, pine, koa, and other trees enhance the trek. There's ample parking near the trailhed, close to restrooms and a picnic pavilion. ✉ *Aiea District Park, 99-350 Aiea Heights Dr., Aiea* ✛ *At the uper east corner of the park, at the top of Aiea Heights Rd.* ☎ *808/587–0300* ⊕ *dlnr.hawaii.gov/dsp/hiking/oahu/aiea-loop-trail.*

Diamond Head Crater. Every vacation has requirements that must be fulfilled, so that when your neighbors ask, you can say, "Yeah, did it." Climbing Diamond Head is high on that list of things to do on Oahu. It's a moderately easy hike if you're in good physical condition, but be prepared to climb many stairs along the way. Also be sure to bring a water bottle, because it's hot and dry. Only a mile up, a clearly marked trail with handrails scales the inside of this extinct volcano. At the top, the fabled final 99 steps take you up to the pillbox overlooking the Pacific Ocean and Honolulu. It's a breathtaking view and a lot cheaper than taking a helicopter ride for the same photo op. Last entry for hikers is 4:30 pm. ⊠ *Diamond Head Rd. at 18th Ave., Diamond Head* ✛ *Enter on east side of crater; there's limited parking inside, so most park on street and walk in* 🕾 *808/587–0300* ⊕ *dlnr.hawaii.gov/dsp/parks/oahu/ diamond-head-state-monument* ⛃ *$1 per person, $5 to park.*

Fodor's Choice
★
Kaena Point Trail. Kaena Point is one of the island's last easily accessible pockets of nature left largely untouched. For more than a quarter century, the state has protected nearly 60 acres of land at the point, first as a nature preserve and, more recently, as an ecosystem restoration project for endangered and protected coastal plants and seabirds. The uneven 5-mile trail around the point can be entered from two locations—Keawaula Beach (aka Yokohama Bay) at the end of Farrington Highway on Oahu's western coastline, or Mokuleia at the same highway's northern coast endpoint. It's a rugged coastline hike without much shade, so bring lots of water and sunscreen (or better yet, start early!). ■**TIP→** Keep a lookout for the Laysan albatrosses; these enormous birds have recently returned to the area. Don't be surprised if they come in for a closer look at you, too. ⊠ *81-780 Farrington Hwy., Waianae* ✛ *Take Farrington Hwy. to its end at Yokohama. Hike in on old 4x4 trail* ⊕ *dlnr.hawaii.gov/dsp/hiking/oahu/kaena-point-trail.*

Makapuu Lighthouse Trail. For the less adventurous hiker and anyone looking for a great view, this paved trail that runs up the side of Makapuu Point in Southeast Oahu fits the bill. Early on, the trail is surrounded by lava rock but, as you ascend, foliage—the tiny white *koa haole* flower, the cream-tinged spikes of the *kiawe*, and, if you go early enough, the stunning night-blooming *cereus*—begins taking over the barren rock. At the easternmost tip of Oahu, where the island divides the sea, this trail gives you a spectacular view of the cobalt ocean meeting the land in a cacophony of white caps. To the south are several tide pools and the lighthouse, while the eastern view looks down upon **Manana** (Rabbit Island) and Kaohikaipu islets, two bird sanctuaries just off the coast. The 2-mile round-trip hike is a great break on a circle-island trip. From late December to early May, this is a great perch to see migrating humpback whales. ■**TIP→** Be sure not to leave valuables in your car, as break-ins, even in the parking lot, are common. ⊠ *Makapuu Lighthouse Rd., Makapuu* ✛ *Take Kalanianaole Hwy. to base of Makapuu Point, then look for the parking lot* ⊕ *dlnr.hawaii.gov/dsp/hiking/oahu/ makapuu-point-lighthouse-trail.*

Fodor's Choice
★
Manoa Falls Trail. Travel up into the valley beyond Honolulu to make the Manoa Falls hike. Though only a mile long, this well-trafficked path, visited by an estimated 100,000 hikers a year, passes through so many different ecosystems that you feel as if you're in an arboretum—and you're not far off. (The beautiful Lyon Arboretum is right near the trailhead, if you want to make another stop.) Walk among the elephant ear ape plants, ruddy fir trees, and a bamboo forest straight out of China. At the top is a 150-foot waterfall, which can be an impressive cascade or, if rain has been sparse, little more than a trickle. This hike is more about the journey than the destination; make sure you bring some mosquito repellent because they grow 'em big up here. ⊠ *3998 Manoa Rd., Manoa* ✛ *West Manoa Rd. is behind Manoa Valley in Paradise Park. Take West Manoa Rd. to end, park on side of road or in parking*

9

DID YOU KNOW?

Manoa Falls is about 150 feet high and is the gem at the end of a mile-long hike. At its top, you'll find a small pool perfect for wading.

TIPS FOR THE TRAIL

■ When hiking the waterfall and rain-forest trails, use insect repellent. The dampness draws huge swarms of bloodsuckers that can ruin a walk in the woods.

■ Volcanic rock is very porous and therefore likely to be loose. Rock climbing is strongly discouraged, as you never know which little ledge is going to go.

■ Avoid hiking after heavy rains and check for flash-flood warnings. Keep in mind that those large boulders in the idyllic pools beneath the waterfalls were carried by torrential flows high up in the mountains.

■ Always let someone know where you're going, and never hike alone. The foliage gets very dense, and, small as the island is, hikers have been known to get lost for a week or longer.

lot for a small fee, follow trail signs ⊕ *www.hawaiitrails.org/trails/#/ trail/manoa-falls-trail/225.*

Maunawili Falls. Want to find a waterfall that you can actually swim in? Then Maunawili Falls is your trip. In fact, even if you don't want to get wet, you're going to have to cross Maunawili Stream several times to get to the falls, and the route is pretty muddy. Along the 1½-mile trek enjoy the ginger, vines, and heliconia before greeting fern-shrouded falls that are made for swimming. The water is not the clearest, but it's cool and refreshing after battling the bugs to get here. ■TIP➜ **On weekends the trail can be very crowded. Prepare to park far from trailhead as regulations are strictly enforced. Be sure to bring mosquito repellant. Walking sticks are helpful—if you don't have any, use the loaner sticks often left by hikers at the trailhead.** ⊠ *1221 Kolowina St., Kailua* ✛ *Take Pali Hwy. (Rte. 61) from Honolulu through the tunnels, then take the third right onto Auloa Rd., then take the left fork immediately. At the dead end, climb over the vehicle gate to find the trailhead.*

Trails at Turtle Bay Resort. When on the North Shore, check out the Turtle Bay Resort, which has more than 12 miles of trails and oceanside pathways. You can pick up a map of the resort property, which includes trail and coastal jogging paths. ⊠ *57-091 Kamehameha Hwy., Kahuku* ☎ *808/293–8811* ⊕ *www.turtlebayresort.com.*

GOING WITH A GUIDE

FAMILY **Hawaii Nature Center.** A good choice for families, the center in upper Makiki Valley conducts a number of programs for both adults and children. There are guided hikes into tropical settings that reveal hidden waterfalls and protected forest reserves. They don't run tours every day, so it's a good idea to get advance reservations. ⊠ *2131 Makiki Heights Dr., Makiki Heights* ☎ *808/955–0100* ⊕ *www.hawaiinaturecenter.org.*

North Shore Eco Tours. Native Hawaiians own and operate this business, the only one allowed to lead guided small-group adventures in private conservation lands. Options range from 2-mile and 3.5-mile roundtrip hikes to pools and waterfalls (lunch included) to an off-road expedition in all-terrain vehicles. Hiking adventures begin at a pickup point in Haleiwa town at North Shore Marketplace; off-road tours begin in Waimea Valley. ✉ *North Shore Marketplace, 56-250 Kamehameha Hwy., Haleiwa* ☎ *877/521–4453* ⊕ *www.northshoreecotours. com* ✉ *From $95.*

Oahu Nature Tours. Guides explain the native flora and fauna and history that are your companions on their various walking and hiking tours on Oahu. This outfitter offers tours to the North Shore, Diamond Head, and Windward Oahu. The company also offers much more expensive private birding tours, perfect for those interested in spotting one of Hawaii's native honeycreepers. Tours include pickup at centralized Waikiki locations and are discounted if booked online in advance. ☎ *808/924–2473* ⊕ *www.oahunaturetours.com* ✉ *From $35.*

HORSEBACK RIDING

A great way to see the island is atop a horse, leaving the direction to the pack while you drink in the views of mountains or the ocean. It may seem like a cliché, but there really is nothing like riding a horse with spectacular ocean views to put you in a romantic state of mind.

Gunstock Ranch. This working cattle ranch encompasses nearly 800 acres on the northeastern shore of Oahu, in the foothills of the Koolau range. Choose among five to ten small-group guided trail rides a day (one to 2½ hours or longer) for riders of all skill levels. Rides are designed to replicate the experience of the *paniolo,* or Hawaiian cowboy. Some climb high enough to view (on clear days) 30 miles of coastline, and sometimes as far as Maui and Molokai. The ranch also offers private 30-minute horse experiences for ages two to seven, private and group advanced trail rides, and private romantic couples tours with picnics. Advance reservations are required. ✉ *56-250 Kamehameha Hwy., Laie* ✛ *2 miles North of the Polynesian Cultural Center, between Laie and Kahuku.* ☎ *808/341–3995* ⊕ *www.gunstockranch.com* ✉ *Trail rides from $82.*

FAMILY **Happy Trails Hawaii.** Take a guided horseback ride above the North Shore's Waimea Bay along trails that offer panoramic views from Kaena Point to the famous surfing spots. Groups are no larger than 10, and instruction is provided. The rides are particularly family-friendly, and children six and older are welcome. You can take either a 1½- or a 2-hour ride, which includes a 15-minute mini-lesson. Reservations are required. ✉ *59-231 Pupukea Rd., Pupukea* ✛ *Go 1 mile mauka (toward mountain) up Pupukea Rd.; the office is on the right* ☎ *808/638–7433* ⊕ *www.happytrailshawaii.com* ✉ *$95 for 1½ hrs, $115 for 2 hrs.*

FAMILY **Kualoa Ranch.** This 4,000-acre working ranch across from Kualoa Beach Park on Windward Oahu offers two-hour trail rides in the breathtaking Kaaawa Valley, which was the site of such movie back lots as *Jurassic Park, Godzilla,* and *50 First Dates.* There is an hour-long option, but it doesn't take you into the valley. Instead, this tour takes you to the scenic northern section of the ranch with its WWII-era bunkers. Kualoa has other activities such as bus, boat, and jeep tours, ATV trail rides, canopy

Continued on page 232

HAWAII'S PLANTS 101

Tropical Hibiscus

Hawaii is a bounty of rainbow-colored flowers and plants. The evening air is scented with their fragrance. Just look at the front yard of almost any home, travel any road, or visit any local park and you'll see a spectacular array of colored blossoms and leaves. What most visitors don't know is that many of the plants they are seeing are not native to Hawaii; rather, they were introduced during the last two centuries as ornamental plants, or for timber, shade, or fruit.

Hawaii boasts nearly every climate on the planet, excluding the two most extreme: arctic tundra and arid desert. The Islands have wine-growing regions, cactus-speckled ranchlands, icy mountaintops, and the rainiest forests on earth.

Plants introduced from around the world thrive here. The lush lowland valleys along the windward coasts are predominantly populated by non-native trees including yellow- and red-fruited **guava**, silvery-leafed **kukui**, and orange-flowered **tulip trees**.

The colorful **plumeria flower**, very fragrant and commonly used in lei making, and the giant multicolored **hibiscus flower** are both used by many women as hair adornments, and are two of the most common plants found around homes and hotels. The umbrella-like **monkeypod tree** from Central America provides shade in many of Hawaii's parks including Kapiolani Park in Honolulu. Hawaii's largest tree, found in Lahaina, Maui, is a giant **banyan tree**. Its canopy and massive support roots cover about two-thirds of an acre. The native **ohia tree**, with its brilliant red brush-like flowers, and the **hapuu**, a giant tree fern, are common in Hawaii's forests and are also used ornamentally in gardens.

Naupaka, Limahuli Garden

Bougainvillea

Guava

Monkeypod

Banyan

Ohia Lehua*

Tulip Tree

Plumeria

Pandanus

Hibiscus

Anthurium

Kukui

Hapuu

*endemic to Hawaii

DID YOU KNOW?

More than 2,200 plant species are found in the Hawaiian Islands, but only about 1,000 are native. Of these, 320 are so rare, they are endangered. Hawaii's endemic plants evolved from ancestral seeds arriving in the Islands over thousands of years as baggage with birds, floating on ocean currents, or drifting on winds from continents thousands of miles away. Once here, these plants evolved in isolation, creating many new species known nowhere else in the world.

zipline tours, and children's activities, which may be combined for full-day package rates. The minimum age for horseback rides is 10. ⊠ *49-479 Kamehameha Hwy., Kaneohe* ☎ *800/231–7321, 808/237–7321* ⊕ *www.kualoa.com* ⊟ *$85 for 1 hr, $130 for 2 hrs.*

FAMILY **Turtle Bay Stables.** Trail rides follow the 12-mile-long coastline and even step out onto sandy beaches fronting this luxe resort on Oahu's fabled North Shore. The stables here are part of the resort but can be utilized by nonguests. The sunset ride is a definite must. A basic trail ride lasts 45 minutes and visits filming sites for ABC's *Lost* and the film *Pirates of the Caribbean.* ⊠ *Turtle Bay Resort, 57-091 Kamehemeha Hwy., Kahuku* ☎ *808/293–6024* ⊕ *www.turtlebayresort.com/things-to-do/sports-recreation/horse-riding* ⊟ *From $85.*

TENNIS

While tennis has given way to golf as the biggest resort attraction, and many of the hotel courts have closed, there are still locations in Waikiki to get your tennis match on. Both sides of Waikiki are framed by tennis complexes, with Ala Moana Park containing a 12-court spread, and two different sets at Kapiolani Park. Play is free at public courts, which are readily available during the day—but they tend to fill up after the sun goes down and the asphalt cools off.

Ala Moana Park Tennis Courts. With ten public courts, those located in Ala Moana Park are the closest to the *ewa* (west) end of Waikiki. ⊠ *Ala Moana Park, 1201 Ala Moana Blvd., Ala Moana* ☎ *808/768–3029.*

Diamond Head Tennis Center. Across the street from Kapiolani Park, this center has ten courts open to the public. ⊠ *3908 Paki Ave., Waikiki* ☎ *808/971–2525.*

Kapiolani Tennis Courts. There are four courts for play here. ⊠ *2740 Kalakaua Ave., Waikiki* ☎ *808/765–4626.*

UNDERSTANDING OAHU

HAWAIIAN VOCABULARY

HAWAIIAN VOCABULARY

Although an understanding of Hawaiian is by no means required on a trip to the Aloha State, a *malihini,* or newcomer, will find plenty of opportunities to pick up a few of the local words and phrases. Traditional names and expressions are widely used in the Islands. You're likely to read or hear at least a few words each day of your stay.

With a basic understanding and some uninhibited practice, anyone can have enough command of the local tongue to ask for directions and to order from a restaurant menu. One visitor announced she would not leave until she could pronounce the name of the state fish, the *humuhumunukunukuāpua'a.*

Simplifying the learning process is the fact that the Hawaiian language contains only eight consonants—H, K, L, M, N, P, W, and the silent *'okina,* or glottal stop, written '—plus one or more of the five vowels. All syllables, and therefore all words, end in a vowel. Each vowel, with the exception of a few diphthongized double vowels such as *au* (pronounced "ow") or *ai* (pronounced "eye"), is pronounced separately. Thus *'Iolani* is four syllables (ee-oh-la-nee), not three (yo-la-nee). Although some Hawaiian words have only vowels, most also contain some consonants, but consonants are never doubled.

Pronunciation is simple. Pronounce *A* "ah" as father; *E* "ay" as in weigh; *I* "ee" as in marine; *O* "oh" as in no; *U* "oo" as in true.

Consonants mirror their English equivalents, with the exception of W. When the letter begins any syllable other than the first one in a word, it is usually pronounced as a V. *'Awa,* the Polynesian drink, is pronounced "ava," *'ewa* is pronounced "eva."

Almost all long Hawaiian words are combinations of shorter words; they are not difficult to pronounce if you segment them. *Kalaniana'ole,* the highway running east from Honolulu, is easily understood as *Kalani ana 'ole.* Apply the standard pronunciation rules—the stress falls on the next-to-last syllable of most two- or three-syllable Hawaiian words—and Kalaniana'ole Highway is as easy to say as Main Street.

Now about that fish. Try *humu-humu nuku-nuku āpu a'a.*

The other unusual element in Hawaiian language is the *kahakō,* or macron, written as a short line (ˉ) placed over a vowel. Like the accent (ˊ) in Spanish, the kahakō puts emphasis on a syllable that would normally not be stressed. The most familiar example is probably *Waikīkī.* With no macrons, the stress would fall on the middle syllable; with only one macron, on the last syllable, the stress would fall on the first and last syllables. Some words become plural with the addition of a macron, often on a syllable that would have been stressed anyway. No Hawaiian word becomes plural with the addition of an *s,* since that letter does not exist in the language.

What follows is a glossary of some of the most commonly used Hawaiian words. Hawaiian residents appreciate visitors who at least try to pick up the local language.

'a'ā: rough, crumbling lava, contrasting with *pāhoehoe,* which is smooth.

'ae: yes.

aikane: friend.

āina: land.

akamai: smart, clever, possessing savoir faire.

akua: god.

ala: a road, path, or trail.

ali'i: a Hawaiian chief, a member of the chiefly class.

aloha: love, affection, kindness; also a salutation meaning both greetings and farewell.

'ānuenue: rainbow.

'a'ole: no.

'apōpō: tomorrow.

'auwai: a ditch.

auwē: alas, woe is me!

'ehu: a red-haired Hawaiian.

'ewa: in the direction of 'Ewa plantation, west of Honolulu.

hala: the pandanus tree, whose leaves (*lau hala*) are used to make baskets and plaited mats.

hālau: school.

hale: a house.

hale pule: church, house of worship.

ha mea iki or **ha mea 'ole:** you're welcome.

hana: to work.

haole: ghost. Since the first foreigners were Caucasian, *haole* now means a Caucasian person.

hapa: a part, sometimes a half; often used as a short form of *hapa haole,* to mean a person who is part-Caucasian.

hau'oli: to rejoice. *Hau'oli Makahiki Hou* means Happy New Year. *Hau'oli lā hānau* means Happy Birthday.

heiau: an outdoor stone platform; an ancient Hawaiian place of worship.

holo: to run.

holoholo: to go for a walk, ride, or sail.

holokū: a long Hawaiian dress, somewhat fitted, with a yoke and a train. Influenced by European fashion, it was worn at court, and at least one local translates the word as "expensive mu'umu'u."

holomū: a post–World War II cross between a holokū and a mu'umu'u, less fitted than the former but less voluminous than the latter, and having no train.

honi: to kiss; a kiss. A phrase that some tourists may find useful, quoted from a popular hula, is *Honi ka'ua wikiwiki!* (Kiss me quick!)

honu: turtle.

ho'omalimali: flattery, a deceptive "line," bunk, baloney, hooey.

huhū: angry.

hui: a group, club, or assembly. A church may refer to its congregation as a *hui* and a social club may be called a *hui.*

hukilau: a seine; a communal fishing party in which everyone helps to drive the fish into a huge net, pull it in, and divide the catch.

hula: the dance of Hawaii.

iki: little.

ipo: sweetheart.

ka: the. This is the definite article for most singular words; for plural nouns, the definite article is usually *nā.* Since there is no *s* in Hawaiian, the article may be your only clue that a noun is plural.

kahuna: a priest, doctor, or other trained person of old Hawaii, endowed with special professional skills that often included prophecy or other supernatural powers; the plural form is *kāhuna.*

kai: the sea, saltwater.

kalo: the taro plant from whose root *poi* (paste) is made.

kamā'aina: literally, a child of the soil. It refers to people who were born in the Islands or have lived there for a long time.

kanaka: originally a man or humanity, it is now used to denote a male Hawaiian or part-Hawaiian, but is occasionally taken as a slur when used by non-Hawaiians. *Kanaka maoli,* originally a full-blooded Hawaiian person, is used by some Native Hawaiian–rights activists to embrace part-Hawaiians as well.

kāne: a man, a husband. If you see this word on a door, it's the men's room. If you see *kane* on a door, it's probably a misspelling; that is the Hawaiian name for the skin fungus tinea.

kapa: also called by its Tahitian name, *tapa,* a cloth made of beaten bark and usually dyed and stamped with a repeat design.

kapakahi: crooked, cockeyed, uneven. You've got your hat on *kapakahi.*

kapu: keep out, prohibited. This is the Hawaiian version of the more widely known Tongan word *tabu* (taboo).

kapuna: grandparent; elder.

kēia lā: today.

keiki: a child; *keikikāne* is a boy, *keiki-wahine* a girl.

kona: the leeward side of the Islands, the direction (south) from which the *kona* wind and *kona* rain come.

kula: upland.

kuleana: a homestead or small plot of ground on which a family has been installed for some generations without necessarily owning it. By extension, *kuleana* is used to denote any area or department in which one has a special interest or prerogative. You'll hear it used this way: If you want to hire a surfboard, see Moki; that's his *kuleana*.

lā: sun.

lamalama: to fish with a torch.

lānai: a porch, a balcony, an outdoor living room. Almost every house in Hawaii has one. Don't confuse this two-syllable word with the three-syllable name of the island, Lāna'i.

lani: heaven, the sky.

lau hala: the leaf of the *hala,* or pandanus tree, widely used in handicrafts.

lei: a garland of flowers.

limu: sun.

lolo: stupid.

luna: a plantation overseer or foreman.

mahalo: thank you.

makai: toward the ocean.

malihini: a newcomer to the Islands.

mana: the spiritual power that the Hawaiian believed inhabited all things and creatures.

manō: shark.

manuwahi: free, gratis.

mauka: toward the mountains.

mauna: mountain.

mele: a Hawaiian song or chant, often of epic proportions.

Mele Kalikimaka: Merry Christmas (a transliteration from the English phrase).

Menehune: a Hawaiian pixie. The *Menehune* were a legendary race of little people who accomplished prodigious work, such as building fishponds and temples in the course of a single night.

moana: the ocean.

mu'umu'u: the voluminous dress in which the missionaries enveloped Hawaiian women. Now made in bright printed cottons and silks, it is an indispensable garment. Culturally sensitive locals have embraced the Hawaiian spelling but often shorten the spoken word to "mu'u." Most English dictionaries include the spelling "muumuu."

nani: beautiful.

nui: big.

ohana: family.

'ono: delicious.

pāhoehoe: smooth, unbroken, satiny lava.

Pākē: Chinese. This *Pākē* carver makes beautiful things.

palapala: document, printed matter.

pali: a cliff, precipice.

pānini: prickly pear cactus.

paniolo: a Hawaiian cowboy, a rough transliteration of *español,* the language of the Islands' earliest cowboys.

pau: finished, done.

pilikia: trouble. The Hawaiian word is much more widely used here than its English equivalent.

puka: a hole.

pupule: crazy, like the celebrated Princess Pupule. This word has replaced its English equivalent in local usage.

pu'u: volcanic cinder cone.

waha: mouth.

wahine: a female, a woman, a wife, and a sign on the ladies' room door; the plural form is *wāhine.*

wai: freshwater, as opposed to saltwater, which is *kai.*

wailele: waterfall.

wikiwiki: to hurry, hurry up (since this is a reduplication of *wiki,* quick, neither *w* is pronounced as a *v*).

Note: Pidgin is the unofficial language of Hawaii. It is a Creole language, with its own grammar, evolved from the mixture of English, Hawaiian, Japanese, Portuguese, and other languages spoken in 19th-century Hawaii, and it is heard everywhere.

TRAVEL SMART
OAHU

GETTING HERE AND AROUND

Visitors to Oahu can navigate by orienting themselves to a few major landmarks. Oahu is made up of three extinct shield volcanoes, which form the island's two mountain ranges: Waianae and Koolau. The Waianae range curves from Kaena State Park, on the island's westernmost point, past Makaha, Waianae, and Nanakuli to Ko Olina on the sunny leeward shore. The extinct craters of Diamond Head and Koko Head are usually visible from anywhere along the island's Leeward Coast. The Koolau range forms a jagged spine that runs from the island's eastern tip along the Windward Coast to the famous surfing center on the North Shore.

▌ AIR TRAVEL

Flying time to Oahu is about 10 hours from New York, 8 hours from Chicago, and 5 hours from Los Angeles.

All the major airline carriers serving Hawaii fly direct to Honolulu; some also offer nonstops to Maui, Kauai, and the Big Island, though most flights to the latter two come from the West Coast only. Honolulu International Airport, although open-air and seemingly more casual than most major airports, can be very busy. Allow extra travel time during busy mornings and afternoons.

Plants and plant products are subject to regulation by the Department of Agriculture, both on entering and leaving Hawaii. Upon leaving, you'll have to have your bags X-rayed and tagged at the airport's agricultural inspection station before you proceed to check-in. Pineapples and coconuts with the packer's agricultural inspection stamp pass freely; papayas and certain other fruits must be treated, inspected, and stamped. But most other fruits are banned for export to the U.S. mainland. Flowers pass except for citrus-related flowers, fruits or parts, jade vine,

and mauna loa. Also banned are insects, snails, soil, cotton, cacti, sugarcane, and all berry plants.

Bringing your dog or cat with you is a tricky process and not something to be done lightly. Hawaii is a rabies-free state and requires animals to pass strict quarantine rules, which you can find online at ⊕ *hdoa.hawaii.gov/ai/aqs.* Most airlines do not allow pets to travel in the cabin on flights to Hawaii (though Alaska Airlines and Hawaiian Airlines are notable exceptions). If specific pre- and postarrival requirements are met, most animals qualify for a five-day-or-less quarantine.

Airline Security Issues Transportation Security Administration. ☎ 866/289–9673 ⊕ *www.tsa.gov.*

Air-Travel Resources in Oahu State of Hawaii Airports Division Offices. ☎ 808/836–6413 ⊕ *www.hidot.hawaii.gov/ airports.*

AIRPORTS

Honolulu International Airport (HNL) is roughly 20 minutes (9 miles) west of Waikiki, and is served by most of the major domestic and international carriers. To travel to other islands from Honolulu, you can depart from either the interisland terminal or the commuter-airline terminal, located in two separate structures adjacent to the main overseas terminal building. A free Wiki-Wiki shuttle bus operates between terminals.

Airport Information Honolulu International Airport (HNL). ☎ 808/836–6411 ⊕ *airports. hawaii.gov/hnl/.*

GROUND TRANSPORTATION

Some hotels have their own pickup and drop-off service, though they may charge a fee, so check when you book accommodations.

Taxi service is available on the center median just outside baggage-claim areas. Look for the taxi dispatchers wearing yellow shirts, who will radio for a taxi. The fare to Waikiki runs approximately $40–$45 plus 60¢ per bag, and tip, with a maximum of four passengers. An oversize baggage fee may apply. Uber and Lyft also serve the airport.

Another option is to take a private shuttle service like Roberts Hawaii. The company will greet you at the arrival gate, escort you to baggage claim, and take you to your hotel. Call ahead for the service, which costs $16 per person for one-way service, $32 round-trip.

TheBus, the municipal bus, will take you into Waikiki for only $2.75, but all bags must fit on your lap or under your legs.

Contacts Roberts Hawaii. ☎ 866/898–2523 ⊕ www.robertshawaii.com. **TheBus.** ☎ 808/848–5555 ⊕ www.thebus.org.

FLIGHTS FROM THE U.S. MAINLAND

From the U.S. mainland, Alaska Airlines, American, Delta, Hawaiian, and United are the primary U.S. carriers to serve Honolulu. Southwest plans to add service to Hawaii in late 2018 or early 2019.

Contacts Alaska Airlines. ☎ 800/252–7522 ⊕ www.alaskaair.com. **American Airlines.** ☎ 800/433–7300 ⊕ www.aa.com. **Delta Airlines.** ☎ 800/221–1212 for U.S. reservations, 800/241–4141 for international reservations ⊕ www.delta.com. **Hawaiian Airlines.** ☎ 800/367–5320 ⊕ www.hawaiianairlines.com. **Southwest.** ☎ 800/435–9792 ⊕ www.southwest.com. **United Airlines.** ☎ 800/864–8331 for U.S. reservations ⊕ www.united.com.

CHARTER FLIGHTS

Mokulele Airlines operates charter flights between Oahu and the Big Island, Maui, Molokai, and Lanai. Several other smaller charter companies service the Neighbor Islands as well.

Contacts Mokulele Airlines. ☎ 866/260–7070 ⊕ www.mokuleleairlines.com/charters.

INTERISLAND FLIGHTS

If you've allotted more than a week for your vacation, you may want to consider visiting one of the other Hawaiian Islands. From Honolulu, flights depart almost hourly from early morning until evening. Since each flight lasts only 30–60 minutes, you can watch the sunrise on Oahu and sunset on the Big Island, Kauai, Lanai, Maui, or Molokai. To simplify your vacation, schedule your return flight to Oahu so that it coincides with your flight home.

In addition to Hawaiian Airlines (⇨ see Flights from the U.S. Mainland), Mokulele Airlines operate regular service between the islands, so be sure to compare prices. Both have frequent-flyer programs that entitle you to rewards and upgrades. A number of wholesalers offer Neighbor Islands packages including air, hotel, rental car, and even visitor attractions or activities.

Contacts Mokulele Airlines. ☎ 866/260–7070 ⊕ www.mokuleleairlines.com.

▌ BOAT TRAVEL

CRUISES

When Pan Am's amphibious *Hawaii Clipper* touched down on Pearl Harbor's waters in 1936, it marked the beginning of the end of regular passenger-ship travel to the Islands. From that point on, the predominant means of transporting visitors would be by air, not by sea. Today, however, cruising to Hawaii is a delightful way to experience the beauty and majesty of the Pacific Ocean and Hawaiian Islands. Several major cruise lines offer seasonal cruises to and from the Hawaiian Islands (typically from Los Angeles, San Francisco, or San Diego) with interisland cruise components. But you can also hop aboard a strictly interisland cruise with Norwegian Cruise Line's ship *Pride of America*, or Un-Cruise Adventures' smaller yacht.

Contacts Norwegian Cruise Line. ☎ 866/234–7350 ⊕ www.ncl.com. **Un-Cruise Adventures.** ☎ 888/862–8881 ⊕ www.uncruise.com.

▮ BUS TRAVEL

Getting around by bus is an affordable option on Oahu, particularly in the most heavily touristed areas of Waikiki. In addition to TheBus and the Waikiki Trolley, Waikiki has brightly painted private buses, many of them free, that shuttle you to such commercial attractions as dinner cruises, garment factories, and the like.

You can travel around the island or just down Kalakaua Avenue for $2.75 on Honolulu's municipal transportation system, affectionately known as TheBus. It's one of the island's best bargains. Buses make stops in Waikiki every 10–15 minutes to take passengers to nearby shopping areas.

Free transfers have been discontinued, but you can purchase a one-day pass for $5.50. Just ask the driver as you're boarding. Exact change is required, and dollar bills are accepted. Monthly passes cost $70.

The company's website has timetables, route maps, and real-time bus tracking, or you can download the free DaBus2 app for your smartphone. You can call to speak with a representative for route advice. Or you also can find privately published booklets at most drugstores and other convenience outlets.

The Waikiki Trolley has five lines and dozens of stops that allow you to plan your own itinerary while riding on brass-trimmed, open-air buses that look like trolleys. The Historic Honolulu Tour (Red Line) travels between Waikiki and Chinatown and includes stops at the State Capitol, Iolani Palace, and the King Kamehameha statue. The Waikiki-Ala Moana Shopping Shuttle (Pink Line) runs from the T Galleria by DFS to Eggs 'n Things, stopping at various Waikiki locations and the Ala Moana Center. The Scenic Diamond Head Sightseeing Tour (Green Line) runs through Waikiki and down around Diamond Head. There's also a south shore coastline tour (Blue Line) and a line that runs to Aloha Stadium and Pearl Harbor

(Purple Line). A one-day pass costs $23 to $45, four-day passes are $36.50 to $74, and seven-day passes are $41 to $79. All passes are discounted when purchased in advance.

Contacts TheBus. ☎ 808/848–5555 ⊕ www. thebus.org. **Waikiki Trolley.** ☎ 808/593–2822 ⊕ waikikitrolley.com.

▮ CAR TRAVEL

You can get away without renting a car if you plan on staying in Waikiki. But if you want to explore the rest of the island, there's no substitute for having your own wheels. Avoid the obvious tourist cars—candy-color convertibles, for example—and never leave anything valuable inside, even if you've locked the car. A GPS will save you on phone data and guide you through Oahu's sometimes-confusing streets.

If you are renting a car, reserve your vehicle in advance, especially when traveling during the Christmas holidays and summer breaks. This will not only ensure that you get a car but also that you get the best rates. Also, be prepared to pay for parking; almost all hotels in Honolulu (and many outside of Honolulu) charge for parking.

Except for one area around Kaena Point, major highways follow Oahu's shoreline and traverse the island at two points. Rush-hour traffic (6:30–9:30 am and 3:30–6 pm) can be frustrating around Honolulu and the outlying areas. Winter swells also bring traffic to the North Shore, as people hoping to catch some of the surfing action clog the two-lane Kamehameha Highway. Parking along many streets is curtailed during these times, and tow-away zones are strictly enforced. Read curbside signs before leaving your vehicle, even at a meter.

Asking for directions will almost always produce a helpful explanation from the locals, but you should be prepared for an island term or two. Instead of using compass directions, remember that Hawaii residents refer to places as being either *mauka* (toward the mountains) or *makai* (toward the ocean). Other directions depend on your location: in Honolulu, for example, people say to "go Diamond Head," which means toward that famous landmark, or to "go *ewa*," meaning in the opposite direction. A shop on the *mauka*–Diamond Head corner of a street is on the mountain side of the street on the corner closest to Diamond Head. It all makes perfect sense once you get the lay of the land.

GASOLINE
Gasoline is noticeably more expensive on Oahu than on the U.S. mainland.

ROAD CONDITIONS
Oahu is relatively easy to navigate. Roads, although their names are often a challenge for the tongue, are well marked; just watch out for the many one-way streets in Waikiki and downtown Honolulu. Keep an eye open for the Hawaii Visitors and Convention Bureau's red-caped King Kamehameha signs, which mark major attractions and scenic spots. Ask for a map at the car-rental counter. Free publications containing helpful maps are found at most hotels throughout Waikiki.

ROADSIDE EMERGENCIES
In case of an accident, pull over if you can. If you have a cell phone, call the roadside assistance number on your car-rental contract or AAA Help. If your car has been broken into or stolen, report it immediately to your rental-car company. If it's an emergency and someone is hurt, call 911 immediately.

Contacts AAA Help. ☎ *800/222–4357* ⊕ *www.hawaii.aaa.com.*

RULES OF THE ROAD
Be sure to buckle up, as Hawaii has a strictly enforced mandatory seat-belt law for front- and backseat passengers. Children under four must be in a car seat (available from car-rental agencies), and children ages four to seven must be seated in a booster seat or child safety seat with restraint such as a lap and shoulder belt. Hawaii also prohibits texting or talking on the phone (unless you are over 18 and using a hands-free device) while driving. The highway speed limit is usually 55 mph. In-town traffic travels 25–40 mph. Jaywalking is not uncommon, so watch for pedestrians, especially in congested areas such as Waikiki and downtown Honolulu. Unauthorized use of a parking space reserved for persons with disabilities can net you a $250–$500 fine.

Oahu's drivers are generally courteous, and you rarely hear a horn. People will slow down and let you into traffic with a wave of the hand. A friendly wave back is customary. If a driver sticks a hand out the window in a fist with the thumb and pinky sticking straight out, this is a good thing: it's the *shaka,* the Hawaiian symbol for "hang loose," and is often used to say "thanks."

CAR RENTALS
Hotel parking garages charge upwards of $20 per day, so if you're staying in Waikiki you may want to rent a car only when you plan to sightsee around the island. You can easily walk or take public transportation to many of the attractions in and around the area.

If you are staying outside Waikiki, your best bet is to rent a car. Even though the city bus is a wonderfully affordable way to get around the island, you'll want the flexibility of having your own transportation, especially if you're planning lots of stops.

■TIP→ Make sure that a confirmed reservation guarantees you a car. Agencies sometimes overbook, particularly for busy weekends and holiday periods.

You can rent anything from an econobox and motorcycle to a Ferrari while on Oahu. Rates are usually better if you reserve through a rental agency's website. It's wise to make reservations far in advance, especially if visiting during peak seasons.

CAR RENTAL RESOURCES

Automobile Associations

AAA	☎ 800/222–4357 for roadside assistance	⊕ www.aaa.com
National Automobile Club	☎ 650/294–7000	⊕ www.nacroadservice.com (CA residents only)

Major Agencies

Alamo	☎ 888/233–8749	⊕ www.alamo.com
Avis	☎ 800/633–3469	⊕ www.avis.com
Budget	☎ 800/218–7992	⊕ www.budget.com
Hertz	☎ 800/654–3131	⊕ www.hertz.com
National Car Rental	☎ 888/826–6890	⊕ www.nationalcar.com
Thrifty Car Rental	☎ 800/334–1705	⊕ www.thrifty.com

Rates in Honolulu begin at about $25 a day for an economy car with air-conditioning, automatic transmission, and unlimited mileage. This does not include the airport concession fee, general excise tax, rental-vehicle surcharge, or vehicle-license fee. When you reserve a car, ask about cancellation penalties and drop-off charges, should you plan to pick up the car in one location and return it to another. Many rental companies offer coupons for discounts at various attractions that could save you money later on in your trip.

In Hawaii you must be 21 years of age to rent a car, and you must have a valid driver's license and a major credit card. Those under 25 will pay a daily surcharge of about $15 to $30. Request car seats and extras such as GPS when you make your reservation. Hawaii's Child Restraint Law requires that all children under four be in an approved child safety seat in the backseat of a vehicle. Children ages four to seven must be seated in a rear booster seat or child safety seat with restraint such as a lap and shoulder belt. Car seats and boosters run about $13 per day.

In Hawaii your unexpired mainland driver's license is valid for rental for up to 90 days.

Be sure to allow plenty of time to return your vehicle so that you can make your flight. Traffic in Honolulu is terrible during morning and afternoon rush hours. Give yourself about 3½–4 hours before departure time to return your vehicle if you're traveling during these peak times; otherwise plan on about 2½–3 hours.

■ TAXI TRAVEL

Taxis cost $3.10 at the drop of the flag and each additional mile is $3.60. Taxi and limousine companies can provide a car and driver for half-day or daylong island tours, and a number of companies also offer personal guides. Remember, however, the rates are quite steep for these services, running $100 to $200 or more per day. Uber and Lyft also serve Oahu, including for airport pick-ups.

Contacts TheCAB Hawaii. ☎ 808/422–2222 ⊕ www.thecabhawaii.com. **Carey Hawaii Chauffeured Services.** ☎ 808/572–3400 ⊕ www.careyhonolulu.com. **Charley's Taxi.** ☎ 808/233–3333 ⊕ www.charleystaxi.com. **Elite Limousine Service.** ☎ 800/776–2098, 808/735–2431 ⊕ www.elitelimohawaii.com.

ESSENTIALS

■ BUSINESS SERVICES AND FACILITIES

The Hawaii Convention Center, located at the entrance to Waikiki, is a gorgeous facility that captures the spirit of Hawaii through its open-air spaces, tropical gardens, and soaring forms that resemble Polynesian canoes. The center also boasts an extensive art collection featuring the work of dozens of local artists. The Hawaii Visitors & Convention Bureau's website has a directory of products and services.

Contacts Hawaii Convention Center. ⊠ *1801 Kalakaua Ave., Waikiki* ☎ *808/943-3500* ⊕ *www.meethawaii.com/ convention-center/.*

■ COMMUNICATIONS

INTERNET
Most of the major hotels and resorts offer high-speed access in rooms and lobbies. In some cases there will be an hourly or daily charge. If you're staying at a small inn or B&B that doesn't have Internet access, ask about the nearest café or coffee shop that does.

■ EMERGENCIES

To reach the police, fire department, or an ambulance in an emergency, dial ☎ *911.*

Longs Drugs (owned by CVS) on Kalaukaua Avenue is open seven days a week, with its pharmacy open from 8 am to 8 pm. Longs also has evening hours at its Ala Moana location and is open 24 hours at its South King Street location (a 15-minute drive from Waikiki). There's also a 24-hour Walgreens near Ala Moana. Pillbox Pharmacy, located in Kaimuki, will deliver prescription medications for a small fee.

■ HEALTH

Hawaii is known not only as the Aloha State, but also as the Health State. The life expectancy here is 82.4 years, the longest in the nation. Balmy weather makes it easy to remain active year-round, and the low-stress attitude seems to contribute to the general well-being. When visiting the Islands, however, there are a few health issues to keep in mind.

The Hawaii State Department of Health recommends that you drink 16 ounces of water per hour to avoid dehydration when hiking or spending time in the sun. Use sunblock, wear UV–reflective sunglasses, and protect your head with a visor or hat. If you're not acclimated to warm, humid weather, you should allow plenty of time for rest stops and refreshments. When visiting freshwater streams, be aware of the tropical disease leptospirosis, spread by animal urine and carried into streams and mud. Symptoms include fever, headache, nausea, and red eyes. If left untreated it can cause liver and kidney damage, respiratory failure, internal bleeding, and even death. To avoid this, don't swim or wade in freshwater streams or ponds if you have open sores and don't drink from any freshwater streams or ponds.

On the Islands, fog is a rare occurrence, but there can often be "vog," an airborne haze of gases released from volcanic vents on the Big Island. During certain weather conditions, such as "Kona Winds," the vog can settle over the Islands and wreak havoc with respiratory and other health conditions, especially asthma or emphysema. If susceptible, stay indoors and get emergency assistance if needed.

The Islands have their share of insects. Most are harmless but annoying, but Dengue fever, a mosquito-borne disease, has been reported in Oahu. When planning to spend time outdoors in hiking areas, wear long-sleeve clothing and pants, and use mosquito repellent containing DEET. In damp places you may encounter the dreaded local centipedes, which are brown and blue and measure up to eight inches long. Their painful sting is similar to those of bees and wasps. When camping, shake out your sleeping bag and check your shoes, as the centipedes like cozy places. When hiking in remote areas, always carry a first-aid kit.

▌ HOURS OF OPERATION

Even people in paradise have to work. Generally local business hours are weekdays 8–5. Banks are usually open Monday–Thursday 8:30–4 and until 6 on Friday. Some banks have Saturday-morning hours.

Many self-serve gas stations stay open around the clock, with full-service stations usually open from around 7 am until 9 pm. U.S. post offices generally are open weekdays from 8 or 10 to 4:30 or 5 and Saturday from 9 to noon or 2. On Oahu, the Ala Moana post office is the only branch to stay open until 4:30 pm on Saturday. The main Honolulu International Airport facility is open until 4 pm on Saturday.

Most museums generally open their doors between 9 and 10 and stay open until 5 Tuesday to Saturday. Many museums operate with afternoon hours only on Sunday and close on Monday. Visitor-attraction hours vary, but most sights are open daily with the exception of major holidays such as Christmas. Check the local newspaper upon arrival for attraction hours and schedules if visiting over holiday periods. The local daily carries a listing of "What's Open/What's Not" for those time periods.

Stores in resort areas sometimes open as early as 8, with shopping-center opening hours varying from 9 to 10 on weekdays and Saturday, a bit later on Sunday. Bigger malls stay open until 9 weekdays and Saturday and close at between 5 and 7

on Sunday. Boutiques in resort areas may stay open as late as 11.

▌ MONEY

⇨ *Prices for Exploring sights are given for adults.* Substantially reduced fees are almost always available for children, students, and senior citizens.

ATMS AND BANKS

ATMs, for easy access to cash, can be found at many locations throughout Oahu, including shopping centers, convenience and grocery stores, and hotels and resorts, as well as outside most bank branches.

CREDIT CARDS

It's a good idea to inform your credit-card company before you travel. Otherwise, the credit-card company might put a hold on your card owing to unusual activity—not a good thing halfway through your trip. Record all your credit-card numbers—as well as the phone numbers to call if your cards are lost or stolen—in a safe place, so you're prepared should something go wrong. Both MasterCard and Visa have general numbers you can call (collect, if you're abroad) if your card is lost, but you're better off calling the number of your issuing bank, since MasterCard and Visa usually just transfer you to your bank; your bank's number is usually printed on your card.

Reporting Lost Cards American Express. 🖾 800/528–4800 in the U.S. ⊕ www.american-express.com. **Diners Club.** 🖾 800/234–6377 in the U.S. ⊕ www.dinersclubus.com. **Discover.** 🖾 800/347–2683 in the U.S. ⊕ www.discover.com. **MasterCard.** 🖾 800/627–8372 in the U.S. ⊕ www.mastercard.us. **Visa.** 🖾 800/847–2911 in the U.S. ⊕ www.usa.visa.com.

▌ PACKING

Oahu is casual: sandals, bathing suits, and comfortable, informal clothing are the norm. In summer, synthetic slacks and shirts, although easy to care for, can be uncomfortably warm.

There's a saying that when a man wears a suit during the day, he's either going for a loan or he's a lawyer trying a case. Only a few upscale restaurants require a jacket for dinner. The Aloha shirt is accepted dress on Oahu for business and most social occasions. Shorts are acceptable daytime attire, along with a T-shirt or polo shirt. There's no need to buy expensive sandals on the mainland—here you can get flip-flops (locals call them slippers) for a couple of dollars and off-brand sandals for $20. Golfers should remember that many courses have dress codes requiring a collared shirt; call courses you're interested in for details. If you're not prepared, you can pick up appropriate clothing at resort pro shops. If you're visiting in winter or planning to visit a high-altitude area, bring a sweater or light- to medium-weight jacket. A polar fleece pullover is ideal and makes a great impromptu pillow. If you're planning on doing any hiking, a good pair of boots is essential.

SHIPPING LUGGAGE AHEAD

Imagine globe-trotting with only a carry-on in tow. Shipping your luggage in advance via an air-freight service is a great way to cut down on backaches, hassles, and stress—especially if your packing list includes strollers, car seats, etc. There are some things to be aware of, though.

First, research carry-on restrictions; if you absolutely need something that isn't practical to ship and isn't allowed in carry-ons, this strategy isn't for you. Second, plan to send your bags several days in advance to U.S. destinations and as much as two weeks in advance to some international destinations. Third, plan to spend some money: it will cost at least $100 to send a small piece of luggage, surfboard, or a golf bag to a domestic destination, much more to places overseas.

Some people use Federal Express to ship their bags, but this can cost even more than air-freight services. All these services insure your bag (for most, the limit is $1,000, but you should verify that amount); you can, however, purchase additional insurance for about $1 per $100 of value.

Contacts Luggage Concierge. ☎ *800/288-9818* ⊕ *www.luggageconcierge.com.* **Luggage Free.** ☎ *866/710-0201* ⊕ *www.luggagefree.com.* **Sports Express/Luggage Forward.** ☎ *866/416-7447* ⊕ *www.sportsexpress.com.*

∎ SAFETY

Oahu is generally a safe tourist destination, but it's still wise to follow the same common-sense safety precautions you would normally follow in your own hometown. Rental cars are magnets for break-ins, so don't leave any valuables in the car, not even in a locked trunk. Avoid poorly lighted areas, beach parks, and isolated areas after dark as a precaution. When hiking, stay on marked trails, no matter how alluring the temptation might be to stray. Weather conditions can cause landscapes to become muddy, slippery, and tenuous, so staying on marked trails will lessen the possibility of a fall or getting lost.

Women traveling alone are generally safe on the Islands, but always follow the safety precautions you would use in any major destination. When booking hotels, request rooms closer to the elevator, and always keep your hotel-room door and balcony doors locked. Stay away from isolated areas after dark; camping and hiking solo are not advised. If you stay out late visiting nightclubs and bars, use caution when exiting nightspots and returning to your lodging.

∎ TIP→ **Distribute your cash, credit cards, IDs, and other valuables between a deep front pocket, an inside jacket or vest pocket, and a hidden money pouch. Don't reach for the money pouch once you're in public.**

Contact Transportation Security Administration (*TSA*). ⊕ *www.tsa.gov.*

TAXES

A 10.25% tax is added onto your hotel bill. A $3-per-day road tax is also assessed on each rental vehicle plus $4.50 a day if you're renting it at the airport.

TIME

Hawaii is on Hawaiian standard time, five hours behind New York, and two hours behind Los Angeles.

When the U.S. mainland is on daylight saving time, Hawaii is not, so add an extra hour of time difference between the Islands and U.S. mainland destinations. You may also find that things generally move more slowly here. That has nothing to do with your watch—it's just the laid-back way called Hawaiian time.

TIPPING

People who work in the service industry rely on tips, so tipping is not only common, but expected.

Tip bartenders ($1–$5 per round of drinks, depending on the number of drinks); bellhops ($1–$5 per bag, depending on the level of the hotel and whether you have bulky items like golf clubs and surfboards); hotel concierges ($5 or more, depending on the service); hotel maids ($1–$3 per day); taxi drivers (15%–20% of the fare); tour guides (10% of the cost of the tour); valet parking attendants ($1–$3, each time you pick up your car); and waiters (15%–20%, with 20% being the norm at high-end restaurants).

TOURS

GUIDED TOURS

One way to manage several Hawaiian Islands on the same trip is to take a guided tour that includes all your travel arrangements in the Islands, including hotels, interisland transfers, and some sightseeing.

Globus has four Hawaii itineraries that include Oahu, two of which are escorted cruises on Norwegian Cruise Line's *Pride of America* that include four days on the island. Tauck and Trafalgar offer several land-based Hawaii itineraries that include nights on Oahu. Both companies offer similar itineraries with visits to the USS *Arizona* Memorial National Park and plenty of free time to explore the island. Tauck offers a 12-night Best of Hawaii itinerary. Highlights of the Oahu portion of the trip include a Waikiki outrigger canoe trip and a private dinner at Iolani Palace. Trafalgar has 8- to 13-night multi-island tours.

Atlas Cruises & Tours sells a couple dozen Hawaii trips running 7 to 13 days, operated by various guided tour companies including Globus, Tauck, and Trafalgar.

Contacts Atlas Cruises & Tours. ☎ 800/942–3301 ⊕ www.atlastravelweb.com. **Globus.** ☎ 866/755–8581 ⊕ www.globusjourneys.com. **Tauck.** ☎ 800/788–7885 ⊕ www.tauck.com. **Trafalgar.** ☎ 866/809–8426 ⊕ www.trafalgar. com.

SPECIAL-INTEREST TOURS

BIRD-WATCHING

More than 150 species of birds live in the Hawaiian Islands. For $5,450 per person double-occupancy, Field Guides has a three-island (Oahu, Kauai, and the Big Island), 10-day, guided bird-watching trip that includes accommodations, meals, ground transportation, and interisland air.

Victor Emanuel Nature Tours, the largest company in the world specializing in birding tours, has two 10-day Fall Hawaii and Spring Hawaii trips to Oahu, Kauai, and the Big Island that cost $4,895 (fall), including double-occupancy accommodations, meals, interisland air, ground transportation, and guided excursions.

Contacts Field Guides. ☎ 800/728–4953 ⊕ www.fieldguides.com. **Victor Emanuel Nature Tours.** ☎ 800/328–8368 ⊕ www. ventbird.com.

CULTURE

Road Scholar (originally called Elderhostel) is a nonprofit educational travel organization offering several guided Hawaii tours targeted at adults 50 and over (with grandparent/grandchild and family trips, too), with in-depth looks into the culture, history, and beauty of the Islands.

Contacts Road Scholar. ☏ 800/454–5768 ⊕ www.roadscholar.org.

HIKING

Sierra Club Hawaii offers regular guided hiking tours, outings, botanical gardens visits, and cleanup and community service efforts on Oahu that you can join in on during your visit.

Contacts Sierra Club Hawaii. ☏ 808/538–6616 ⊕ sierraclubhawaii.org.

▮ TRIP INSURANCE

Comprehensive trip insurance is valuable if you're booking a very expensive or complicated trip (particularly to an isolated region) or if you're booking far in advance. Comprehensive policies typically cover trip cancellation and interruption, letting you cancel or cut your trip short because of illness, or, in some cases, acts of terrorism in your destination. Such policies might also cover evacuation and medical care. Some also cover you for trip delays because of bad weather or mechanical problems, as well as for lost or delayed luggage.

Another type of coverage to consider is financial default—that is, when your trip is disrupted because a tour operator, airline, or cruise line goes out of business. Generally you must buy this when you book your trip or shortly thereafter, and it's available to you only if your operator isn't on a list of excluded companies.

Always read the fine print of your policy to make sure that you're covered for the risks that most concern you. Compare several policies to be sure you're getting the best price and range of coverage available.

Insurance Comparison Info InsureMyTrip. ☏ 800/487–4722 ⊕ www.insuremytrip.com. **Squaremouth.** ☏ 800/240–0369 ⊕ www.squaremouth.com.

Comprehensive Insurers Allianz Global Assistance. ☏ 866/884–3556 ⊕ www.allianztravelinsurance.com. **Generali Global Assistance (formerly CSA Travel Protection).** ☏ 800/874–2442 ⊕ www.generalitravelinsurance.com/. **Travel Guard.** ☏ 800/826–5248 ⊕ mvp.travelguard.com. **Travelex Insurance.** ☏ 800/228–9792 ⊕ www.travelexinsurance.com. **Travel Insured International.** ☏ 800/243 3174 ⊕ www.travelinsured.com.

▮ VISITOR INFORMATION

Before you go to Hawaii, contact the Oahu Visitors Bureau (OVB) for a free vacation planner and map. The OVB website has an online listing of accommodations, activities and sports, attractions, dining venues, services, transportation, travel professionals, and wedding information. For general information on all the Islands, contact the Hawaii Visitors & Convention Bureau. The HVCB website has a calendar of local events that will be taking place during your stay.

Contacts Hawaii Visitors & Convention Bureau. ☏ 800/464–2924 for brochures ⊕ www.gohawaii.com. **Oahu Visitors Bureau.** ☏ 800/464–2924 ⊕ www.gohawaii.com/oahu.

ONLINE RESOURCES

Contacts Hawaii Beach Safety. ⊕ hawaiibeachsafety.com. **Hawaii Department of Land and Natural Resources.** ⊕ dlnr.hawaii.gov. **Hawaii Tourism Authority.** ⊕ www.hawaiitourismauthority.org.

INDEX

PHOTO CREDITS

NOTES

NOTES

ABOUT OUR WRITERS

Powell Berger lives in the heart of Honolulu's Kakaako neighborhood, where she's ever in search of the best poke bowl. Her wanderlust has taken her to more than 50 countries around the world, and her writing appears in numerous state and regional publications, AAA magazines, *The Atlantic*, and various websites, in addition to Fodor's. She updated Where to Eat and Where to Stay for this edition.

Tiffany Hill has lived on Oahu's Leeward and Windward sides, but today she calls Honolulu home. She is a freelance writer whose work is regularly published in regional and national publications, as well as online. When she's not on assignment, you can find her playing roller derby. She updated Exploring Oahu and Nightlife and Performing Arts for this edition.

 Trina Kudlacek fell in love with Hawaii while on vacation 20 years ago. She now has the best of all possible worlds as she splits her time between her home in Hawaii, where she is a lecturer at the University of Hawaii, and Italy, where she is a tour guide. She updated all coverage of Beaches; Water Sports and Tours; and Golf, Hiking, and Outdoor Activities for this edition.

U.K.-born **Chris Oliver** has been a resident of Oahu for 30 years. As a reporter and travel editor for the *Honolulu Advertiser* she wrote about the Hawaiian Islands, as well as national and international destinations, with an eye for what visitors would most enjoy on a visit to Hawaii. Coming from a different country, climate, and culture has given her an enthusiasm for the exotic. She currently edits a newsletter, writes for *Hawaii* magazine, and divides her time between Hawaii and the United Kingdom. She updated Shops and Spas for this edition.

Writer and multimedia journalist **Anna Weaver** is a sixth-generation *kamaaina*, born and raised in Kailua, Oahu. She can never get enough Spam *musubi*, *malassadas*, or hiking time in her home state. Anna has written for *Slate*, as well as such Hawaii publications as the *Honolulu Advertiser* (now *Star-Advertiser*), *Honolulu Magazine*, and *Pacific Business News*. She updated Experience Oahu and Travel Smart for this edition.